Money Without Boundaries

How Blockchain Will Facilitate the Denationalization of Money

Thomas J. Anderson

WILEY

Published by John Wiley & Sons, Inc., Hoboken, New Jersey.
Published simultaneously in Canada.

For general information on our other products and services or for technical support, please contact our
Customer Care Department within the United States at (800) 762-2974, outside the United States at
(317) 572-3993, or fax (317) 572-4002.

Wiley publishes in a variety of print and electronic formats and by print-on-demand. Some material
included with standard print versions of this book may not be included in e-books or in
print-on-demand. If this book refers to media such as a CD or DVD that is not included in the
version you purchased, you may download this material at http://booksupport.wiley.com. For more
information about Wiley products, visit www.wiley.com.

Library of Congress Cataloging-in-Publication Data is Available:

ISBN 9781119564065 (Hardcover)
ISBN 9781119564041 (ePDF)
ISBN 9781119564058 (ePub)

Cover Design: Wiley
Cover Image: © RamCreativ / iStockphoto

Printed in the United States of America

V10012290_071819

To Allison

Thank you for your love and support.

"When the people find that they can vote themselves money, that will herald the end of the Republic."

– Benjamin Franklin

Contents

Preface

"All money is a matter of belief."

– Adam Smith

*M*oney *Without Boundaries* is about the creation of a new global currency. Unlike traditional currencies, such as the dollar, yen, or euro, this currency strives to be a risk-free store of value. And unlike bitcoin, which tethers to a finite number of units, this store of value tethers to zero risk. As a result, it is constrained not by an arbitrary number of units, but by market forces of supply and demand.

The foundational ideas are not new and are not unique. A privately controlled, market-based currency striving for zero risk is arguably the holy grail of multiple influential thinkers and Nobel laureates and the basis for many monetary and investment theories. What is new is that advancements in capital markets, when combined with new technologies, make it possible for society to facilitate old ideas in new ways. *Money Without Boundaries* is about bringing some of the greatest economic theories to reality. This book is a bridge connecting old ideas to new technologies.

The Paradox of Money

If you've studied any economics, you're probably familiar with the concept that money has three different roles in society:

1. A unit of value (how much something costs)
2. A medium of exchange (a way to transact)
3. A store of value (a safe place to store your earnings)

For as important as money is in our society, these concepts are surprisingly abstract. What, exactly, is a dollar, a euro, or a yen? Why can't anyone, from my friends to economic commentators, agree about whether gold is valuable or worthless? Is bitcoin a bubble waiting to crash, or is it the future of money? And what about other cryptocurrencies?

This is a paradox beyond paradoxes. People not only work hard for and fight over, but also beg, steal, and cheat to obtain something that really is an abstract concept. The deeper I dive, the more I realize I have dedicated my career and studies to something that has a fundamentally flawed foundation. I came to realize I don't know what money is, that I can't truly define it. Explain to me, what, exactly, makes that piece of paper in your wallet or that digital figure in your online bank account something unique – something special?

Our inability to easily define "money" is in some ways thousands of years old and in some ways a relatively new phenomenon. Neither Julius Caesar, Christopher Columbus, George Washington, Abraham Lincoln, nor Franklin Roosevelt would have found the question "What is money?" all that challenging. In large part, this is because throughout much of time, money tied to a gold standard and as such the unit of value, medium of exchange, and store of value were all closely related. As recently as the 1920s, our dollars were in fact bearer notes, convertible into gold and silver. However, once the world cut the cord to that tether, we began to drift endlessly in an open sea, with no anchor and no clear path ahead. What was a relatively abstract concept increasingly became much more abstract. So, I began a personal quest to understand "money" in this new world.

> "There is no answer in the available literature to the question why a government monopoly of the provision of money is universally regarded as indispensable.... It has the defects of all monopolies."
> — Friedrich Hayek, *Denationalisation of Money*
> "Underlying most arguments against the free market is a lack of belief in freedom itself."
> — Milton Friedman

Breaking Down My Quest

There are hundreds of countries around the world with hundreds of corresponding currencies. Perhaps much like you, I have visited several of them. I've never had any concern about my ability to travel or my ability to quickly and easily convert my dollars into any unit of value when I do. People in different countries use different monies, which they exchange to buy things at different prices. These prices can be converted quickly and easily from one currency to another. There are good reasons that many, if not most, governments choose to create a common unit of value for their territory. The concept of a unit of value is simple enough and does not preoccupy me.

Similarly, I have traveled to many countries for a short period of time and put the vast majority of my expenses on my credit card. Cash is not needed much these days, and if it is, I can get it quickly and easily at an ATM most anywhere in the world. As such, I have no problem understanding that my primary medium of exchange is my credit card or my debit card, which I use to access cash and buy goods and services around the world. Here again, while there are some complexities behind the technologies that make this possible, the concept itself is simple enough. I have had no sleepless nights worrying if my credit card will work in Paris, Tokyo, or Tulum.

As I peeled back the onion, I realized the paradox for me − what keeps me up at night −has to do with money as a store of value. What is it that makes a certain currency valuable to a certain group of people? Why, exactly, is the $100 bill in my wallet worth more than the $5 bill? And what about when these pieces of paper move into the digital world as bits and bytes? What then, exactly, is in your checking account, and who, exactly, determines its value or purchasing power?

Equally importantly, I wanted to understand when and why the role of money breaks down in society. Throughout time, paper money has been valued one day and then, virtually the next day, wheelbarrows of cash are not enough for a simple trip to the grocery store. There are multiple examples of hyperinflations throughout the world − in this century − in which money as it was known became as worthless as trash, wiping out the savings of the people. Something so important should not be so fragile.

I had a goal of what I wanted to understand, but first I had to ask a more important question: If a risk-free store of value − a new "money" − could be created, does it matter, and would anybody care? My intuition said this is an important and timely topic, and after taking the deep dive, I'm increasingly confident that *it does not matter*, in the *short term*, to society, if money is a good store of value.

There are two reasons society generally cares little about the value of currency:

1. It is generally viewed as a social construct upon which people believe they have little to no control.
2. They are not incentivized to care because most people do not have much "money."

Most people have a view that large and complex systems are simply out of their control. Bystanders, we are. My view is that large, rigid social constructs are their own paradox, the hardest and easiest things to change. While some constructs, such as language, evolve over long periods of time, others, like empires, rise and then fall very quickly. I believe a revolution is underfoot and this rigid construct of a government monopoly on money will change, and when the change takes place, it will happen quickly. This is in part facilitated by new technologies that add considerable value to society, which are being adapted at stunningly fast rates.

The second point is more nuanced. The basis of people's lack of incentive to care about money is a function of perspective, depending on whether they're spenders or savers. While some people, and some societies, save at high rates, most people rely on income (from a job, a pension, or Social Security), which they primarily consume month to month. Globally, most people live paycheck to paycheck. If people spend most of the money they earn, they likely don't see why they would need to worry about money as a store of value. In the United States, a relatively wealthy society, as much as 78 percent of people live paycheck to paycheck, and the majority saves less than $100 per month, according to a survey conducted by Career Builder.[1]

Not only does the majority of the population live paycheck to paycheck, but they also have some form of debt. According to the same Career Builder survey, 71 percent of all US workers are in debt.[2] Because of these debts, "money" as a store of value is viewed negatively when netted against credit cards, student loans, car loans, mortgages, and most other forms of debt. Typically, money is a holding that destroys value because, in most cases, borrowers earn less on their money than their cost of borrowing. Borrowers are generally seeking to be debt free more than they are seeking a safe store of value.

Few people live primarily off of their savings, though there are some. I confidently, and naively, thought this group must care about "money" as a store of value. However, I cannot find much evidence that a risk-free store of value or even the value of the dollar remaining high is on their list of concerns. Statistical data suggests this group tends to hold little "money" as a percentage of their overall net worth. They tend to convert what was "money" into other assets like stocks, bonds, real estate – you name it – everything except "money." Those who do hold large amounts of "money" tend to do so as a part of a broader strategy such as going to "cash" in anticipation of being able to buy other assets at a lower price in the future.

Individuals who hold money tend to have an objective to maximize the return on that money, versus maximize the safety of that money. If there are two equally insured bank deposit accounts, all things equal, most individuals would choose the one that pays the most interest. Similarly, if there are two money market funds, most individuals would choose the one that pays, higher rate of interest. Let's leap forward and assume we could create a risk-free asset that pays no interest because it's risk free. If you consider the risk of a bank failure to be de minimis, the rational choice is to hold a higher-paying bank deposit than an asset that pays "zero."

Both groups generally tend to believe that as long as their money is safe – which they would define as safe from loss (theft, bank failure, etc.) – and present at the time of consumption, there is no need for a risk-free asset, a safe store of value. This might be a rational view. After all, why care about something you don't have, don't need, don't want, and that destroys value?

I spent time considering that perhaps society doesn't need (or want) a stable store of value. We seem to have existed surprisingly well, and much better than the naysayers forecast at the time of the demise of the gold standard, without a safe store of value. Somehow, and for some reason – even though inflation has decimated the dollar's purchasing power – people continue to consider the dollar or US Treasuries to be "risk free."

Well, if it doesn't matter, then perhaps it just doesn't matter. If the Federal Reserve can create a $4 trillion stimulus package, why not do an $8 trillion package? If the US government can have $20 trillion of debt, why not have $100 trillion? Why stop there? Why not have the government just wire each of us $50,000? $100,000? What is the limit? And what is money?

I understand why people could think money doesn't matter, and I beg to differ. If you feel like you are working harder and harder and not getting ahead, it is because chances are, you're not. Your purchasing power is gradually being stolen from you. This is about something bigger than just preserving purchasing power. This could be, perhaps, the most important issue facing our society. Significant disruptions and collapses in economic systems have led to terrible things throughout history – wars and arguably the deaths of tens of millions, if not hundreds of millions, of people. I believe the current system is surprisingly fragile, but we can leverage old ideas and new technologies, working together, to create a stronger foundation today and prevent disaster and collapse in the future.

A Part of a Broader Movement – Cryptocurrency

A small but growing movement is underfoot in something called cryptocurrency. It is much bigger than bitcoin; hundreds of thousands of people across the world have engaged in various cryptocurrency communities. Billions of dollars have been invested into entities, ideas, and concepts that are collectively valued at hundreds of billions of dollars. If money doesn't matter as a store of value, why the significant interest in cryptocurrency?

Cryptocurrency includes a few different camps of people with varying motivations.

- **Bad Guys.** Criminals can move money for drugs, weapons – most anything – in an untraceable way while preserving its underlying value.
- **Get Rich Quick.** People looking to make a quick buck on a new trend. While that sounds disparaging, nothing could be further from the truth. Speculation is the basis of capitalism and has directly or indirectly fueled most, if not all, societal advancements.
- **Decentralists.** People who believe new technologies can lead to more efficiency (and lower costs) by facilitating more direct connections with fewer (or no) intermediaries.
- **Doubters.** From conspiracy theorists to Nobel laureates, there are people who believe that without sound money, and without a strong foundation in a solid store of value, we would create a house of cards upon which society can (and will) collapse. This group includes cryptocurrency, gold, and sound money advocates. Many in this group believe we are destined for a global hyperinflation like the one that occurred in the German Weimer Republic or recently in Zimbabwe. As one friend put it rather bluntly, "It is all a bunch of made-up bullshit."

Money Without Boundaries has nothing to offer bad guys and very little that would directly affect speculators, other than perhaps a different perspective to help speculate more efficiently. People in either of the latter two camps – or who, like me, find truth in both –should find this book's quest for a decentralized, risk-free asset quite fascinating.

Technologies, Theories, and Capital Markets

Developing a risk-free store of value is problematic because most people perceive they do not need or want it, and the people who do have a combination of knowledge gaps and predisposed bias that influences their receptivity to some of the concepts we will talk about in this book. I have met theorists who don't understand the underlying technology and technologists who are unfamiliar with monetary theory. Many blockchain and crypto enthusiasts are unaware that the fascination with money is in fact a well-studied, old topic –not an emerging Reddit meme.

Our quest relies on three pillars:

1. Technologies
2. Theories
3. Inner workings of banking and capital markets

In this book, I'll introduce you to some of the godfathers of the conversation about money, Nobel-winning economists like Milton Friedman, Friedrich Hayek, Irving Fisher, and James Tobin, who were considered quite radical for works like *The Denationalization of Money; The Optimum Quantity of Money; The Theory of Interest, Money, Credit and Capital,* and many other thought-provoking – sometimes even mind-bending – works. I'll also introduce you to some key concepts, including blockchain, securitization, and collateralized debt obligations, and bridge them together into a common framework. A Glossary, Resource Guide, and Bibliography are at the end of the book for quick reference and deeper learning. I encourage you to turn to these resources to better calibrate and understand each of the ingredients in this pot.

The Bottom Line: Money Is Credit and Credit Is Money

For much of history, money was gold and gold was money. However, the world has moved from commodity money to fiat money, a system of "full faith and credit." Under A. Mitchell Innes's *Credit Theory of Money,* money is credit and credit is money – they are different sides of the same coin. *Money Without Boundaries* is an application of this theory to create a new currency that is always a proven, known, and transparent store of value.

In the future, money will be decentralized, community-managed money market accounts operating in a nonprofit structure, similar to credit unions today, and leveraging technology and securitization to infinitely sort, segment, and group pools of borrowers into pure commodities and then route them via direct connections, with no intermediary, to pools of lenders. The Credit Theory posits that borrowers create money, a store of value, as the byproduct of direct transactions. The epicenter of this sorting, segmenting, and grouping is "zero," the fulcrum point where borrowing costs zero and lenders receive zero. Both parties engage in this transaction because they mutually benefit; one group receives a pure store of value, and the other side receives capital (money) at zero cost.

This may sound revolutionary, but it is in fact an old idea. The concept of borrowing and lending at the risk-free rate is a cornerstone of Harry Markowitz's Modern Portfolio Theory, and zero nominal return is the backbone of the Friedman Rule and conforms to Hayek's non-interest-bearing ducat in *Denationalization of Money*. What's exciting in the evolution of this concept is that today we have the technology – blockchain – that can play a pivotal role in facilitating this vision. Blockchain, especially when combined with other technologies, not only facilitates community management, but also delivers unprecedented transparency and solves the "trust gap" in transactions that impedes decentralization. Blockchain filters out all the challenges so all the good can rise to the top.

Democratized Borrowing on a Leveled Playing Field

A better store of value is made possible for one group of citizens while another group will get vastly lower interest rates made possible through decentralized, direct, fully transparent connections. The implications of this simple concept are vast. This vision facilitates a future where borrowing is completely democratized, with governments, companies, and

people competing equally, all on the same field, for "full faith and credit."
In fact, once the playing field is leveled, people who are in a better financial position than, for example, the US government (a relatively low bar),
will borrow at rates less than the government.

Don Quixote Meets Copernicus

Like Nicolaus Copernicus, the Renaissance astronomer and mathemati-
cian who turned the world on its head when he revealed that the sun,
not the earth, is the center of the universe, this is a story about a different way of looking at an old problem, an inversion of our current
assumptions and how we approach the world.

Our global society is facing significant challenges with respect to debt
and demographics. (See my commentary in Appendix B, "A House of
Cards." I am obviously not alone in this view. "The Coming Crisis"
section of the Resource Guide will direct your attention to a number
of books that outline in frightening detail the potential size, nature, and
impact of our financial position. Themes include crisis, collapse, ruin,
war, bubble, failure, panics, and even enslavement.)

While some argue our global financial system isn't a complete house
of cards, any reasonable person must at least recognize that we are on very,
very shaky ground. We have cut our ties to a stable store of value, and for
almost 50 years we've been playing with fire, increasing the stakes every
day. History shows that high levels of debt get solved with some form
of a combination of growth, inflation, or a devaluation of the underlying currency. We are not seeing enough growth to solve the underlying
challenges. The challenges are just too big. This is true not just in the
United States, but in many places around the world like Europe and Japan
that are facing similar challenges with debt and demographics. The math
simply does not work.

There is no easy way out. History has shown that change is abrupt,
and the related crises are severe. There has perhaps never been a more
important time for society to work together on a common quest for a
stable store of value. The world certainly does not have it today.

Acknowledgments

My co-workers from my time in "fin" and "tech" inspired this book. I have learned so much from each of you.

Robyn Lawrence, you turned my initial ideas and writing forays into a structured manuscript, and I can't thank you enough for your thoughtful research and editing skills.

I would like to thank the fabulous team at Wiley, including Michael Henton, Editor; Richard Samson, Project Editor; Beula Jaculin, Production Editor; and Mike Isralewitz, Copy Editor; along with the rest of the team. This book would not be possible without you. I appreciate your incredible attention to detail, and any remaining mistakes are my own.

Kids, thank you for your patience as I took on another project. Your fresh perspective and ideas about how money can transcend time and space helped shape this project more than you can imagine. I love who you are and who you are becoming, and I am proud to be your father.

Allison, you make me so happy and I am so lucky. I never thought it would be possible to love somebody as much as I love you.

Introduction

"As a rule, political economists do not take the trouble to study the history of money; it is much easier to imagine it and to deduce the principles of this imaginary knowledge."

– Alexander Del Mar

From the wealthiest business owner to the poorest worker, the global financial crisis of 2008 brought fear and panic to our society. Over a decade later – after trillions of dollars of debt, trillions of dollars of monetary stimulus, trillions of dollars of deficits, and virtually trillions of pages of regulation – do we believe the world is in a more sustainable place? Does the little guy have an equal chance? Is the system materially more stable, more stable at the margin, or perhaps less stable with respect to governments, banks, and markets?

You may have doubts that your country is on a sustainable path or that your government is being fiscally responsible, concerns about money creation and your currency's value, or concerns that you are paying and receiving your fair share. If you are in the middle or lower class, you likely have concerns that the cards are stacked against you and you will not have enough resources to pursue your dreams – or even feed your family. The global wealth gap between the "haves" and "have-nots" continues to grow at an extraordinary pace; the global middle class feels trapped. In 2017, 82 percent of the wealth generated went to the richest 1 percent of the global population while the poorest half of the world saw little or no increase in their wealth.[1] If you are not in the top 1 percent, chances are you feel this pain.

You're certainly not immune from financial distress even if you're a 1 percenter. You likely have concerns about how you can protect and grow your wealth. Tens of trillions of dollars of cash and savings are at historic low interest rates. Many stock markets are trading at or near record highs, and real estate prices are also nearing record highs – against a backdrop of an unprecedented global monetary experiment in quantitative easing, in which central banks buy securities to lower interest rates and increase the money supply to pump up lending and liquidity.

It's a precarious house of cards, and it begs a big question: What is a safe store of value?

What Is Money?

Money, traditionally, has been a safe store of value. But what exactly is money? Most people think of it as a way to buy things, and it goes well beyond physical cash in your pocket. Chances are high you aren't paid in physical cash and you don't make your mortgage, rent, car, cell phone, or utility payment in cash. You do not use cash with Venmo, Uber, Amazon, Netflix, or Airbnb. In 2014, most Americans carried less than $50 in their wallets and half carried less than $20, and by 2016, most people in the United Kingdom carried less than £5.[2] Most business-to-business transactions are cashless. Even some large financial services firms – some of the biggest banks in the world, like Morgan Stanley and State Street – are largely cashless.

From how we get paid to how we pay the bills to how we typically go out to dinner, our transactions rarely take place in physical cash. If money is a series of digital widgets that we rely on for our day-to-day life, what exactly is it? How is it made? Why do we value it? Is it safe, and how do we know it is worth anything?

Money typically serves three roles:

1. A unit of value
2. A medium of exchange
3. A store of value

Historically, these three roles were very interconnected. Today and in the future, however, these roles can be looked at independently. A unit of value is the way in which people process and understand money, typically defined by the currency of their home country. Most Americans consider the US dollar their unit of value. When traveling in Europe, they will typically purchase a cup of coffee with euros and then convert the cost of that cup of coffee from euros to dollars so they have a sense of what it costs. Dollars, euros, or yen as legal tender are simply a measure of value: a way in which parties can quickly and easily agree to how debts and obligations (like your paycheck) will be settled. Legal contracts typically refer to money as a unit of value. If you borrow "30,000" for a car or "300,000" for a house, the contracts typically are in US dollars, euros, or pounds. You cannot repay the "300,000" mortgage with 300,000 seashells or even 300,000 bars of gold. Gold and seashells may be worth more or less, but transactions take place in a unit of value to facilitate commerce.

As a medium of exchange, money is a way to buy things. When you do, merchants generally don't care whether you pay cash or use credit; the most important thing to them is completing the sale. Historically, the vendor may have had a slight preference toward cash because of lower transaction fees, but an increasing number of stores and vendors are choosing to go cashless. Cash now accounts for a mere 13 percent of payments in stores, and half of all merchants expect to stop dealing with it by 2025.[3] Cash payments may save on some fees, but merchants have to deal with the hassle of storing, moving, and managing that cash, not to mention the risk of being robbed. As innovations like Square credit card processing pushes transaction fees even lower, it is easy to envision a world where no cash is ever required for any transaction.

Most people in the developed world make the majority of their purchases with a credit card. Many, if not most, of my friends carry small amounts of physical cash on them, even when we're headed out for a night on the town. Some of my friends are using debit cards, and some are using credit cards. It doesn't matter to the owners of the restaurants and clubs we frequent. Debit or credit is easy and secure. There's absolutely no reason for us to risk losing our cash or getting robbed.

But what about transacting in other countries? Credit or debit cards are much more conducive to travel than cash because they don't recognize borders or boundaries. If you have a Visa card, you can have lunch at the airport in Los Angeles and dinner in New York before you board your flight to Frankfurt. You could then spend a day in Frankfurt and continue on to Dubai, India, China, Japan, and back to Los Angeles. Along the way you could buy virtually anything anywhere – all on the same card – transacting in virtually any currency, anywhere in the world. Just as you can do a night out in your home town with less than $20 in cash, you can travel the world with one credit card, never taking out cash in any country along the way. Nearly any citizen in nearly any country has access to similar services.

As a result of our global preference to transact in a method other than physical cash, payments is a big, competitive business. McKinsey & Company predicts in a whitepaper that global payments will generate $2.2 trillion in revenue by 2020[4] and also warns that digitization will be a hugely disruptive factor. In a 2017 study, consultancy Capgemini and the bank BNP Paribas found that noncash transactions rose 11.2 percent between 2014 and 2015 and predicted that global digital payments would reach $726 billion by 2020, driven by connected homes, contactless bank cards, wearable devices, and augmented reality.[5] In the United States, Juniper Research predicts that mobile payments will be worth $282.9 billion by 2021.[6]

Perhaps nowhere is this shift away from cash more apparent than in China, which historically has been a very cash-based society and as recently as ten years ago had very little credit infrastructure. I was recently in the city of Hangzhou visiting a rural tea farm, and merchants were literally crabby with me when I tried to pay with cash. They didn't want cash because they had no way to get it into their Alipay system. In China, where $5.5 trillion in mobile payments are made every year,[7] it's almost difficult, and certainly annoying, for most vendors when you pay in cash. Everyone from street vendors to taxi drivers to the largest stores conducts the majority of their business via credit or virtual transactions, typically WeChat Pay and Alipay – and it's stunningly simple. Everybody and anybody with a smartphone and a QR code – a mega-bar code that can hold massive amounts of information, including a unique footprint that lets them send and receive money with perfect security – can handle payments. (With the introduction of facial recognition-based Smile to Pay at a Hangzhou KFC, people don't even need the phone.) "Super apps" like Alipay not only handle payments but also allow users to book medical appointments and open money market accounts. Though most people's codes are on their phone, it's possible to print out images of the codes for other people to scan, which is how many Chinese street beggars seek handouts these days. Alipay, which goes by the slogan "trust makes it simple," is one of the most valuable companies in world.

Today, most people are able to make monetary transactions quickly, securely, and effortlessly with all conversions taking place behind the scenes. We are fortunate that money as a medium of exchange and a unit of value already exists, but society lacks a universal store of value. This is the holy grail in our quest for global prosperity and peace.

Money as a Store of Value

Let's assume you're renting an apartment. Shortly after you renew your one-year lease, you inherit $500,000. You would like to set this money aside to purchase a home when your lease is up, but where should you store this money? Under your mattress? In a bank? Convert it to gold, bonds, stocks, or bitcoin? How do you know it will be safe?

Well, first, what is "safe"? It means different things to everyone, of course, but for our purposes, it can be defined as:

1. Safe from being stolen
2. Safe from financial crisis
3. Safe with respect to purchasing power

When you look at it that way, it turns out that neither the mattress, bank, gold, stocks, bonds, or bitcoin are risk-free stores of value. In fact, there is no such thing. While the world is exceptionally efficient at using money as a medium of exchange and has defined many units of value, we do not have an agreed-upon risk-free store of value. Governments have all sorts of mechanisms for controlling units of value, but they have no way to control a store of value, or place where people can safely hold their earnings for future consumption, the last – and most essential – function and purpose of money.

A safe store of value is a standardized, fixed constant that can be measured in any unit of value and take place via any medium of exchange. The purpose of this book is to help the world envision and create something that doesn't yet exist: a market-based, self-stabilizing global currency, the risk-free rate.

Demise of the Gold Standard

Throughout history, people have used everything from cowrie shells to glass beads to salt as stores of value. (Cowrie shells, used on every continent at some point in early history, actually competed with metal currencies in many societies.[8]) Most of these "commodity currencies" died out when people discovered there was virtually unlimited supply of them (what's the value in that?), and people began looking for an alternative. Humans turned to gold, valued primarily because we understand it to be an element with special characteristics that cannot be duplicated and is in limited supply. (This is why gold, though it has been the default store of value for centuries, could not be the standard for all of space and time. All it would take is the discovery of a planet dripping with gold ore and the ability to mine it – a stretch in today's world but not throughout time – and the mineral's value plummets on Earth.)

Gold coins and bars with standardized sizes and weights became the medium of exchange in Greece, Rome, and Byzantium about 2,500 to 2,600 years ago.[9] For centuries, humans relied on gold as their store of value. It was the only form of money that held value as Roman emperors continuously debased their currencies to pay for wars and lavish lifestyles. Julius Caesar conquered nations for gold, and Christopher Columbus set sail to find more of it. When the United States of America was created, its new currency, the dollar, was backed by gold. Long before he became a Broadway star, our nation's first Treasury Secretary, Alexander Hamilton, recognized that a stable national currency was key to building a prosperous, powerful nation – wisdom that prevailed even up to and following the Civil War.

In the 1900s, the definition of "money" in the United States began to change quite radically because of President Franklin Roosevelt's move to partially eliminate citizens' ability to convert dollars into gold and the debasement of the greenback in the 1930s combined with the fractional reserve system, in which people put their money into banks, but banks didn't have to keep that money (or gold) on deposit. Each phenomenon was stunning on its own but had some historical precedent. All these events working together were significant, and as we will see, the system began to drift. These changes caused many scholars not only to question the stability of the underlying system, but also to ask the fundamental question, *What is money?* Approximately 100 years ago, many people predicted the drift and ultimate collapse of a system built on such a weak foundation.

As we know, collapse was not imminent, and the international convertibility of gold did provide a remaining tether. In some ways, the dollar was in fact further strengthened by World War II. After World War II, the Bretton Woods Agreement pegged all nations' currencies to the dollar, which was fully convertible to gold internationally. A breakthrough in global financial history took place on August 15, 1971, when US President Richard Nixon interrupted one of the most popular shows on TV, *Bonanza,* to announce that US dollars would no longer be redeemable for gold. The United States had only about a third of the gold bullion it needed to cover the dollars it had printed.[10] Nixon's primetime announcement launched the world into the "just trust us" era of money supply and the instability, inefficiency, and vulnerability that plague the global financial system today.

"H.J. Res. 192, approved by President Roosevelt on June 5, 1933, provided that obligations payable in gold or specific coin or currency are contrary to public policy, and that those obligations could be discharged dollar for dollar in legal tender. After that resolution was adopted, currency of the United States could not be converted into gold by United

States citizens, but the Treasury would convert dollars into gold for foreign governments as a means of maintaining stability and confidence in the dollar. Because the dollar was no longer freely convertible, one could consider that the United States was no longer on the gold standard at that time. If, however, one considers the gold standard as a monetary system in which the unit of money is backed by gold even if the monetary unit cannot be converted into gold, one could argue that the United States went off of the gold standard on August 15, 1971, when President Nixon announced that the US dollar would no longer be convertible into gold in the international markets. The President was able to suspend the ability to convert the dollar into gold because there was no legal requirement that the United States exchange gold for dollars. On December 18, 1971, the President devalued the dollar, and even though the devaluation was effective immediately, only Congress could officially change the gold value of the dollar. Early in 1972, Congress passed Public Law 92-268, which gave formal approval to the December 1971 devaluation."

> – "Gold & Silver," Federal Reserve
> Bank of Richmond[11]

The United States, in effect, backs the dollar with the country's economic might, in turn backed by the government's right to tax citizens. The problem is that there is no clear control on supply. The government has a virtually *unlimited printing press* and a *Federal Reserve, which is not mandated to create a constant store of value* but instead to maximize employment – which is actually very likely to be in direct conflict with creating a constant store of value.

IS THE DUAL MANDATE WORKING?

The Federal Reserve's Dual Mandate refers to its simultaneous goals of price stability and maximum sustainable employment. How's that going? You be the judge.

The unemployment rate in 1969 was 3.5 percent. The unemployment rate in late 2018 was approximately 3.8 percent. In 1969, the price of a Big Mac was $0.49. The price of a Big Mac in late 2018: $4.79.[12]

Our currency has underlying economic value, but it ultimately holds no value if there is unlimited supply. If the Fed decided to give every citizen a trillion dollars in an effort to maximize employment tomorrow, those dollars would immediately be worth nothing as mass inflation is triggered. It happened in the Weimar Republic when Germany suspended the gold standard and began printing money to pay for the cost of World War I and in Zimbabwe in the 1990s and 2000s when the Robert Mugabe government began printing money to finance the country's involvement in the Second Congo War. In Germany, people fed their stoves with marks because money was cheaper than wood,[13] and Zimbabweans abandoned their currency for US dollars – which eventually began running out, prompting that country's evolution into a nearly cashless economy.[14]

Planting the Seed for the Denationalization of Money

Nobel Prize–winning economists like Irving Fisher predicted the fractional reserve system would bring disaster, while Milton Friedman and Friedrich Hayek pondered the existential question, *What is money?* Hayek envisioned a system of banks that would issue "fiat" money, inconvertible paper that the entities had to maintain in order to stay in business. He advocated for private competing currencies in his 1978 book, *Denationalization of Money*, claiming the "invisible hand" of competition and market forces would determine the dominant world currencies. That idea seemed somewhat preposterous forty years ago –before the rise of bitcoin. Today, technology is making it possible to use theories and ideas from some of the greatest economic thinkers in history – Plato, Adam Smith, Irving Fisher, Milton Freidman, Friedrich

Hayek, Harry Markowitz, James Tobin, William Sharpe – to transform money as we know it.

Cryptocurrency is a movement that touches millions of people and billions of dollars in investment, market capitalization, and exchanged value. But the world can now use the same technology used for bitcoin to create an infinite number of items of limited supply. If you could have bitcoin, fitcoin, litcoin, pitcoin, etc., is supply truly limited? What are coins versus tokens, and what are securities versus utilities? And how does this relate to being a currency and a store of value that transcends time? Billions of dollars are riding on answers to these questions.

The true value in bitcoin is that it gave us blockchain technology, which digitally secures the ownership of an item and its full history, allowing the full transparency necessary to implement Hayek's vision of private competing currencies. However, with blockchain technology, we can now take Hayek's vision to the next level. With blockchain, money can be fully commoditized – just like corn or wheat – in a fully decentralized, self-regulating, not-for-profit, free-market system. Everyone – not just governments and banks – may have the opportunity to compete "on full faith in credit," making secure, anonymous financial transactions without any gaps in trust. Blockchain will facilitate a new way, a new approach, to a decentralized, safe, and secure store of value for all. Doing so will revolutionize banking, currency, and consumer lending as we know them.

Part One

THE FOUNDATION

Chapter 1

Money Through Time – A Different Perspective

"The term money has two very different meanings in popular discourse. We often speak of someone 'making money,' when we really mean that he or she is receiving an income. We do not mean that he or she has a printing press in the basement churning out greenbacked pieces of paper. In this use, money is a synonym for income or receipts; it refers to a flow, to income or receipts per week or per year. We also speak of someone's having money in his or her pocket or in a safe-deposit box or on deposit at a bank. In that use, money refers to an asset, a component of one's total wealth. Put differently, the first use refers to an item on a profit-and-loss statement, the second to an item on a balance sheet."

– Milton Friedman

Before humans had, or even considered having, a universal medium of exchange, they traded one commodity directly for another – two goats for an ox or wheat for labor – but they had no real means of measuring the relative value of what they were trading. So began the search for a universal medium of exchange – money –and throughout history, humans tried everything from cowrie shells to cigarettes. But cowrie shells, used in ancient times on the African coast,[1] broke and wore down, and more and more of them kept washing ashore. How valuable could they be if there was a seemingly limitless supply? Cigarettes, used as currency in Germany just after World War II ended,[2] were certainly scarce enough, but inevitably they got smoked (for after all, their value lay in the relief they provided people during terrible times).

People in the ancient Mediterranean were the first to use metals, including gold, electrum, silver, iron, and copper, as money. Some of these metals were so abundant and easy to procure that they never became valued. Of them all, gold, silver, and copper stood out as precious and worth pursuing as currency, but gold rose to the top for its rarity, durability, malleability, near indestructibility (it doesn't tarnish or burn), and sheer beauty. Throughout the ages, gold has carried with it an almost mystic quality, which is why it became the precious metal most favored by kings.[3] In *The Power of Gold: The History of an Obsession*, Peter L. Bernstein writes that gold rose to the top for practical reasons as well. It is so dense that small amounts can serve as large denominations, and every piece – in the earring, applied to the halo in a fresco, on the dome of the Massachusetts State House, in the flecks on Notre Dame's football helmets, in the gold bars hidden away at Fort Knox – reflects the same qualities.[4]

But it is gold's scarcity – only 125,000 tons exist, as far as we know[5] – that has given it enduring value. Empires have been built and destroyed throughout the ages, and countless lives have been lost in the pursuit of gold. "The history of humankind – sometimes not so human – would have been different without the wars and invasions that had, as a basic aim, the pursuit of power by the possession of gold," Thomas Hoving and Carmen Gómez-Moreno wrote in a Metropolitan Museum of Art Bulletin in 1972,[6] just a year after the United States went off the gold standard. The museum curators went on to point out, poetically, that "with incredible effort it is extracted from the depths of the earth, and much of it is buried again in bank vaults as bullion."[7]

Neolithic humans first discovered gold nuggets carried by rivers during the sixth millennium BC, but they were too soft to be of much use to make the tools and weapons that primitive people needed in their fight for survival. Eventually, as life got easier and cultures grew more sophisticated, gold's allure began to grow. In the fifth century BC, the Greek poet Pindar said gold was "a child of Zeus, neither moth or rust devoureth it, but the mind of man is devoured by this supreme possession."[8] Ancient Egyptians considered it solidified fire, like the sun, and made it a symbol of their sun god Ra,[9] and during the Bronze Age (2200–1100 BC), they began using gold as money, in the form of rings or pellets of fixed weight for small transactions and by weight for larger ones. As the Egyptians' trade routes took them south to Crete and Cyprus, where people still traded in oxen, they adjusted their gold money system to work with oxen as the standard – but instead of trading the animals themselves, they represented them with an oxhide-shaped copper ingot or a small gold ring or pellet called a *talanton*.[10] Gold was the preferred metal as coinage became established everywhere, mining engineer and metallurgist Zay Jeffries wrote, because it was "the most beautiful metal, the heaviest substance known until the platinum metals became available, easy to fabricate, difficult to counterfeit, scarce but not too scarce, durable, dividable into small units without impairment of its value, easy to evaluate by weight and assay, valuable per unit of weight, transportable and storable."[11]

Silver and copper were used along with gold in early coinage, but from the beginning it was clear to everyone that silver, which blackens and changes over time, and copper, which can be ruined by moisture in a matter of days, were inferior metals.[12] Croesus, the last king of Lydia from 560 until 546 BC, was the first to acknowledge the lesser value of silver in relation to gold when he decreed that one gold coin was equivalent in value to twenty silver coins – an equation that would influence gold and silver value ratios for millennia. After Persia defeated Croesus as it built the Achaemenid Empire, Darius the Great began issuing gold *darics* and silver *sigloi* that were minted in the millions by Achaemenid kings for the next two centuries. Those coins influenced a huge swath of history, from the downfall of Athens to the corruption of Sparta to the Sicilian wars.[13]

Rulers, as they will, learned early on how to manipulate the money system to their best advantage. In the fourth century, for example, Dionysius of Syracuse was heavily indebted to his citizens, so he forced everyone to bring him every one of their one-drachma coins, which he promptly had re-stamped as two-drachma coins.[14] That was just one of the tricks early world leaders employed when they needed money. They also debased coins by alloying, short weighting, and even clipping off the edges to melt into new ones. In a cycle that would repeat itself again and again down through the ages, their debasements inevitably triggered inflation, sometimes so massive that nations had to start again with new currencies.[15] Many would even argue that continuous currency debasement and runaway inflation is what took down the Roman Empire.

Romans used rough, broken lumps of bronze or copper as currency until the first silver coins were minted in 187 BC.[16] In 49 BC, when Julius Caesar arrived in Rome to begin his reign, one of the first things he did – without senate approval – was issue coins with elephants on them in his own name.[17] As the empire grew, so, too, did Rome's need for new sources of gold to pay the soldiers and mercenaries who were building it, while also satisfying the upper classes' insatiable need to adorn themselves and their buildings with gold. The Romans took Dionysius's classic method of currency debasement and ran with it, making it standard procedure for centuries. Silver coins lost 60 percent of their metal between 27 BC, when Augustus became the first emperor, and 260 AD, when Gallienus took the reign. With Rome under pressure from invasions, civil war, plague, and economic depression, Gallienus steadily debased Roman coins until silver made up only 4 percent of them. The coins were so flimsy they could only be imprinted on one side. In addition to staggering inflation, Rome lost its purchasing power and respect with the rest of the world.[18]

Worried about losing their gold to calamity or thieves, people began depositing it with goldsmiths for safekeeping and using the receipts for that storage as money. Goldsmiths soon realized they didn't actually need to keep enough gold on hand to cover the sum total of all those receipts. The seeds of modern banking were planted.

"The Holy Gift of Free Gold"

When Christopher Columbus set sail in 1492, he was looking not so much for a New World as he was for a New World with abundant sources of gold – and in the beginning, it looked pretty promising. After he landed in North America, Columbus ran the Pinta aground at a spot in Haiti that he called La Isla Espanola because he thought it resembled Spain,[19] and he befriended the natives by trading them red bonnets, beads, and bells for cotton, parrots, spears, and gold. Columbus was convinced that La Espanola was dripping with the precious metal after one of the island's caciques gave Columbus five pieces of gold and a gold mask. In his official letter announcing the discovery, Columbus wrote that La Espanola embodied "the holy gift of free gold."[20] He returned from his first voyage in May 1493 and presented to King Ferdinand and Queen Isabella, at the royal court in Barcelona, a procession of naked Indians adorned with gold and accompanied by parrots, representing the fertile lands and great gold mines he claimed to have discovered.[21] With promises to return with much more where that came from, Columbus immediately set sail again with seventeen caravels to colonize La Espanola on September 25, 1493, promising the "taking of the Indies and all that they contain"[22] (but mostly gold).

Unfortunately for everyone involved – and tragically for the natives – Columbus's promises that he was sending Ferdinand and Isabella a map with the location of gold and spices had no basis. There actually was very little gold on La Espanola. In 1494, still claiming La Espanola was home to rich mines, Columbus said he was unable to deliver the gold because the colonists who were supposed to be mining it were too sick and hungry. Instead of gold, he sent to Ferdinand and Isabella a group of cannibals and their alleged concubines, a handful of castrated young males, and parrots that he suggested the House of Castile could give away to other kings to show off Spain's colonial achievements. The relief fleet that delivered this spectacle did not hesitate to let the monarchs know there was no gold on the island, but the king and queen refused to believe their investments would never be recovered.[23]

Columbus was spectacular with words. In letter after letter, he convinced Ferdinand and Isabella that "there are many wide rivers of which the majority contain gold"[24] in La Espanola, while beseeching them for more money. Desperate and knowing that his time was running out, Columbus decreed that every three months, every native had to bring the colonists a hawk's bell filled with gold dust (chiefs had to bring about ten times that amount). The decree led to gruesome consequences, Hans Koning wrote in *Columbus: His Enterprise: Exploding the Myth*. "Once the Indians had handed in whatever they still had in gold ornaments, their only hope was to work all day in the streams, washing out gold dust from the pebbles. It was an impossible task, but those Indians who tried to flee into the mountains were systematically hunted down with dogs and killed, to set an example for the others to keep trying." Within two years, up to half of the Arawak population of La Espanola – estimates run from 125,000 to 500,000 – killed themselves with cassava poison.[25]

In the end, Columbus never delivered much gold. He delivered spectacle – cannibals, Amazons, and naked Indians – instead, and he created a masterful model for how to manipulate people through money and desire. "By promising providential gold and giving New World wonders, Columbus produces the scarcity that automatically increases the desire to enjoy both," Duke University Romance Studies Professor Elvira Vilches wrote in *Columbus's Gift: Representations of Grace and Wealth and the Enterprise of the Indies*. "The interstice that the spectacle of the marvelous creates between abundance and scarcity, satisfaction and desire produces a 'metaphoric thirst' which seeks satisfaction in comparable things and signs. The yearning for something else is consequently associated with lack and disappearance, since they are effective means to entice desire. Gold is almost absent; New World wonders are equally scarce in the Old World."[26]

National Debt, National Blessing?

Three hundred years after Columbus landed on North American shores, the United States of America rose from the ashes of the Revolutionary War and began functioning as a sovereign nation. The new country's finances were in tatters. The freshly written Constitution made the federal government responsible for securities issued during the revolutionary era, and those securities were selling on the market for ten to twenty cents on the dollar.[27] Making matters worse, the Continental Congress and several colonial states had followed the lead of Massachusetts in 1690 and printed paper money to make up for tax shortfalls. From 1774 to 1779, the Continental Congress had issued so many bills of credit that they were virtually worthless, referred to as "not worth a continental." Dismayed at this practice, the authors of the Constitution very clearly banned it.[28]

In 1781, Alexander Hamilton, the nation's first Secretary of the Treasury under President George Washington, wrote to financier and fellow founding father Robert Morris that the United States was in the same predicament as England after King William's long, expensive wars in the seventeenth century drained the country of all its specie (gold and silver) and devastated commerce. "The administration wisely had recourse to the institution of a bank; and it relieved the national difficulties," Hamilton wrote. "We are in the same, and still greater, want of a sufficient medium."[29] Hamilton was one of the world's first macroeconomic planners and a spectacular orator, and he used all his skills to gather support for his proposed national bank.

Conveniently, the Treasury Secretary believed that "the most important measures of every government are connected with the Treasury," and he was convinced that the key to building a stable government and an expansive economy was creating a sound base of public credit.[30] Hamilton saw the lack of adequate money supply as one of the fledgling economy's biggest problems, so he created large blocks of new government securities, in effect monetizing the United States' debts. As historian Thomas K. McGraw explained, Hamilton was way ahead of his contemporaries in seeing "that a new money supply could simply be created out of government instruments, that a positive psychology of money was wrapped up with prospects for business confidence, and that both were essential for economic growth."[31]

In 1790, Hamilton presented his Report of Public Credit and broached his plans for creating a mint that would coin silver and gold at a ratio of 15 to 1 and the Bank of the United States, which would generate revenue for the new government. Hamilton capitalized the bank with $10 million, $8 million from individual subscriptions – one-quarter in gold and silver and three-quarters in 6 percent public debt – and $2 million in cash borrowed from abroad.[32]

He believed that guaranteeing regular interest payments would raise and stabilize security prices and drive away speculators who were diverting investment from commerce and agriculture and aggravating the specie shortage.[33] "A national debt if it is not excessive will be to us a national blessing; it will be a powerful cement of our union," Hamilton wrote. "It will also create a necessity for keeping up taxation to a degree which without being oppressive, will be a spur to industry."[34] Historians Donald F. Swanson and Andrew P. Trout wrote that Hamilton "saw his funding system as basically a contract, a promise to the nation's creditors that revenues would be sufficient to cover all government spending, especially interest on the debt. The penalty for failure to live up to that promise was more than just passing a debt to one's children; it was tantamount to bequeathing them a nation lacking credit and financial economic soundness."[35]

Thomas Jefferson, who was famously no friend of Hamilton, vigorously opposed the national debt and the central bank. He feared that relying on bank notes would create economic instability and a permanent creditor faction that depended on taxpayers, and instead, he wanted taxes to be payable in non-interest-bearing bills of credit to fund the new government. Jefferson was appalled at what he considered Hamilton's use of the bank as an "engine of influence" to create a "moneyed aristocracy" that would get rich by speculating, stockjobbing, and other financial manipulations. "No one has a natural right to the trade of a money lender, but he who has the money to lend," Jefferson said.[36]

Hamilton prevailed, and when the books were opened on the $8 million in capital stock, available to "any person, co-partnership, or body politic," on July 4, 1791, the securities were heavily oversubscribed within an hour as wealthy merchants, prominent professionals and speculators, and influential politicians snapped them up. Harvard College, Massachusetts Bank, and the State of New York were among the subscribers.[37] Until its non-recharter and dissolution in 1811 (following a campaign under President Jefferson's administration charging that the bank was constraining economic development), the Bank of the United States functioned and flourished as the engine of business and finance that Hamilton promised.[38] Hamilton's financial revolution put into place all the components of the modern financial system: public finances and debt management, a stable monetary unity, a central bank, a banking system, securities markets, and more accessible charting provisions for business corporations.[39]

Hamilton's bimetallic standard, or bimetallism, in which the government recognizes fixed ratios of gold and silver as legal tender, would provide fodder for heated debate well into the next century and beyond.

Following the Yellow Brick Road

Wars take their toll on national treasuries, and the US Civil War was no exception. In 1861, the year the war broke out, bankers were sent into a panic after the Treasury issued a particularly bleak budget report and became convinced that investors would lose confidence in bank notes and begin to demand a massive gold outflow. On December 30, they suspended their notes' convertibility into gold, and the US government immediately suspended the right to convert Treasury notes into specie. Just like that, the notes had become worthless pieces of paper – but Unionists kept the faith. When Congress passed the first Legal Tender Act authorizing the government to issue US Notes, an inconvertible currency that came to be known as greenbacks, in February 1862, the public accepted the paper as good money. Even as the greenbacks' value in gold fluctuated wildly with speculation about future war costs, most people believed they would indeed be able to redeem their greenbacks for gold at some point after the war.[40]

There were still plenty of people who weren't quite sure that greenbacks would ever be redeemable for gold, of course, and that's why the notes never did hold parity with gold coins. As people hoarded gold coins throughout the war, their circulation plummeted from more than $200 million when the war broke out in 1860 to a low point of $65 million in 1875. That year, Congress passed legislation pledging full resumption of greenback convertibility by January 1, 1879, and authorizing the Treasury to borrow the money to acquire a gold reserve if it had to.[41] Just like that, the United States was no longer on the bimetallic standard that Hamilton had created nearly a century earlier. It was officially on the international gold standard, where it remained until World War I, and the premium on gold disappeared.[42]

The move away from bimetallism had been all but cemented two years earlier, when Congress, with huge majorities in both the House and the Senate, passed the Coinage Act of 1873, listing various denominations of gold and silver coins the Treasury would mint. Whether by design or oversight, the list did not include the standard silver dollar that Hamilton had established in the United States' first coinage. Bimetallists were outraged, as were farmers and laborers who wanted devalued dollars backed by silver as well as gold to reduce their debt burdens.[43] Senators called it the "crime of the nineteenth century" and "the greatest legislative crime and the most stupendous conspiracy against the welfare of the people of the United States and of Europe which this or any other age has witnessed."[44]

OZ AS ALLEGORY

Many people believe Frank Baum's 1900 book *The Wonderful Wizard of Oz* was a critique of US monetary policy and a parable for the Populists. Dorothy was the average American, her magic slippers represented the free silver movement, the Scarecrow was the farmer, the Tin Woodman the factory worker, and the Cowardly Lion was William Jennings Bryan.

This anger gave rise to the Populist movement and its leader, William Jennings Bryan, "the boy orator from the Platte," who ran unsuccessfully as the Democratic presidential nominee in 1896, 1900, and 1908. Jennings will always be remembered for his rousing "cross of gold" speech railing against the Eastern bankers' and industrialists' "hard money" policy and calling for unlimited silver coinage at a ratio to gold of 16 to 1. "Having behind us the commercial interests and the laboring interests and all the toiling masses, we shall answer their demands for a gold standard by saying to them, you shall not press down upon the brow of labor this crown of thorns," he famously said. "You shall not crucify mankind upon a cross of gold."[45]

The US government wasn't swayed. In 1900, President William McKinley used a new gold pen to sign the Gold Standard Act[46] establishing gold as the only standard for redeeming paper money, at 25.8 grains of 90 percent purity gold to the dollar.[47] Silver would be used only as tokens. "By this bill, the declaration for the gold standard is made clear and strong," the New York *Times* reported.[48] The act also created a $150 million redemption fund to be used for no other purpose than the redemption of greenbacks and Treasury notes and gave the Treasury Secretary power to sell bonds to replenish the fund should it drop below $100 million. Finally, it set the stage for greater expansion of bank credit and money supply by making it easier for national banks to open branches in small towns and rural areas and to issue credit,[49] which would have far-reaching implications in the century to come.

The US economy was chugging ahead full steam at the turn of the century, but the financial system was often disrupted by currency panics, which were triggered when business and agriculture needs outstripped supplies and exacerbated by incentives for people and banks to hoard liquidity during the shortfalls.[50] Many influential people began calling for a central US bank, like England and France had (and the United States briefly had), which they believed could stop the panics by providing liquidity through an "elastic" currency that could be increased or decreased as the economy demanded. These voices won out, and the Federal Reserve System was founded in 1913 to "provide a means by which periodic panics which shake the American Republic and do it enormous injury shall be stopped."[51] Specifically charged with meeting business and industry's liquidity needs as a means of keeping the financial system and the economy stable, the Fed was given the power to supply liquidity to banks when credit was needed and reduce liquidity when the economy needed to retract. It would issue notes that were to be secured 100 percent with commercial paper and an additional 40 percent reserve in gold. Member banks could obtain the notes by rediscounting their customers' paper with local federal reserve banks.[52]

The currency panics subsided, but very soon it wouldn't matter. All national and international monetary systems were destroyed during World War I, and the Fed was not able to hold back the economic devastation of the Great Depression. "Tragically, the Fed failed to meet its mandate to maintain stability," Ben S. Bernanke, who served as Fed chairman from 2006 until 2014, wrote in 2013. "In particular, although the Fed provided substantial liquidity to the financial system following the 1929 stock market crash, its response to the subsequent banking panics of the 1930s was limited at best; the widespread bank failures and the collapse in money and credit that ensued were major sources of the economic downturn."[53]

"Breaking of the Gold Fetters"

At the turn of the twentieth century, nearly every nation in the modern industrial world was on the gold standard. Great Britain, the world's industrial and mercantile superpower, relied on the standard to keep trade free and secure foreign investments until the outbreak of World War I caused banks in London to stop the flow of credit and start calling in loans, triggering financial chaos as international gold shipments were halted and free gold markets closed down. After the war, Britain was a mere shadow of the financial powerhouse it had been, and the world's financial systems were yet again in shambles. A backlog of consumer and business demand and the expansion of money in circulation during the war fueled runaway worldwide inflation. Currencies' exchange rates, without a fixed gold parity, were allowed to float relative to other currencies.[54]

From 1925 to 1928, most European countries and the United States followed Britain's lead and went back on the gold standard in hopes that it would hasten economic and financial reconstruction. It was a big mistake, wrote Adolph C. Miller, a member of the Federal Reserve Board, in 1936. "Events soon proved that the world was not yet ready for the restoration of the gold standard," he wrote. "It was with difficulty and only with the liberal assistance of the United States that the newly restored gold currencies of Europe and elsewhere were able to maintain themselves. ... The world was too disorganized, on both the economic and the financial side, to provide the conditions essential for the satisfactory operation of the gold standard."[55]

As uncertainty about the stability of key currencies mounted, central banks began liquidating their foreign-exchange balances and replacing them with gold reserves, and the share of foreign exchange in global monetary reserves fell from 37 percent at the end of 1928 to 11 percent by the end of 1931.[56] Interest rates skyrocketed, banks closed, credit dried up, and deflation ruled the day. Britain, besieged by gold outflows and sterling weakness during the Great Depression, went off the standard in fall 1931, in a move that First National Bank of New York President Jackson E. Reynolds said was "like the end of the world." Tom Johnston, a former parliamentary secretary for Scotland, quipped, "Nobody told us we could do that."[57] John Maynard Keynes, then an up-and-coming economist, claimed that "there are few Englishmen who do not rejoice in the breaking of the gold fetters."[58] A mass exodus of countries followed, until the United States and a small European "gold bloc" were the only countries left adhering to it[59] – but not for much longer.

In November 1932, Franklin Roosevelt was elected president. The next spring, in one of his first official acts, he pushed through the Emergency Banking Act of 1933, suspending specie payments in hopes of triggering domestic price increases. He used that law and the 1917 Trading with the Enemy Act to prohibit banks from paying out or exporting gold coin and bullion, making international gold flows impossible and terminating any immediate link between gold and the money supply.[60] With the Gold Reserve Act of 1934, Roosevelt raised the mint price of gold by 59 percent, abolished gold coin as a component of the monetary system, and had all gold coins withdrawn from circulation and melted into 27-pound ingots that would be stored three floors deep in the ground[61] in fortified vaults at the soon-to-be-built United States Bullion Depository at Fort Knox, Kentucky. Gold would be a commodity rather than money. Newly authorized to regulate or prohibit exporting and hoarding of gold and silver, Roosevelt issued executive orders requiring all persons to exchange all gold coin, gold certificates, and bullion for paper currencies or bank deposits and for the banks to deliver the goods to the Federal Reserve.[62]

Conservatives, financiers, politicians, and academics were scandalized – some even called it the end of the world – but by most accounts, Roosevelt's nationalization of gold did what he wanted it to. In 1933, Jesse H. Jones, a member of the Reconstruction Finance Corporation and Roosevelt's future Commerce Secretary, wrote: "In spite of pessimistic predictions before the step was taken, the feeling engendered by the suspension of gold in 1931 was one of newly found freedom. The fall in the external value of our currency actually stimulated trade."[63] From 1933 to 1937, industrial production in the United States increased by 60 percent, wholesale prices rose 31 percent, and unemployment fell from 25 percent to 14 percent. From its low point of 40 in 1932, the Dow Jones Industrial Average surged to 200 in 1937.[64]

By then, sinister forces had begun to take hold in Europe, however, and World War II would again throw the world financial system into total chaos. Shortly after the war ended, on July 1, 1944, 730 delegates from 44 nations spent three weeks at the Mount Washington Hotel in Carroll, New Hampshire, an area known as Bretton Woods, creating a postwar economy out of the ashes.[65] The system they came up with during the United Nations Monetary and Financial Conference was a weak variant of the gold standard in which only the United States fixed the price of the dollar in terms of gold and all other convertible currencies were pegged to the dollar.[66] The dollar was defined as one thirty-fifth of an ounce of gold, and the United States kept the anchor stable by being willing to buy and sell gold to other Treasuries and Central Banks for a completely unrealistic $35 per ounce.[67]

In establishing the International Monetary Fund to promote financial stability and monetary cooperation, economist Milton Friedman wrote, the delegates gave gold an even smaller role, requiring convertibility into gold only for the United States and only for external purposes.[68] He called it a "pseudo-gold standard and not a real one" because there was no direct relation between US gold holdings and the money supply.[69] He and several others predicted the system would fail, and sure enough, by the 1960s it was collapsing under the strain of the United States' trade and budgetary deficits[70] and the cost of funding the Vietnam War.[71]

WILL PAY TO THE BEARER UPON DEMAND

A gold-standard 1928 dollar bill identified as a "**United States Note**" rather than a **Federal Reserve note**. The words "Will Pay to the Bearer on Demand" do not appear on today's currency.

Source: Public Domain; https://commons.wikimedia.org/wiki/File:One_dollar_1928.jpg

Table 1.1 The Price of Gold 1840–1970[72]

Year	Gold Price $/ozt
1840	$20
1900	$20
1920	$20
1940	$33
1960	$35
1970	$35

"Let Me Lay to Rest the Bugaboo ... "

The official price of gold had been relatively stable from 1840 through 1970, as shown in Table 1.1. However, by 1971, the Vietnam War was causing runaway inflation in the United States, and the world was losing faith in its ability to anchor the Bretton Woods system. Gold was selling for far more than $35 per ounce in the commodities market, and international speculators were pressuring foreign governments to buy gold from the United States at $35 per ounce and make a profit by selling it on the open market. More and more western European nations were demanding that the United States exchange gold for their dollar assets,[73] and in early August 1971, the British economic representative went in person to the Treasury and asked for $3 billion in gold. Trouble was, the United States didn't have it. In fact, it had only about a third of the gold bullion it needed to cover the dollars in foreign hands.[74] On Friday the 13th, President Richard Nixon flew his sixteen major economic policymakers in his helicopter to a top-secret meeting at Camp David, where they could figure out what to do.[75]

Paul W. McCracken, who was at the Camp David summit, described a mission "launched with cloak-and-dagger stealth." Participants were told to come with clothes for the weekend, tell no one (including families) where they would be, and while there were allowed no contact with the outside world. When they emerged with a plan on August 15, McCracken wrote, "a man fundamentally committed to the superiority of a liberal, market-organized economic system (as were his principal advisers) launched a 'New Economic Policy' (NEP) calling for quite detailed government controls of economic life." (The slogan and acronym NEP were quickly nixed after Nixon's speech writers discovered Lenin had used it in the 1920s.[76]) The NEP closed the gold window and put the international economic order on a floating rate basis while placing a mandatory, comprehensive freeze on prices and wages for 90 days.

In what became known as the "Nixon shock," on Sunday night the president interrupted *Bonanza* to announce that he had directed Treasury Secretary John Connolly to suspend the convertibility of the dollar into gold or other assets. (Aides who were there said the discussion about whether or not to interrupt one of the most popular shows on television took up nearly as much time as discussing the speech and how the economic program would work. Nixon didn't want to do it, but his aides convinced him the speech had to be delivered before the markets opened on Monday morning.[77]) Nixon went on TV and laid out the plan. "What does it mean for you?" he asked. "Let me lay to rest the bugaboo of what is called devaluation. If you want to buy a foreign car or take a trip abroad, market conditions may cause your dollar to buy slightly less. But if you are among the overwhelming majority of Americans who buy American-made products in America, your dollar will be worth just as much tomorrow as it is today. The effect of this action, in other words, will be to stabilize the dollar."[78]

Critics predicted that without the discipline of tying money to gold, the United States would create money on an inflationary scale – and it did. By the third quarter of 1974, the consumer price index was 23 percent above where it had been in the third quarter of 1971.[79] Prices in the United States rose by 157 percent over 11 years in the greatest inflationary event in the country's history since the Revolutionary War.[80] President Ford declared inflation the nation's number one problem in 1974, a year before economist C. Lowell Harris wrote:- "Today the United States as well as the rest of the world is struggling with massive inflation, which seems to threaten the very foundations of society. Economists and political leaders do not agree on how it can be controlled, but they do believe that it poses a problem of the first magnitude."[81]

The overheated economy boiled over in 1980. Inflation was running over 12 percent,[82] and the prime interest rate hit 21.5 percent.[83] Many believed the United States was on the brink of financial disaster. Paul Volcker, the Federal Reserve chairman, pledged to stop the inflation by restricting the money supply, and he pushed the interest rate to near 20 percent in 1980, triggering a painful recession in which unemployment rose to nearly 11 percent and the banking system nearly went insolvent.[84] Though many people questioned whether the draconian means were worth the end, Volcker's plan did accomplish what he said it would. By the end of 1981, inflation dropped to 9 percent, then 6 percent, then 4 percent, where it has hovered for more than three decades.[85] Volcker and his supporters had won – but at a severe cost. "In retrospect," said economist Dean Beker, "I find it hard to say that the best thing we could've done is push the unemployment rate up to 11 percent and have that really whack inflation. It did do that. But it was at a really terrible cost."[86] One way to measure the destruction of the purchasing power of a currency is relative to gold. As shown in Table 1.2 The Price of Gold 1970–2010 once the tether was broken, the purchasing power of the United States dollar plummeted as measured in gold.

Table 1.2   The Price of Gold 1970–2010[87]

Year	Gold Price $/ozt
1970	$35
1990	$383
2010	$1,225

Chapter 2

The Fundamentals
of Money

"It is well enough that people of the nation do not understand
our banking and monetary system, for if they did, I believe
there would be a revolution before tomorrow morning."

– Henry Ford

As we saw in Chapter 1, human culture's obsession with money
has been a determining factor in so much of our history, a constant subject of manipulation and the cause of so much brutality.
But what, exactly, is money? That question can send you into a rabbit
hole that could swallow you right up. As Robert A. Leonard writes in
Money and Language, "Money and language are both highly abstract social
conventions. Although we deal with them daily on what appears to be a
concrete level, they both really exist only as social contracts; money and
language are, if you will, all in our minds."[1]

When most people Google *what is money?*, Wikipedia is one of the first entries to pop up with this definition: "Money is any item or verifiable record that is generally accepted as payment for goods and services and repayment of debts, such as taxes, in a particular country or socio-economic context. The main functions of money are distinguished as: a medium of exchange, a unit of account, a store of value, and sometimes, a standard of deferred payment. Any item or verifiable record that fulfills these functions can be considered as money." Wikipedia further defines a country's money supply as "currency (banknotes and coins) and, depending on the particular definition used, one or more types of bank money (the balances held in checking accounts, savings accounts, and other types of bank accounts). Bank money, which consists only of records (mostly computerized in modern banking), forms by far the largest part of broad money in developed countries."[2] We'll want to pay particular attention to these references to a "verifiable record," as they'll become very important when we talk about blockchain technology in later chapters.

But let's just say aliens came down to Earth from somewhere out there in space and demanded all the money on the planet. Even if we wanted to give it to them, how would we comply? For now, let's start with the basic premise that money is the paper bills printed by the government. According to the Federal Reserve, there are actually a stunningly low number of legal tender bills in circulation when you consider the number of financial transactions that take place; in 2017, there were 21.1 billion $1 bills, 1.2 billion $2 bills, 3 billion $5 bills, 2 billion $10 bills, 9.2 billion $20 bills, 1.7 billion $50 bills, and 12.5 billion $100 bills, for a total of 41.6 billion bills.[3]

We could give the aliens all the paper bills in the world, but we all know there's more to money than paper bills. There also are checking accounts, savings accounts, money markets, and other short-term deposits such as bank notes and certificates of deposit. But it doesn't stop there. In 2016 the World Economic Forum counted $7.9 trillion in gold and silver reserves, $7.6 trillion in commercial real estate investments, and $70 trillion in global stock markets in its estimates of how much "broad," or easily accessible, money is in the world. And this is just the beginning of the money equation. Debt is a form of money. Short-term Treasury bonds are quickly and easily convertible to money for purchasing power. All bonds and loans that can be sold and converted to money quickly and easily are another form of money. It is estimated that there are $1.2 quadrillion in funds invested in derivatives (contracts that derive their value from underlying entities' performances),[4] which can be converted to money.[5] To make things even more complicated, available but unused credit is a form of money. Even if you had no money in your checking account, you could use your credit card as "money" to make virtually all of your day-to-day purchases.

To say today's global money market supply is complicated is an understatement. At best, money is an illusion, a conversation, and once you start to peel back the layers, it starts to get very abstract and weird – especially when you consider how important the whole concept is in our society. Finances are consistently found to be the leading cause of stress in relationships and one of the leading causes of divorce, and one poll even found that 40 percent of American adults thought more often about money than about sex.[6] In a well-publicized 2013 study, a group of psychology researchers suggested that people hold onto money as a way to deal with the anxiety of knowing they will inevitably die. "We conclude that, beyond its pragmatic utility, money possesses a strong psychological meaning that helps to buffer existential anxiety," they wrote.[7] Their studies were inspired by the work of American anthropologist Ernest Becker, who wrote that "in its power to manipulate physical and social reality, money in some ways secures one against contingency and accident."[8]

We say that money talks, is the root of all evil, is power, can't buy happiness or love (or can it?), and makes the world go 'round. It is an integral part of our lives and our psyches – and yet, we don't have a good collective definition of what it is and who is overseeing it. "Money is one of the most important pieces of 'social technology' ever developed," economist Geoffrey Ingham writes, "but as an object of study in its own right it is neglected by the dominant or mainstream traditions not only in modern economics but also in sociology."[9]

Narrow Money versus Broad Money

The biggest delineating factor in economists' debates about what comprises money is the line between narrow money, which is easily convertible into cash, and broad money, which generally includes anything of value that resembles money. The debate stretches back for centuries – even to Aristotle, who said "money is as it were our surety; for it must be possible for us to get what we want by bringing the money."[10] Seventeenth-century economist Rice Vaughan wrote in 1675 that money was a pledge protecting people from "the corruption of man's nature" and giving them confidence to conduct transactions based on quid pro quo.[11]

Narrow money proponents, or functionalists, generally echo the views of eighteenth-century British philosopher David Hume, one of the earliest proponents of the narrow money argument, who stated, "Money is not, properly speaking, one of the subjects of commerce, but only the instrument which men have agreed upon to facilitate the exchange of one commodity for another. It is none of the wheels of trade: it is the oil which renders the motion of the wheels more smooth and easy."[12] Probably the most famous advocate of this idea was eighteenth-century economist Adam Smith, who compared money to a road that all produce must pass over to get to market. "Nobody would be so foolish as to expect to eat a road, yet man is always being surprised afresh by the discovery that he cannot eat money," D.H. Robertson wrote in the book *Money* in 1922. "He is so pleased with his ingenious invention that he is always expecting too much of it."[13]

In 1880, just as fiat paper money was beginning to replace gold and silver coins, British economist Bonamy Price expanded the definition of money, pointing out, "Other things can buy besides coins – a piece of paper with writing on it, a promise, will often make a purchase as easily as a sovereign. If the inquirer has recourse to the language of the City, in the counting-house and the daily press, the puzzle will grow darker. He will find money said to be abundant or scarce, and yet there may not be an ounce more of gold and silver in the country. He will hear of it as dear or cheap, and yet not a particle more or less of any commodity in any shop or warehouse is being given in exchange for it. New senses of the word will be pressing in upon him from every side; mere lines in banking ledgers will be spoken of as money."[14]

In the late nineteenth century, the notion that precious coins were the only "true money" was being replaced with a much broader view, paving the way for A. Mitchell Innes's *Credit Theory of Money*, published in 1913, asserting that sales and purchases are the exchange of a commodity for credit, and their value depends on debtors' rights to release themselves from debts by tender of equivalent debts owed by creditors and creditors' obligation to accept this tender in satisfaction of their credit. This theory posits we're all at the same time both debtors and creditors of each other, with banks as the clearinghouse through which our debts and credits are centralized and set against each other. "In practice, therefore, any good credit will pay any debt," Innes wrote.[15] Innes believed that as an entire community's debts and credits were set out against each other, every merchant who paid for purchases with bills and every banker who issued notes or authorized drafts to be drawn on them were in effect issuing money. "Of all the false ideas current on the subject of money none is more harmful than that which attributes to the government the special function of monopolizing the issues of money," Innes wrote.[16]

Innes traced the flaw in the functionalist argument to Adam Smith, "backed up by a few passages from Homer and Aristotle and the writings of travelers in primitive lands." Smith had cited the use of nails as money in Scotland and dried cod in Newfoundland, but in reality, the Scottish villagers sold materials and food to the nail makers and charged the value of nails they bought against that debt, and Newfoundland fishermen sold dried fish to traders for credit to pay for supplies. "A moment's reflection shows that a staple commodity could not be used as money, because *ex hypothesi*, the medium of exchange is equally receivable by all members of the community. Thus, if the fishers paid for their supplies in cod, the traders would equally have to pay for their cod in cod, an obvious absurdity." Smith thought he had discovered currency, Innes continued, but he had merely found credit.[17] And credit could actually be better than gold, because it was a good or value someone could deliver to you in the future.

The Theory of Money and Credit

In 1912, the year before Innes released his *Credit Theory of Money*, Ludwig von Mises published *The Theory of Money and Credit*. Some of the pillars of this seminal work help establish our foundation for understanding money, particularly the importance of sound money.

The principle of sound money that guided nineteenth-century monetary doctrines and policies was a product of classical political economy. It was an essential part of the liberal program as developed by eighteenth-century social philosophy and propagated in the following century by the most influential political parties of Europe and America. ... It is impossible to grasp the meaning of the idea of sound money if one does not realize that it was devised as an instrument for the protection of civil liberties against despotic inroads on the part of governments. Ideologically it belongs in the same class with political constitutions and bills of rights. The demand for constitutional guarantees and for bills of rights was a reaction against arbitrary rule and the nonobservance of old customs by kings. The postulate of sound money was first brought up as a response to the princely practice of debasing the coinage. It was later carefully elaborated and perfected in the age which —through the experience of the American continental currency, the paper money of the French Revolution and the British restriction period — had learned what a government can do to a nation's currency system. ... Thus the sound-money principle has two aspects. It is affirmative in approving the market's choice of a commonly used medium of exchange. It is negative in obstructing the government's propensity to meddle with the currency system.[18]

Von Mises went on to explain that money has a use or purpose with respect to managing wealth.

What is called storing money is a way of using wealth. The uncertainty of the future makes it seem advisable to hold a larger or smaller part of one's possessions in a form that will facilitate a change from one way of using wealth to another, or transition from the ownership of one good to that of another, in order to preserve the opportunity of being able without difficulty to satisfy urgent demands that may possibly arise in the future for goods that will have to be obtained by way of exchange.[19]

He also discusses the quantity of money.

In the first place, it must be recognized that from the economic point of view there is no such thing as money lying idle. All money, whether in reserves or literally in circulation (i.e. in process of changing hands at the very moment under consideration), is devoted in exactly the same way to the performance of a monetary function. The stock of money of the community is the sum of the stocks of individuals; there is no such thing as errant money.[20]

Von Mises gives us another piece of our foundational pillar: a view that "money" is required to be a sound asset where one can store wealth to protect against the future and that the "stock of money of the community is the sum of the stocks of individuals." Fiat money, while capable of obtaining this objective, may in fact have another long-term incentive.

Full Faith and Credit: Money Is the Government's Debt

It's fascinating to note that Innes published his theory the same year the Federal Reserve was established. If Innes and his followers woke up from the dead today, they would be absolutely amazed – and likely horrified – at where our conversation about money has gone. Today, money is created when the Fed, in its own words, writes a check "drawn on itself" by issuing Treasury bills.[21] (If you or I tried to write checks based on nothing but good faith in ourselves, we'd likely end up spending time in prison.) Treasury bills are interest-bearing monetary liabilities, and money is basically the monetary system's debt to the public. (Get your head around that one.) MIT civil engineer Edward S. Shaw wrote in *Money, Income, and Monetary Policy* in 1950: "The monetary system creates and destroys money – expands and contracts the money supply. It is a money factory, setting up new monetary liabilities to pay for assets or to pay off nonmonetary claims against itself. It is also a money incinerator, retiring monetary liabilities by disposing of assets or by incurring nonmonetary obligations."[22]

What we've seen over the decades is that the system is set up to continue as a money factory. Since 1917, when the President and Treasury were given authority to borrow, the legal limit was raised about 90 times, from $49 billion in 1940 to 5,950 billion in 2000.[23] By 2019, the US national debt was hovering around $21 trillion, according to USDebtClock.org. Continued debt is built into the system, and the government doesn't have a lot of incentive to put a lid on it. When the Fed purchases and sells Treasury bonds through regularly scheduled "open market operations," it creates a demand for more government-issued debt and the money to buy it.[24] It's a cycle that can only continue to spiral up, up, up – until it can't anymore, and that's a probability that keeps a lot of economists up at night. Against this backdrop of "full faith and credit," the US government uses a shady accounting method to report its debt – a system that would likely send the CFO of any publicly traded company straight to jail if they used it.

Quite simply, the Treasury leaves entitlement programs – $14.1 trillion in unfunded Social Security liabilities and $32.5 trillion in unfunded Medicare liabilities in 2017 –off its balance sheet.[25] Economists Laurence Kotlikoff and Scott Burns predicted in 2012 these unfunded liabilities would "result in significant economic upheaval as the US government fights both the laws of economics and mathematics in a futile attempt to fulfill its financial obligations."[26] Kotlikoff estimates the unfunded liabilities are closer to $210 trillion,[27] and the US Debt Clock puts them at $126 trillion[28], but even the reported $46.7 trillion is a confounding number. All the government's gold ($300 billion worth) and land ($1.8 trillion in holdings) would not come close to covering its debt. In fact, all of its $3 trillion in assets would not even cover 2 percent of its obligations.[29] "So," Kingston University London economics professor Steve Keen concluded in a 2015 *Forbes* article, "the mighty US dollar is not backed by gold or silver or anything at all; it's simply an accounting trick."

That should keep us all up at night. As Randall Wray points out in *Credit and State Theories of Money: The Contributions of A. Mitchell Innes*, the government has no liability with respect to its money. "When it prints a bill or creates money, it is not obligated to do anything but accept that form of money as a payment for taxes," he writes. "And herein lies the problem: lacking a tether, governments have an incentive to facilitate inflation much more than they have an incentive to maintain stable prices. We see this reflected not only in policy, and in actions, but in prices over time. As Milton Friedman said, "Inflation is taxation without representation."[30]

M1 AND M2

Just how closely money supply is linked to bank accounts and how monetary supply is a function of the banking system is evident in the way the Federal Reserve System tracks the money supply in the United States based on two types of "money." M1 is money that can be used immediately to facilitate transactions and does not need to be converted, like cash and traveler's checks. M2 includes M1 plus things that can easily be converted to M1, like savings accounts, money market funds (multiple investors' deposits pooled and invested safely), and CDs – all of which are often referred to as "near money."

SLANG TERMS FOR MONEY THROUGH THE YEARS

Dough, jack, spondulics, rhino, simoleans, mazuma, gingerbread, kale, moss, long green, salt, dust, insect powder, tin, chink, blunt, brass, dibs, chips, beans, rocks, clinkers, plunks, horse nails, iron men, mopuses, bucks, bones, wad, oof, ooftish, yellow boys, thick 'uns, shekels, barrel (political), velvet (gained without effort), palm oil (bribe), the needful, the ready, the actual, corn in Egypt, plum ($100,000), grand ($1,000), monkey ($500), century ($100), pony ($25), tenner ($10), ten spot, fiver, five spot, cart wheel (silver dollar), bob (shilling), tanner (sixpence), two bits (quarter), moolah, greenbacks, fin, sawbuck ($10), double sawbuck ($20), two bits (25 cents), four bits (half dollar), six bits (75 cents).[31]

Chapter 3

Banking – An Overview

"I sincerely believe … that banking establishments are more dangerous than standing armies."

– Thomas Jefferson

"We should not have a system that's this fragile, that causes this much risk to the economy."

– Tim Geithner

One of our founding fathers, Thomas Jefferson, believed banking was an inherently dangerous establishment, one he hardly put any faith into. He would be appalled, then, if he could see the global banking system today, a house of cards so fragile that a Treasury Secretary some 200 years later would declare it a risk to the economy. Since humans learned to institutionalize transactions with each other's money, the practice of banking has been marked by cunning and ignorance, reverence and revolt.

Banking is an institutional pillar in virtually every culture on this planet, older than most religions and often more revered, practiced in some form since the earliest civilizations. In ancient Mesopotamia, repayments for commodities that had been deposited at palaces and temples were recorded on transferable clay tablets that paid (sometimes compounded) interest with rates based on agricultural measures.[1] In the eighth century in China, shops that stored people's valuables for safekeeping issued deposit receipts that eventually became circulated like money. By the ninth century, unscrupulous shopkeepers had discovered they could issue and hand out more of these receipts than they had valuables on deposit,[2] and they invented one of the most important tenets of banking known as fractional reserve–a system economist Murray N. Rothbard, one of its most vocal critics, calls a "form of theft known as *embezzlement*."[3]

As banking evolved from the Jews of Venice, who did their business while seated on benches behind tables on ghetto streets, to the Medici family of Italy, which amassed enormous power by creating the first decentralized banking system, the practice of fractional reserves continued. In the seventeenth century, European banks including the Swedish Riksbank and the Dutch Wisselbank were known as Lanebanks, meaning they lent amounts in excess of the metallic reserves they held for people.[4]

Rothbard explains that in fractional reserve banking, the bank is not borrowing from depositors and pledging to pay it back on a future date but is pledging to pay it back at any time, on demand. Banks are vulnerable because their liabilities are instantaneous but their assets aren't. "The bank creates new money out of thin air and does not, like everyone else, have to acquire money by producing and selling its services," Rothbard wrote. "In short, the bank is *already* and at all times bankrupt; but its bankruptcy is only *revealed* when customers get suspicious and precipitate 'bank runs.' No other business experiences a phenomenon like a 'run.' No other business can be plunged into bankruptcy overnight simply because its customers decide to repossess their own property. No other business creates fictitious new money, which will evaporate when truly gauged."[5]

At the end of the seventeenth century, the cash-strapped throne in England had come to realize that banking could be a very lucrative enterprise, and it took things a step further, establishing the Bank of England to help finance its war by converting government debt into bank shares in 1694. In 1742 this precedent-setting central bank was granted a partial monopoly on the issue of non-interest-bearing banknotes.[6] This was precedent-setting because, as Niall Ferguson explains in *The Ascent of Money*, it changed the definitions – indeed, the very nature – of money and banking. "No longer was money to be understood, as the Spaniards had understood it in the sixteenth century, as precious metal that had been dug up, melted down, and minted into coins," Ferguson writes. "Now money represented the sum total of specific liabilities (deposits and reserves) incurred by banks. Credit was, quite simply, the total of banks' assets (loans). Some of this money might indeed still consist of precious metal, though a rising proportion of that would be held in the central bank's vault. But most of it would be made up of those banknotes and token coins recognized as legal tender along with the invisible money that existed only in deposit account statements."[7]

In the more rebellious United States, the central Federal Reserve System was established in 1913 only after decades of periodic financial panics, crises, and bank failures, and it has been a subject of much debate and controversy ever since. The Fed is the central authority that loans money to all other banks, primarily through advances backed by US government securities that it buys every week from an elite group of private dealers. When it wants to encourage banks to borrow, the Fed lowers the interest rate it charges, known as the rediscount rate, and it does the opposite when it wants to slow down borrowing. Under the Federal Reserve Act of 1913, reserve requirements – the amount of money banks must keep on hand to cover their loans – were lowered from 21.1 percent to 11.6 percent. Banks were suddenly free to create twice as much money as they could before – and by 1917, they had doubled the money supply in the United States.[8] Decades of financial engineering and tinkering would ensue.

A System That Multiplies Money

Banks hold less in reserves than they owe against their deposit liabilities, which, today, are considered money. To be sure we are on the same page of understanding, when you deposit money at a bank, you might think that you "deposited money at a bank" and may have the perception that it is "safe." What you have in fact done through your deposit is made a loan to the bank. And, like any loan, it might be safe, and it might not be. Banks take your money and lend it out to others, acting as an intermediary. They are not required to keep your money, specifically, segregated, and you do not have a specific claim against any specific asset. Instead, the depositor has a general claim against the bank. Because banks can lend out more than they have on deposit, the system creates more "money" than the money initially created by the central bank.

Giving central banks the authority to create and issue money also, naturally, gives them the ability to stimulate inflation. When banks grant loans at less than the natural interest rate to stimulate the economy, it causes an overall expansion in the economy, including credit expansion and price increases. When lots of cheap money is available, firms will reinvest and trigger cumulative inflation, during which prices increase and purchasing power falls.

Fractional reserve banking exacerbates this because it multiplies the base money supply by the amount that banks can "pyramid" new deposits on top of reserves —what is called a money multiplier (MM). Remember those M1 and M2 money supply measurements from the previous chapter? M is now defined as cash plus total bank reserves multiplied by MM, or M = Cash + (Total Bank Reserves × MM).[9] Under ordinary circumstances, inflation increases about 1 to 3 percent every year, but in hyperinflationary situations when prices spiral out of control as people's fears of prices going up cause them to raise their own prices in anticipation, it can spike as high as 70 percent, 80 percent, and, in some instances much higher. At this point, money stops serving two of its primary functions as a store of value and a unit of value.

Inflation, in essence, penalizes people who save their money and encourages people to take on debt that they can repay with degrading dollars, and it demeans the standard of living for just about everyone. "It should be clear that by printing new money to finance its deficits, the government and the early receivers of the new money benefit at the expense of those who receive the new money last or not at all: pensioners, fixed-income groups," Rothbard writes in *The Mystery of Banking*.

"The expansion of the money supply has caused inflation; but, more than that, the essence of inflation is the process by which a large and hidden tax is imposed on much of society for the benefit of government and the early receivers of the new money. Inflationary increases of the money supply are pernicious forms of tax because they are covert, and few people are able to understand why prices are rising."[10]

Money Is Credit, and Credit Is Money

Economist A. Mitchell Innes floated his Credit Theory – that a sale and purchase is the exchange of a commodity for credit independent of the value of any metal and based only on the debtor's obligation to pay and the creditor's right to acquire payment and accept the tender – in the *Banking Law Journal* in 1913. He believed credit existed before any other common medium of exchange did and all other forms simply reflected that. "Credit and credit alone is money," Innes wrote. "The monetary unit is an abstract standard for the measurement of credit and debt. It is liable to fluctuation and only remains stable if the law of the creation of credits and debts is observed."[11]

Innes's colleague Ludwig von Mises used this theory to justify his assumption that civilization would eventually forego narrow money altogether and move to a "pure credit" system. "If there were no artificial restriction of the credit system at all, and if the individual credit-issuing banks could agree to parallel procedure, then *the complete cessation of the use of money* would only be a question of time," Mises wrote.[12]

"Not for Profit, Not for Charity, but for Service"

Another important building block to our foundation is the evolution and existence of credit unions, which prove that banks do not have to be for-profit institutions. Originating as cooperative banks or "people's banks" in Germany in the 1850s, credit unions began cropping up in the United States at the turn of the century as formerly agrarian communities began to need access to unsecured loans, which most financial institutions didn't offer. In credit unions, people banded together in groups based on a common bond, perhaps working for the same company, so they could use their knowledge of each other's creditworthiness as collateral. Members received low-interest loans and were also owners, so failing to repay a loan would damage their reputation.[13]

St. Mary's Cooperative Credit Association, the first credit union in the United States, opened in Manchester, New Hampshire, in 1909. The credit union movement's patron saint at the time was Edward Filene, who created the Filene's Basement chain of retail stores. During his travels in India, Filene had seen how beneficial it could be when agricultural cooperative lenders gathered small deposits from Indian farmers and made small-value loans with them to members.[14] The movement's mission, as described by the League of Southeastern Credit Unions & Affiliates, couldn't sound more different than that of the corporate titans: "The credit union movement began with a simple idea – that people could achieve a better standard of living for themselves and others by pooling their savings and making loans to neighbors and co-workers. The philosophy of the credit union movement is 'Not for Profit, Not for Charity, But for Service.'"[15] The movement grew, and today about one in every three Americans relies on their local credit union to handle their finances.[16]

Credit unions are an important model to understand, but they were certainly not immune when the 2008 housing crisis went down. Severely overleveraged in subprime mortgage investment, the two largest corporate credit unions failed. As Aaron Klein wrote in *American Banker*, it was " a stark reminder that even within the nonprofit credit union world, the desire for greater return on investment can translate into risky behavior."[17]

Chapter 4

The Denationalization
of Money

"I do not think that it is an exaggeration to say that history is
largely a history of inflation, and usually of inflations
engineered by governments and for the gain of governments."

– Friedrich Hayek

During a recent trip to Paris, I went to two museums in one
day. The Crypte Archeologique de Notre-Dame is a sprawl-
ing archaeological dig that provides fascinating insights into
Parisian living from Gallo-Roman times (27 BC to 14 AD) through the
twentieth century. As I wandered through the crypt under the square
in front of Notre Dame checking out relics from 2,000 years of archi-
tectural and cultural evolution, I was struck by the stunning number of
exhibits in that museum centered around money and coins. Gold coins

47

were not only currency throughout the centuries, but they also helped people date different events throughout time. Their progressions and debasements mark the march of history.

Next, I visited the Musee d'Orsay, which undoubtedly has the world's largest and best collection of Impressionist and post-Impressionist masterpieces by painters including Oscar-Claude Monet, Edouard Manet, Pierre-Auguste Renoir, Paul Cezanne, Paul Gauguin, and Vincent Van Gogh. Seeing all their works together made it crystal clear how much Renoir inspired Monet, and in fact how all the artists fed off each other to create and drive the Impressionist movement. The painters steadily built off of the huge legacy left by the painters who came before them until Pablo Picasso came along and ripped through Impressionism's soft strokes with increasingly bold Cubism, Surrealism, and Realism.

I had plenty of time to hang out in cafes during my stay in Paris, and I reread Friedrich Hayek's 1976 classic *The Denationalization of Money* while I sipped my espresso. Hayek's call for competing private currencies was – and still is –considered Picasso-level radical, but just as Picasso evolved from Monet, he was building on the ideas of economists who had come before him. This legacy chain of economic theory starts with the father of economics, Adam Smith, who advocated for private money issuance in the eighteenth century,[1] and includes Irving Fisher, the first economist to call out fractional reserve banking as a scam, and Nobel Prize–winning economist Milton Friedman, who called for abolishing the US Federal Reserve and implementing an automatic rule for monetary growth rather than letting the central bank control interest rates and the money supply.[2]

Amazingly enough, Friedman also saw cryptocurrencies coming. "The one thing that's missing, but that will soon be developed, is a reliable e-cash, a method whereby on the internet you can transfer funds from A to B, without A knowing B or B knowing A," he said in 1999,[3] many years before anyone had ever heard of bitcoin.

Irving Fisher: Abolish Fractional Reserve Banking

The Great Depression was one of history's most epic economic fails, and it sent the economists of the day into major bouts of thinking, writing, and debating about how and why it happened and how to make sure it never happened again. In the early 1930s, at the height of the Great Depression, a group of leading US economists including Irving Fisher of Yale University published a monetary reform proposal that became known as the Chicago Plan (because many of the economists were from the University of Chicago), calling for separation of the banking system's monetary and credit functions by requiring 100 percent reserve backing for deposits. Fisher claimed eliminating sudden increases and contractions of bank credit and bank-created money supply would allow for much better control of a major source of business cycle fluctuations and eliminate bank runs while no longer having to create debt in order to create money would dramatically reduce both public and private debt.[4]

Fisher, the most prominent American economist of the early twentieth century, argued the "essence of the depression" came when "check-book" money fell from $22 billion in 1929 to $14 billion in 1933, and the "essence of the recovery" was when money expanded to $23 billion in 1937. He considered this "see-saw" inevitable as long as commercial banks could destroy and create money by lending and investing and called instead for "the outright abolition of deposit banking on the fractional reserve principle."[5] Under a 100 percent reserve system, Fisher wrote, "no action of the banks could alter the circulating medium in the least." Initially, he proposed the government could issue banks bonds that it would progressively acquire, adding 5 percent to the nation's money supply each year and bringing about "a complete divorce … between money as a governmental function and loaning as a banking function."[6]

Fisher and others were in contact with President Franklin Roosevelt about the plan, and FDR is said to have seriously considered it.[7] The economists didn't stand a chance against the powerful banking interests, however, and the fractional reserve system survived – though not without controversy. Our "just trust us" financial system that lets banks hold only a fraction of their deposits as reserves and lend the rest at interest has more than its share of critics, many of whom call for Chicago Plan–style reform.

In a 2012 International Monetary Fund working paper, Jaromir Benes and Michael Kumhof write that keeping money and credit quantity completely independent would make control of credit growth more straightforward because "banks would no longer be able, as they are today, to generate their own funding, deposits, in the act of lending, an extraordinary privilege that is not enjoyed by any other type of business. Rather, banks would become what many erroneously believe them to be today, pure intermediaries that depend on obtaining outside funding before being able to lend."[8]

Milton Friedman and Setting the Nominal Interest Rate to Zero

Milton Friedman, considered by many the most prominent American economist in the second half of the twentieth century, never studied directly with Fisher but was highly influenced by his ideas while a graduate student at the University of Chicago, where he spent most of his career. Like Fisher, Friedman believed inflation occurs when money supply rapidly outpaces output and asserted that a drop in the money supply caused the Great Depression.[9] "Just as banks all around the country were closing, the Fed raised the discount rate; that's the rate they charge for loans to banks," he told *Playboy* in 1973. "Bank failures consequently increased spectacularly. We might have had an economic downturn in the thirties anyway, but in the absence of the Federal Reserve system – with its enormous power to make a bad situation worse – it wouldn't have been anything like the scale we experienced."[10]

When inflation raged in the 1970s, Friedman blamed it on "excess demand" due to monetary ease,[11] and he spent much of his career meticulously documenting the failures of the Fed's discretionary monetary policy. He believed price stability could be preserved by expanding the money supply at a steady and known rate sufficient to finance the growth of real output allowing for a trend in velocity.[12] In *The Life and Times of Milton Friedman: Remembering the 20th Century's Most Influential Libertarian,* Brian Doherty explains: "The juicy libertarian implication of Friedman's dry and scientific work is that government stabilization attempts, whether through fiscal or monetary policy, are bound to fail, since the effects of money on the economy work only through a lag that's both long and variable. Any attempt to respond to an economic ailment by increasing or decreasing the money supply is apt to be either too little, too late or too much, too soon. When the Federal Reserve jiggers with the money supply, it is as likely to exacerbate problems as solve them."[13]

In 1969, Friedman proposed the Friedman Rule setting the nominal interest rate to zero so the marginal benefit to society of holding money would equal the marginal cost to society of producing it.[14] Friedman believed optimal policy would eliminate incentives to economize on using money, which makes it easier and more convenient for consumers to execute transactions. Under Friedman's Rule, the nominal interest rate equals the real interest rate plus expected inflation. If the real interest rate were around 2 to 3 percent, the central bank would seek to deflate at that same rate by reducing the nominal quantity of money.[15]

Friedman's theory became known as monetarism, and like the Chicago Plan, it has fierce critics and just-as-fierce disciples to this day. When he died in 2006, the *Wall Street Journal* wrote that Friedman "helped to shift the center of the debate in the US and abroad about the proper role of government in managing a nation's economy." Friedman's theory that policymakers couldn't maintain low unemployment by permitting higher inflation "holds sway at major central banks today, including the Fed, and helped to defeat the inflation of the 1970s and set the stage for the low inflation and low unemployment of the 1990s and today," the article stated.[16]

Friedrich Hayek: Denationalize Money

Of all the theories, from reactionary to radical, that were aired during the "econ wars" of the 1970s and 1980s, Friedrich Hayek's assertion in *Denationalization of Money* that "as soon as one succeeds in freeing oneself of the universally but tacitly accepted creed that a country must be supplied by its government with its own distinctive and exclusive currency, all sorts of interesting questions arise which have never been examined"[17] is perhaps the most extreme. Just as Nicolaus Copernicus revolutionized astronomy and science with his model of the universe placing the sun, not the earth, at the center during the Renaissance, Hayek broke open a monumental conversation with his radical theory about the center of money.

Blaming governments' monopoly over money issuing for recurrent periods of depression and unemployment, Hayek asserted that private enterprise should provide the public with a choice of currencies[18] that would be traded against each other and against commodities at floating exchange rates on the open market.[19] "When one studies the history of money one cannot help wondering why people should have put up for so long with governments exercising an exclusive power over 2,000 years that was regularly used to exploit and defraud them," he wrote. "This can be explained only by the myth (that the government prerogative was necessary) becoming so firmly established that it did not occur even to the professional students of these matters (for a long time including the present writer!) ever to question it. But once the validity of the established doctrine is doubted its foundation is rapidly seen to be fragile."[20]

Hayek, along with Friedman and many other economists, was appalled when President Nixon dumped the gold standard. He'd never put much stock in it, calling it a "very wobbly anchor," but he wrote that "any anchor is better than a money left to the discretion of government."[21] Like Adam Smith, Hayek believed private institutions were better equipped to provide stable currencies because that would be best for their businesses, just as it would for any commodity. "Blessed indeed will be the day when it will no longer be from the benevolence of the government that we expect good money but from the regard of the banks for their own interest," he wrote.[22]

Hayek called government monopoly over the issue and control of money "the source and root of all monetary evil."[23] Consumers' and producers' valuations, preferences, and knowledge, not government intervention, are what would create sound money, he believed. In a nutshell, Hayek believed money could and should be issued by competing private interests. Hayek broadened the definition of the term "currencies" to include not only paper and other sorts of "hand-to-hand money" but also "bank balances subject to cheque and other media of exchange that can be used for most of the purposes for which cheques are used." This, Hayek believed, "would create the conditions in which responsibility for the control of the quantity of the currency is placed on agencies whose self-interest would make them control it in such a manner as to make it most acceptable to the users."[24]

This proposal was shocking to people, Hayek wrote, because they've been programmed to believe that government control of "legal tender" is an indispensable aspect of daily business. "This is a survival of the medieval idea that it is the state which somehow confers value on money it otherwise would not possess," he writes.[25] But the strictly legal definition of "legal tender" simply states that it is a kind of money creditors cannot refuse in discharge of a debt due to them..[26] "If we want free enterprise and a market economy to survive ... we have no choice but to replace the government currency monopoly and national currency systems by free competition between private banks of issue. ... We have always had bad money because private enterprise was not permitted to give us a better one," he concluded.[27]

In a fascinating chart, Hayek showed how government destruction, or debasement, of paper money decreased the purchasing power of people in about 50 countries from 1950 until 1975. During that quarter century, people in Chile, Uruguay, Argentina, Brazil, Bolivia, South Korea, and Vietnam saw their purchasing power drop an astonishing 99 percent in free market value vis-a-vis the US dollar while the cost of living increased astronomically – 11,318,874 percent, in Chile's case – as their currencies depreciated based on the skyrocketing price of gold after the United States went off the gold standard. Free market gold prices rose from the official $35 per ounce price in 1950 to $141 per ounce at the end of 1975.[28] (The value of the US dollar collapsed after the United States closed the gold window, recovered some of its value due to high interest rates and tax reductions in the 1980s, and has fallen more than 80 percent since the free-money 1990s ended in 1999.[29])

In an example of how this would work in action, Hayek describes a scenario in which a major Swiss joint stock bank announces the issue of non-interest-bearing certificates or notes and the readiness to open current checking accounts in terms of a unit called a ducat, which would be made available to the public by short-term loans or sale against other currencies. Ducats could be benchmarked to a basket of currencies or commodities, though Hayek didn't believe that was desirable or necessary, and the bank would also announce its intention to regulate ducat quantity to keep their purchasing power as constant as possible.[30]

Hayek's vision was that private currencies would have a mission to protect a stable store of value and that everything else in the world would fall in value relative to that stable core. Assurance that a currency's value remained stable would be the chief attraction issuers would have to offer in Hayek's world, though the expected value would determine how much the public might wish to hold. Maintaining a currency's value would require continuous adjustments of the quantity in circulation; an "incautious increase" could cause the flow back to the bank to grow faster than the public demand to hold it.[31]

"The kind of trust on which public money would rest would not be very different from the trust on which today all private banking rests (or in the United States rested before the governmental deposit insurance scheme!)," Hayek wrote. "People today trust that a bank, to preserve its business, will arrange its affairs so that it will at all times be able to exchange demand deposits for cash, although they know that banks do not have enough cash to do so if everyone exercised his right to demand instant payment at the same time. Similarly, under the proposed scheme, the managers of the bank would learn that its business depended on the unshaken confidence that it would continue to regulate its issue of ducats so that their purchasing power remained approximately constant."[32]

To maintain the public's trust, Hayek suggested banks would need to publish their balance sheets in the newspaper, providing full transparency. Daily decisions about lending and selling and purchasing currencies on the exchange would be the result of constant computer calculation utilizing current information about commodity prices and rates of exchange.[33] Constant scrutiny by the financial press would make competition between issuing banks very acute, Hayek believed. This is where the theory falls apart a bit, because people will never trust banks to self-report. (Back in the 1970s, people trusted the government more than they trusted the press; today, very few people trust either of them.) They chose to stick with the "legal tender" dollar, thank you very much.

Without transparency and trust, Hayek's vision had a weak foundation. But he wrote *The Denationalization of Money* in 1976, when computers were just being invented. As we move forward in *Money Without Boundaries*, we will see that today it is possible not only to have full transparency on a micro-second basis, but also to have full decentralization.

Chapter 5

The Rise of
Cryptocurrency

"It is very attractive to the libertarian viewpoint if we can
explain it properly. I'm better with code than words, though."

– Satoshi Nakamoto

In 2008, an important development occurred in the digital
world. Just a month after the stock market crashed, a writer
using the pseudonym Satoshi Nakamoto released a whitepaper,
"Bitcoin: A Peer-to-Peer Electronic Cash System," proposing a "purely
peer-to-peer version of electronic cash" that would allow parties to send
online payments directly without going through a financial institution.
Nakamoto described a network of nodes, or computers running the
Bitcoin protocol, that would timestamp, or verify, transactions between
anonymous public keys by hashing them into an ongoing chain of

hash-based proof-of-work to create a permanent, unchangeable record. A timestamp server would widely publish a block of items to be time-stamped, and every node on the network would collect them and work on finding a difficult proof-of-work in a process called "mining." The node that found it first would broadcast it to all other nodes, which would accept the block by using its hash as the previous hash when it began creating the next block in the chain. As a reward for finding the proof-of-work, the winning node would get a newly minted "bitcoin," providing a means of initially distributing this new form of money into circulation.[1]

> *For readers who are new to bitcoin, blockchain, and proof-of-work, a lot of this jargon may look like a foreign language. If that is the case, don't worry about the specific mechanics at this time; we will break down these concepts in the next section of the book.*

In 2009, Nakamoto sent an obscure piece of code based on his algorithm, called bitcoin, to cryptographer Hal Finney, and bitcoin became a reality. Bitcoins were traded for pennies as coders refined the open-source system, then their value climbed to about $1 in February 2011 and nearly $30 four months later before they stabilized around $8.16 from July 2011 to February 2012.[2] Copycat cryptocurrencies almost immediately followed bitcoins onto the market, and more than 500 were trading with a combined market capitalization of roughly $4.89 billion by 2015, though bitcoin continued to dominate with 85.6 percent of the market[3] and market capitalization exceeding that of many national currencies.[4]

The method of creating new bitcoins is mathematically controlled, with supply growing at a pre-set, limited rate, never to exceed 21 million.[5] Miners receive 25 new bitcoins when they add a block to the chain, and by 2140 all bitcoins are expected to be mined out.[6] "In the absence of any central authority, bitcoins are created at a predetermined, knowable rate, and no self-interested individual or entity may change that," Jonathan B. Turpin wrote in the *Indiana Journal of Global Legal Studies* in 2014. "Quantitative easing and other mechanisms used by central banks are simply not possible. It is this stability and predictability that attracts many to the system."[7]

This concept of a "tether" based on a limited value of 21 million units is one gift bitcoin has given us, and it's a very special one because it never existed before. People want this tether, or backing, for their currency – which is why so many were shocked and unhappy when the United States yanked the dollar's tether by moving from the gold standard to "full faith and credit." This is exciting. Tyler Winklevoss of the Facebook Winklevoss Twins, who were early bitcoin proponents, explained, "Our basic thesis for bitcoin is that it is better than gold" because it "matches or beats gold across the board" when compared with the nine foundational traits that make gold valuable, including scarcity, durability, and portability. "We see bitcoin as potentially the greatest social network of all," Tyler said.[8]

Without a doubt, the world's first cryptocurrency has been successful – and very lucrative for some. In 2018, less than a decade after Nakamoto wrote that first piece of code, bitcoin saw the largest, quickest rise in asset value in the history of the human race, jumping from a starting point of $0.003 to $7,432.[9] (As much as 90 percent of bitcoin transactions are believed to be speculative.[10]) Not everyone was so impressed. "Boosters say that bitcoin is the currency of the future," *New York Times* columnist Adrian Chen wrote in 2013. "I'd argue that the phenomenon is a digital gold rush perfectly emblematic of the present."[11]

Coins and Tokens

There are two types of digital currencies: coins and tokens. Coins are generally distinguished by their defined quantity, which is typically made possible via blockchain technology. Bitcoin, for example, has a defined number of 21 million units. A potential concern with bitcoin is that it has no economic value other than the value people ascribe to it. It has no intrinsic value. It is simply a unit of limited supply, which is why it is considered to be valuable. This is not completely irrational. Gold, at least, has some – though relatively limited – underlying economic value. For thousands of years, people have ascribed value to it and considered it to be "money," not because of underlying economic value, but because it has limited supply.

Coins are not typically designed to do anything specifically other than focus on being a limited store of value. Coins use blockchain technology to create transparency and decentralized engagement in an activity centered on sending, receiving, and creating something of limited supply (like bitcoin). The network's activity is centered on and around the coin itself.

Tokens are different, and it creates confusion when people put coins and tokens into the same category. If you are like me, chances are you use tokens all the time. I use a token to pick up a Divvy bike in Chicago or a Citi Bike in New York and to access certain computer systems. I use a token (a key card) to access the front door to my office building, a different token to access the office, and a different token to access my elevator at home. A ticket to a movie theater or sports event is a form of token/access right. Virtual tokens are the same thing – another form of unique access rights.

Platforms such as Ethereum enable the creation and facilitate the use of tokens. Inspired by bitcoin and its underlying blockchain technology, Ethereum enables smart contracts or applications that, according to its website, "run exactly as programmed without any chance of fraud, censorship, or third-party interference."

Ethereum allows users to:

1. Design and issue their own cryptocurrency.
2. Create a tradable digital token that can be used as a currency, a representation of an asset, a virtual share, a proof of membership, or anything at all.
3. Set the total amount of tokens in circulation to a simple fixed amount or fluctuate based on any programmed rule set.
4. Build a tradable token with a fixed supply, a central bank that can issue money, a puzzle-based cryptocurrency.[12]

Well, that is pretty cool. If limited supply is valuable (as in the case of bitcoin) and Ethereum will let me create something of limited supply using the same technology, then I should just make my own coin, the tomcoin. I did, in fact, work with a friend to create a kevincoin, just to understand the process. In our case, the token had no use or purpose. We just wanted to see if we could create something of limited supply. The premise was that if bitcoin is worth $100 billion because it has a limited supply of 21 million units, our kevincoin should be more valuable with a limited supply of 10 million units.

BLOCKCHAIN GOES MAINSTREAM

In February 2019, after years of bashing bitcoin as a "fraud," JPMorgan CEO Jamie Dimon announced the bank had created JPM Coin, a digital token to be used to instantly settle wholesale payment transactions. JPMorgan will use blockchain technology to transfer money at lightning speed as smart contracts are closed.

"So anything that currently exists in the world, as that moves onto the blockchain, this would be the payment leg for that transaction," Umar Farooq, head of JPMorgan's blockchain projects, told CNBC. "The applications are frankly quite endless; anything where you have a distributed ledger, which involves corporations or institutions can use this."

Note the term "coin" is confusing. JPM Coin is actually a token facilitating a role – transactions – and providing access rights to an underlying blockchain technology.[13]

To be sure, there's no shortage of crypto-competitors out there vying to take bitcoin's share. Alt-coins burst onto the scene shortly after bitcoin made its mark, and by 2015 more than 500 cryptocurrencies were trading.[14] By 2018, there were more than 1,600 cryptocurrencies in a market capitalized at just under $269 billion.[15] This market briefly hit a combined market capitalization of approximately $830 billion.[16] Following a significant correction throughout 2018, as of March 2019, there were still over 2,100 cryptocurrencies with a total market capitalization of approximately $140 billion with bitcoin comprising approximately $71 billion of that total.[17] The market does not value all cryptocurrencies the same. The top 20 cryptocurrencies account for 89 percent of that market, giving you a sense of just how top-heavy it is.[18] Some estimate that 95 percent of bitcoin's wealth is held by 4 percent of its owners, and even more alarmingly, about 94 percent of bitcoins are held by males.

As Nellie Bowles suggested in the *New York Times* in 2018, "There are only a few winners here, and, unless they lose it all, their impact going forward will be outsize."[19]

So, why is my kevincoin worth nothing while some coins are worth tens of millions, hundreds of millions, and in some cases, billions of dollars? That we never marketed, sold, or distributed it because it was simply an experiment we stopped before full completion could have something to do with it. But what if we had moved it forward and marketed it across the world as the next bitcoin? Would it have been worth anything? As billions of dollars have poured into coins with little regulatory oversight, these have become key questions for regulators: What exactly are people buying, and what exactly was being promised?

CRYPTOCURRENCY GLUT

Before the cryptocurrency boom, the world had hundreds of currencies. With cryptocurrency as a potential solution, the world now has approximately 2,100 "currencies" with growth averaging almost a new currency per day. Does that seem sustainable or logical?

The end state is one of two things: a world of infinite currencies or a world in which each person, business, or asset is tied to a unique currency that converges around a central currency, a known and common store of value. I do not think these concepts are exclusive, and in fact, I think they are one and the same — as we will see, different sides of the same coin. Convergence is inevitable.

Is It a Security or a Utility? The Howey Test

Tokens have been broadly divided into two groups: utility tokens and securities. The term "security" refers to an investment security, like a stock. (To make this differentiation clear, I will refer to security coins as security/investment tokens.) The division between the two is determined by something called the Howey Test, formulated by Justice Frank

Murphy as a part of a 1946 Supreme Court decision about how to determine if something is a security and therefore subject to registration and oversight by the Securities and Exchange Commission. Murphy wrote:

> An investment contract for purposes of the Securities Act means a contract, transaction, or scheme whereby a person **invests his money** in a common enterprise and is **led to expect profits** solely from the efforts of the promoter or a third party, it being immaterial whether the shares in the enterprise are evidenced by formal certificates or by nominal interests in the physical assets employed in the enterprise. ... If that test be satisfied, it is immaterial whether the enterprise is speculative or non-speculative or whether there is a sale of property with or without intrinsic value"[20]

Emphasis is added to highlight what are commonly referred to as the four main pillars of the test. For a segment of tokens, investors expect to earn money or share in the profit of a project, platform, or entity. Another segment of tokens exist for the sole purpose of being a utility. They have no underlying economic value, share of ownership, or direct or indirect participation rights in profits related to a venture. These tokens primarily serve for access, governance, and operations of the decentralized communities they support.

It gets a bit more complicated because early network participants aren't necessarily devoid of expectations of profit or appreciation. In the late 1990s I purchased a speculative utility token for $100: VIP access to a new club, no line, no cover. If the club became successful, my access right could be very valuable. If the club was a bust, my access right could be worthless. I had no right to profit in the club; I simply had access to it, which was valuable to me. My contribution benefited me, and every similar contribution created a higher probability of the club's success. As the club grew in popularity, so did the cost of the access right. The card I purchased for $100 was soon being sold for $200, then $500. If I remember correctly, the price went as high as $1,000. (Today the club is closed, and my access rights are worth $0.) I had a similar experience later in life with a yoga studio, where I could access unlimited yoga through a special early member promotion. The same concept applies to health clubs, country clubs, and many other organizations.

Clubs have a lot in common with utility tokens. Let's imagine the club decided to outsource all operating decisions to token holders. This is what a utility token could look like in the decentralized organization.

1. DJ playlists would be determined by a democratic voting process.
2. There would be no bouncers, no host, and no bartenders. People who help run and police the club would be paid in tokens valid for free admission.
3. Before anyone was let into or kicked out of the club or served a drink, their actions would have to be verified by a majority of members.
4. Members' actions would be monitored and verified to determine if they qualified for the free admission token.

Stablecoin: Establishing Trust and Stability

The Winklevoss Twins began their cryptocurrency journey with bitcoin and evolved to co-found the digital currency exchange Gemini Trust Co., which created the world's first regulated stablecoin pegged 1:1 to the US dollar, in late 2018. Claiming part of their mission was to "build the future of money," Tyler Winklevoss explained that the twins saw stablecoin as "the missing link between the traditional banking system and the crypto economy."[21] "The Gemini dollar – the world's first regulated stablecoin – combines the creditworthiness and price stability of the US dollar with blockchain technology and the oversight of US regulators, namely the New York Department of Financial Services (NYDFS),"[22] states a Gemini blog post. "Stablecoins are becoming increasingly popular with proponents of decentralized technology because they alleviate some of cryptocurrencies' shortcomings, including trust and volatility."[23]

The Gemini "dollar" is not the first cryptocurrency to target being pegged to the US dollar. Tether, one of the first large projects in the cryptocurrency space, is tethered to a value of $1. Stablecoin offers multiple advantages, allowing people to set up virtual wallets that work like anonymous, secure, decentralized bank accounts. A coin that maintains a store of value equal to $1 is valuable because it lets you store money and transact digitally and, in theory, securely. A problem with "stable value coins" is that they rely on a third party to keep and store the money.

How and where is this money kept, and how do you know it is secure? Without going into the drama, this was (and I believe remains) a challenge for Tether. The Winklevoss twins are addressing this problem by issuing a regulated coin, designating financial services and bank holding company State Street as the custodian, and hiring BPM Consulting and Auditing. In theory, holders of this coin can feel a higher degree of safety because an independent custodian is holding the assets and an independent third party is vouching that those assets are there.

However, there is a deeper question: If the return on stablecoin is zero (it pays no interest) and the asset backing the stable coin is the dollar (which is an unsecured claim backed by nothing), then what is the actual value of the stablecoin? Is it truly stable?

How Should We Value Coins and Tokens?

An unlimited supply of money with no real economic value has generally been proven to lack societal value. For thousands of years, society centered on money of limited supply, such as bartering and commodity money – primarily a gold standard. We then moved to "full faith and credit" currencies, or an unlimited money supply backed by government's ability to repay it with future taxation. The value derived or perceived from these currencies is primarily tied to beliefs related to the underlying economic value of the currency issuer.

Bitcoin brought us blockchain, a technology that gives the world the ability to create items of limited supply. We are witnessing the creation of a virtually infinite number of currencies based not on economic value, but on the fact that they are in limited supply. But if the world can create an infinite number of items with limited supply, then limited supply by itself is no longer valuable. Similarly, an unlimited supply of items with economic value is also worthless in the long run. The goal for society is to have both limited supply and economic value.

With respect to stablecoin, tethering to something that is not valuable in the long term means it, too, is not valuable in the long term – that's how a tether works. In the short term, these coins may play a role in facilitating a number of transactions —many, like a Venmo, for legitimate purposes. Some people will inevitably seek out stablecoin's security, anonymity, and ease of use for illicit transactions. How, or even if, society can protect against money laundering and other illicit activity will be briefly addressed later in this book but is a broader topic for another discussion.

Security/Investment Tokens

Some tokens will be valuable in the long term. Ironically, if a central authority like the SEC deems that a token is a security, it is expressing a view that the token *does not* pass the Howey Test, implying that a person is investing in a common enterprise and expecting profits from the efforts of others. This "endorsement" could be considered great news because it recognizes that some of these tokens may in fact have considerable long-term value. Investment in profit-seeking ventures is what has facilitated the creation of virtually every great product and service you use today.

The challenge is that there is little difference in the risk/reward characteristics between security/investment tokens and many other forms of investing such as stocks or start-up companies. The fact that it may have value does not make it a stable form of value. These investments are far from, and anything but, "risk free."

Many of the tokens raising money before 2019 were not yet profitable, did not have revenue, and had considerable expenses related to their underlying business plans. Some were little more than an idea on a sheet of paper, with little in terms of an actual business plan or even management team. A few operated in a gray area where critics would argue there was no credible path to profitability. Some were outright fraud. With little regulation for a wide variety of business plans, it was like the Wild West and full of speculation.

Are tokens an early stage Twitter? It's too early to tell the long-term size, scale, and monetization opportunities they'll bring. That they are not proven is not necessarily a bad thing; it's what happens with all early stage technologies. Speculative investments continue to drive pharmaceutical drugs and biotechnology, the early stages of the Internet, social media, and even the early stages of the Industrial Revolution. Regulators point out that investors may not fully understand the risks and may be risking more than they can afford to lose. Based on the activity in the space, it would be hard to argue against that belief. Some might be over-speculating.

I believe society will value investment tokens in the long term on the same risk/reward scale as any other investment on earth. Across planet Earth there are countless pre-revenue, money-losing ideas with no clear line of sight into when, let alone how, they will ever turn a profit. Some estimates indicate 97 percent (and more) of new companies don't make it, and I would anticipate a similar trend with investment tokens – but my estimate for the likelihood of failure is even higher. I would be surprised if 10 out of 1000 security/investment tokens are around in 10 years.

It is also somewhat ironic that some of these investments seek a quest toward more transparency and more visibility yet provide less visibility and less transparency than public investments. Those that provide less transparency should trade at a discount, not a premium, to their peers in other markets.

Utility Tokens

Utility tokens are similar to the decentralized night club I described earlier, but potentially on a much bigger scale. In some cases, they have a much better purpose, but often they have more in common with a club than you might imagine: marginal societal value with a high risk of here today, gone tomorrow.

Valuation is much more difficult in this space because it is a new frontier. Traditional approaches to valuation, such as valuing a company, look at some combination of anticipated revenue minus anticipated expenses to calculate the anticipated profit over time. That anticipated profit is factored over time / growth and a variety of other factors to determine a present value.

Utility tokens have little in common with traditional companies. Some of the platforms never anticipate revenue, might be not-for-profit entities, may have expenses related to ongoing support and maintenance, or may in fact be able to exist solely from the efforts of volunteers – contributors to the community – and have no expenses. Those that do have expenses may be able to cover them in their own currency, others require outside capital for support, and some operate in a combination. What is the value of something that has the possibility of no revenue, no profit, and no expenses and might handle revenue or expenses in its own currency? Making matters more complicated, some tokens are associated or affiliated with for-profit entities but do not participate in the profits.

Using traditional valuation models is not particularly helpful because the value can range between infinity and zero. If it is very difficult to move to another platform or network ("switching costs" are exceptionally high), and if the value received by the participants in the network is high, then it is likely the value of the tokens is high. More users are likely to participate in maintaining a network's functionality if the reward for providing services – the payment (from activities like mining) – is high. If the price drops to a low level and the task is difficult to execute, few people are likely to be willing to do the work required. If it's easy to change to another provider, users will switch providers.

In theory, there should be a natural tug of war that makes these tokens a lot like other utilities such as electricity, cable, and cell phones, but with more competition and less of a monopoly. But even if the network is valuable, is the underlying token affiliated with that network valuable? It depends, and not always. The reasons for this will become clearer as we get a better understanding of the different components of the blockchain ecosystem.

A NEW CURRENCY FOR THE NEW REPUBLIC?

Let's say we wanted to create a new country called the United States, with a Treasury and a Treasury Secretary. We might issue our own currency, which could be backed by something (like gold) or could simply be a claim on our ability to tax the people who live in or transact with our country, or perhaps a combination. If the value we provide as a country is greater than the price of the tax, people might stay and transact with us. If the tax is too high and the value is too low, people might move elsewhere. For our new currency to be valuable, we must provide compelling value, securely.

The functions of government are remarkably similar to the functions of utility tokens and the belief in their underlying values. It is incongruent to believe in one and to doubt the other. Both of them face the same problems of scale, and both can be a form of self-fulfilling prophecy of success or destruction. By reframing utility tokens as the ability to tax a network and comparing that to the ability of a government to tax its people, we can perhaps see that, while not exactly the same, the two have a lot in common.

What does that mean with respect to valuation? I believe a segment of these tokens will in fact be exceptionally valuable, because their networks will be valuable. However, just because they could be valuable does not mean that I believe they will be a "risk-free store of value" – that is something different. The two concepts need to be separated and looked at independently. *Money Without Boundaries* is not about the value to society of coins, security/investment tokens, stablecoin, or even utility coins. It is about a quest for a store of value – the risk-free rate.

Chapter 6

The Role Model

"Almost certainly, however, the first essential component of social justice is adequate food for all mankind."

– Norman Borlaug

I was going to school at Washington University in St. Louis in the 1990s, just after the collapse of the Soviet Union, and I had a friend who was from Russia. One night over beers, we got to talking about what it was like there during this historic event, and it was fascinating. Sure, people were excited about all the new possibilities and freedoms that would come with the USSR's fall, but they also had all sorts of doubts about how capitalism could possibly work. The whole concept was in fact literally terrifying to many Russians.

My friend could not understand, at the time, how money-seeking companies could be trusted to run grocery stores, which supplied the population's most basic of all needs. "What happens if they just say, 'We're not going to carry milk and eggs.' What if milk goes to $20 a gallon because all the stores have colluded, so they have fewer products for higher prices?" He got really worked up about this, and I was moved.

We then discussed what we had learned in economics classes, that controlling prices, as the Communists did in the USSR, is actually what amplifies them and causes products to be of lower quality.[1] It's probably not intuitive to a lot of people, not just those who have lived in Communist regimes, but capitalism provides more choices at less cost.

Like a good Iowan, I explained to him that because our food system is so completely decentralized, it can withstand nearly any shock to its system. I wouldn't have used this analogy back then, because most of us hadn't heard of it yet, but our food system is a lot like the Internet, which was designed to withstand a nuclear strike. If one part of the system goes down, there are several others that can step in to take its place. Similarly, if either the largest farmer in my home state of Iowa or Quaker Oats, one of the largest food producers based in my home town, went bankrupt, it wouldn't likely impact the price of anything in the grocery store. When the local chain Dominick's went bankrupt in my neighborhood in Chicago in 2013, a Whole Foods moved in. When Hostess Brands went bankrupt that same year, an investment firm stepped in to keep Twinkies on the shelves.

This is not at all what our financial system is like. Who can forget "too big to fail," when many banks in the United States basically went bankrupt (or perhaps better said, were "technically insolvent") and had to be bailed out to the tune of $700 billion in emergency funds and trillions in additional assistance from the US Treasury Department and the Federal Reserve?[2]

Since then, the banking system in the United States has grown even more concentrated, stunningly concentrated. Today, the five largest banks (JPMorgan Chase, Bank of America, Wells Fargo, Citigroup, and US Bancorp) control 44 percent of the $15.3 trillion in assets held in the United States.[3] As Matt Taibbi explained in *Rolling Stone* in 2013: "It was all a lie – one of the biggest and most elaborate falsehoods ever sold to the American people. We were told that the taxpayer was stepping in – only temporarily, mind you – to prop up the economy and save the world from financial catastrophe. What we actually ended up doing was the exact opposite: committing American taxpayers to permanent, blind support of an ungovernable, unregulatable, hyper-concentrated new financial system that exacerbates the greed and inequality that caused the crash."[4]

The food system is unlikely to get a bailout like the 2008 Troubled Asset Relief Program, hastily signed into law as the subprime mortgage crisis threatened to take down the entire system, because it would never need it. Unlike financial services, the food system has much less leverage and is much more decentralized –completely the opposite of the financial system.

Everything the Banking System Is Not

I'm well aware that there have been plenty of farm crises throughout time – which in my view were driven by either a lack of stable money, inflation, and/or debt – and the government has stepped in to "bail out" farmers. I am also aware that an astronomical amount of government subsidies are paid to support farmers. The degree to which those are necessary and the pros and cons of those arrangements are topics for another day. My point here is that while the system certainly is not perfect, there are many lessons we can learn from the good and the bad aspects of our farm-to-table food network.

We have plenty of choices in our food system, in which commodities from many producers are efficiently sorted, standardized, and sold in bulk. If the price of raspberries goes up because of a drought, people can eat another kind of berry or fruit. A decentralized system has substitutions and redundancy, and you can look at it like a bucket of water. If you reach into the middle of the bucket and take out water, more water immediately fills the gap. There is no reasonable possibility of a long-term structural hole. If demand is there, then products are supplied. If consumer preferences shift, then manufacturers change their product mix (so long, Cherry Vanilla Coke!).

Commoditization levels the playing field. Goods of a certain quality may be sold to the market at the same price, regardless of producer. Goods may be distributed globally. The costs of the commodity plus storage and transportation create a market price that transcends all locations on earth (absent government intervention with tariffs or subsidies). Large producers have the advantages of economies of scale. Small producers win with better quality. But in a decentralized system, how do you know whether farmers are sending good corn or bad corn to the market? To address this challenge, the grain elevator was created. Before it was invented, farmers mostly sold grain in bags, which was not efficient for the producer nor the buyer. The grain elevator enables both sides to transact in bulk. It receives, tests, measures, sorts into similar qualities, and stores grain, then moves the sorted grain into containers for bulk shipment. This intermediary makes the market much more efficient for both the farmer and the grain purchaser.

When farmers grow corn in Iowa, they take it to grain elevators so it can be weighed, sorted, and measured for quality, then dried and made to conform to standards before it's sold in bulk. This is much more efficient than each and every farmer hauling bags of their corn to Quaker Oats and asking if the company might want to buy some. Quaker Oats gets the benefit that it can specify an exact quality, a characteristic that it desires, and order corn by the trainload. As long as the corn conforms to its specifications, the company doesn't care about who produced it and has almost no knowledge of whether the goods came from a farmer with 200 acres or a farmer with 20,000 acres.

This "technology" of the late 1800s, when combined with other emerging technologies like railroads, containers, and mechanized farming, led to the second agricultural revolution (the first being the movement from hunting and gathering to planting and sustaining), which is generally characterized by an increase in productivity and an increase in market areas because of better transportation. One plus one equals three.

The key to the revolution was not a single technology that lead to explosive growth, but a combination of advancements within multiple technologies. Before the revolution took place, certain aspects would seem completely unrelated. Trains, after all, were to haul coal and people. What could they have to do with farming?

As mechanized farming combined with grain elevators and railroads, productivity began to increase dramatically. This alone was a foundation for significant global change in the supply and production of food and set the stage for a truly explosive Green Revolution led by Norman Borlaug, who received the Nobel Peace Prize in 1970. As the father of the Green Revolution, he is credited with saving over one billion people from starvation. Borlaug's contribution was a more disease-resistant, higher-yielding wheat, which, when combined with advancements in other technologies (planting, harvesting, sorting, storing, and shipping) dramatically increased the ability of countries like Pakistan, India, and Mexico to improve, maintain, and enhance food security and stability.

LESSONS FROM THE GLOBAL FOOD INDUSTRY

The global food industry offers some key traits the financial services industry should admire and embrace.

Production is decentralized with thousands of inputs. Food production starts with the farmer. Thousands of farms grow pigs, cows, and corn. If one farmer goes out of business, you will still have milk on your table. If 100 farmers go out of business, you will still have milk on your table but the price may be higher. Droughts and floods impact prices regularly, but you can pretty much count on always being able to have a steak and potato with a glass of milk.

Producers and consumers have freedom of choice. You can walk into any grocery store and purchase 10 boxes of Fruity Pebbles or vegetables, milk, and meat. Similarly, a farmer can produce only corn or grow soybeans or raise cows. You have complete freedom to choose what you buy and what you produce.

The system is extremely efficient for consumers. Grocery stores have vast selections and generally run at margins of less than 3 percent before interest and taxes. Consumers also have choices in the way they consume their food. They can eat at home or in a restaurant.

The system is based on commodities. Investopedia defines commodities as "basic goods that are interchangeable with other commodities of the same type. ... Commodities are basic because they have simply been grown or extracted from their natural state and brought up to a minimum grade for sale in a marketplace – there is no extra value added to them by the producer. Although the quality may differ slightly between producers, commodities by definition are very similar no matter who produces them. All commodities of the same grade are priced equally and are interchangeable."[5] Food commodities are shipped to centralized nodes such as grain elevators or slaughterhouses, where they're grouped, standardized, graded, packaged, and sold to manufacturers such as Quaker Oats or ADM, whose products are then shipped to grocery stores.

Prices are dynamic and driven low by powerful market-based forces. When the price of corn is low and the price of beans is high, farmers will see the prices and plant more beans, leading to an increase in the bean supply and a reduction in the corn supply. This pushes down the price of beans and pushes up the price of corn. Consumers might look at the high price of corn and select edamame instead. As demand for high-priced goods falls, supply increases; as demand for low-priced goods increases, supply decreases. The market is powerful and self-correcting.

There is always a market. When farmers plant corn, they do not know who will buy the corn or the price they'll get for it. They simply know that consumers want corn. They typically do not sell directly to the end consumer but to a central location that groups their goods with goods of similar quality from other producers. This lets people operate in bulk and is efficient for buyers and sellers.

Regulation and government involvement are relatively minimal. Grocery stores and restaurants provide an essential service to consumers throughout the world, distributing food through 36,571 supermarkets[6] and 660,755 restaurants[7] in the United States alone, with a relatively low level of regulation based largely on inspections.

Critical infrastructure is easily taken over. While there are critical players in the food industry, their roles and infrastructure can quickly and easily be taken over by other entities if necessary. If Quaker Oats goes bankrupt, the facilities do not go away. The creditor takes over the plant and either operates it or sells it to a company that can operate it.

The food system is everything the banking system is not: decentralized, full of choice, efficient, and based on commodities. As such, it's a perfect role model for the financial system. The principles of global food, from farm to table, could easily be applied to financial markets, banking, and currency (money). We have a highly regulated, centralized, and concentrated financial system with limited transparency, high barriers to entry, high levels of leverage throughout the system, and high counterparty risk.

What if instead we had a decentralized system based on freedom of choice for producers and consumers with light regulation and relatively little government involvement? What if prices were dynamic and based on market forces and critical infrastructure could quickly and efficiently be taken over in a transparent system? Consumers would have lower costs, positive feedback loops, and more safety, transparency, and choice. The financial "grocery stores" of the world would have much lower margins – 2 percent instead of 20 percent (and more!).

While the focus of this book is how the contribution of one new technology will lead to explosive change, it is in fact possible because we're sitting on a tinderbox for the convergence of technologies, much like the convergence witnessed in agriculture in the last century. Blockchain is the catalyst for a true revolution, but it is built upon and relies upon a foundation of technologies that came before it as well as a strong ecosystem of complementary technologies.

Part Two

THE FOUR PILLARS – OUR BUILDING BLOCKS

Chapter 7

Pillar 1 – Modern Portfolio Theory and the Risk-Free Asset

"The circulation of confidence is better than the circulation of money."

— **James Madison**

Before we move on and start putting these pieces together, let's review what we've learned so far.

In Chapter 1, we learned that since 1971, when President Richard Nixon announced the US dollar would no longer be convertible into gold in international markets, currency has been backed only by the considerable power of the US economy, or "full faith and credit." While our currency has underlying economic value, it doesn't have any real value because there's no limit on supply, and this "just trust us" era brought on the instability and inefficiency that make the global financial system so vulnerable today.

In Chapter 2, we learned that "full faith and credit" suffers because it has no anchor, and the dollar has therefore drifted endlessly. We saw that money is nothing more than an illusion or a conversation about much more than currency and dollars. We learned the difference between narrow money, which is easily convertible into cash, and broad money, generally anything of value that resembles money. And we learned about A. Mitchell Innes's Credit Theory of Money, which asserts we're all both debtors and creditors of each other and that if an entire community's debts and credits could be set out against each other, every merchant who paid for purchases with bills and every banker who issued notes were in effect issuing money.

In Chapter 3, we learned about fractional reserve banking and how it makes banks vulnerable because they're pledging to pay back loans from their depositors immediately, on demand. We saw how giving central banks authority to create and issue money by granting loans at less than the natural interest rate to stimulate the economy also gives them the ability to stimulate inflation because banks can "pyramid" new deposits on top of reserves. We also learned about credit unions, in which people banded together based on a common bond such as a place of employment or higher education in a not-for-profit structure for their mutual benefit. .

In Chapter 4, we looked at the groundbreaking work of Nobel laureates who envisioned control of money and the ability to create it taken away from central banks. Irving Fisher's Chicago Plan called for separation of the banking system's monetary and credit functions by requiring 100 percent reserve banking to better control business cycle fluctuations and eliminate bank runs without having to create debt. Milton Friedman also blamed the Fed for the country's economic woes – including the Great Depression – and proposed stabilizing prices by expanding the money supply at a steady and known rate. The Friedman Rule, which became known as monetarism, set the nominal interest rate to zero, which he believed would eliminate incentives to economize and make it easier for consumers to execute transactions. Friedrich Hayek took this a step further, blaming government monopoly over money issuing for recurrent periods of depression and employment and suggesting private enterprises should issue currencies that could be traded against each other and against commodities at floating exchange rates on the open market. Private currencies would have a mission to protect a stable store of value, and everything else in the world would fall relative to that stable core. We saw that the biggest roadblock to Hayek's vision was that the public didn't trust banks to be transparent about their books and balance sheets.

In Chapter 5, we learned about the rise of cryptocurrency and the formation of bitcoin. We identified a growing movement of people globally seeking a safe and transparent store of value that is decentralized and out of governments' control. We learned about the difference between coins and tokens, utility and security (or investment) tokens, and stablecoin.

In Chapter 6, we looked at how the decentralized food system in the United States provides a role model for the financial system: efficient, full of choice, and based on commodities. We saw how multiple technologies converged to fuel a Green Revolution, and we looked at one piece of the system, the grain elevator, that measured, assessed, sorted, segmented, and grouped commodities so both producers and users of a given commodity could transact in bulk with a known underlying good.

These chapters form the foundation for understanding our vision. From this foundation, we'll now move into the building blocks, the four pillars, that will form the framework of understanding the creation of money without boundaries, a new decentralized currency as a stable store of value that transcends space and time. We will create "absolute safety" where there is no default, no creditor risk, and no theft. These building blocks include the following:

1. The concept of a "risk-free asset" and the idea of borrowing and lending at the risk-free rate.
2. How the risk-free asset, and private money, can be created in a private, peer-to-peer transaction through borrowing.
3. Blockchain technology: what it is, what it does, and how it works.
4. Money markets and the inner workings of capital markets: what they are and how they work.

Once we frame out these ideas, we will pull them together in a sketch of what a decentralized peer-to-peer risk-free asset can look like. While my goal is to begin with a framework – a simple understanding – we do have to take a slightly deeper dive into some complex topics on theory, technology, and capital markets. Some readers may be very familiar with the inner workings of "repurchase agreements" but have never heard of a "hash." Others are focused on how super-computers can create the demise of "consensus" but are unfamiliar with Modern Portfolio Theory.

Whether you are "fin," "tech," or neither, we can set a table from which we can all approach a common goal: the creation of a constant store of value. We'll look at the big picture as we dive into key concepts, and readers who want more detail should turn to the reference guide. I will freely admit that I'm not entirely certain *how* these ideas will converge, and we'll discuss this in Part 3. However, I believe with the highest conviction that the pillars we'll explore in Part 2 definitely *will* converge.

What we've seen is that centralized banking and government monopoly of currency based on no tether other than "trust us" has set the system adrift. Many very smart people have spent their careers seeking a better way, and now technologies are emerging to make their dreams possible – but we still need to define exactly what we're trying to build. To do that, let's look at how a few more Nobel laureate economists who were also consumed with finding a better way picked up and ran with the philosophies of Fisher, Friedman, and Hayek. Like the Impressionists, these economists built upon Fisher, Friedman, and Hayek and evolved each other's philosophies.

WHO CAME FIRST?

During a recent visit to the Musee d'Orsay in Paris, I spent a lot of time checking out an exhibit that I interpreted as focusing on which Impressionist artist inspired which Impressionist artist to do what. It's a fascinating concept, but it's not my focus with this book. I would rather focus on a radical movement in economics, and I'm focused much less on who did what first or who inspired whom; that is a topic for other books. Harry Markowitz, James Tobin, and William Sharpe all had ideas that preceded Friedman and Hayek

relative to the risk-free rate, but they were more focused on portfolios and investments than "money." I believe they were looking
at the same problems from different perspectives. I'm playing DJ,
mixing the ideas of these Nobel laureates. The correlation and
interdependence of their works, to me, is not self-evident. The
point is to embrace the "shoulders of giants" to build the foundation upon which a truly revolutionary movement can be built.

Evolving Modern Portfolio Theory and the Risk-Free Asset

In 1952, Harry Markowitz and a handful of colleagues introduced
Modern Portfolio Theory, in which a combination of assets is referred
to as efficient if it has the best possible expected return for its risk level
so that every possible combination of risky assets can be plotted to reveal
an "efficient frontier" offering the highest expected return for any given
risk level. Markowitz was the first to bring risk into the picture, whereas
before him, the focus had been almost entirely on return and reward.
Markowitz showed that putting together non-correlated investments,
which don't rise and fall in lockstep, in a portfolio decreases the risk
investors take without very much negatively affecting the financial
return. Markowitz would write in an article he co-authored 50
years later that Modern Portfolio Theory "introduced a whole new
terminology which now has become the norm in the area of investment
management."[1]

William Sharpe took Markowitz's theory and ran with it in the
1960s, using it as a basis for his Capital Asset Pricing Model, a theory
of price formation for financial assets. Sharpe suggested investors could
choose their exposure to risk through a combination of lending and borrowing and an optimal portfolio of risky securities based on the investor's
assessment of the future prospects of different securities rather than the
investor's attitude toward risk. In the Capital Asset Pricing Model, risks
can be shifted to the capital market, where they're bought, sold, and
evaluated so that risky asset prices are adjusting, keeping portfolio decisions consistent.[2] The Sharpe Ratio shows how much excess return an

investor gets for the extra volatility that holding a riskier asset brings. Sharpe uses a risk-free rate of return, or theoretical investment of zero risk, to determine if investors are properly compensated for the risk they take on.

Then, James Tobin upped the efficiency of this approach even more by combining risk-free assets with risky assets in a concept he called Separation Theorem for its departure from Markowitz's approach of dividing an entire portfolio between risky and risk-free assets.[3] Tobin believed investors should determine their appetite for risk, which could be met using Markowitz's Modern Portfolio Theory. Then they would have two buckets to divide assets between based on liquidity needs and their risk-reward profiles. "You would choose the same portfolio of nonsafe assets regardless of how risk-averse you were," Tobin explained. "Even if you wanted to change the amount of risk in the portfolio, you'd do it by changing the amount of the safe assets, relative to the nonsafe assets but not by changing the different proportions in which you held the nonsafe assets relative to each other."[4] He showed that a portfolio of risky assets at the tangent point of a line emanating from the risk-free rate is the optimal risky-asset portfolio, called a market portfolio, and that all investors hold stakes in the risk-free asset and the market portfolio based on their risk tolerance. The risk-free asset and the market portfolio would determine the portfolio's expected return and risk while lenders would lend and borrowers borrow at a risk-free rate – another important step in Modern Portfolio Theory's evolution and another block in our foundation for money without boundaries. While the goal of this book is not to get too technical, it's important to understand the theoretical foundation upon which the ideas are built.

Summary of Pillar 1

The key building block is understanding that multiple Nobel laureates have worked with the following ideas:

1. There should be a risk-free asset.
2. People should be able to borrow and lend at the risk-free rate.
3. People should not be a borrower and a lender (they should be one of the two).

These ideas are more than 50 years old. Today we live in a world where:

1. A risk-free rate does not exist; in fact, the world has drifted further away from, not closer to that goal.
2. People cannot borrow and lend at the risk-free rate and typically are losing on both ends; borrowers typically pay a rate much higher than inflation, and savers typically receive a rate much lower than inflation.
3. Most people are both borrowers and lenders. They hold cash at a low rate and debt at a higher rate. For example, they have $5,000 in a checking account and $5,000 on a credit card. They are receiving $0 on their cash and paying 15 percent on the credit card. In aggregate, this inefficient allocation of capital in which people are both borrowers and lenders costs society tens of billions of dollars per year.

New technologies are about to enable old theories to converge, creating a new reality.

Chapter 8

Pillar 2 – The Credit Theory of Money

"When the people find that they can vote themselves money, that will herald the end of the Republic."

– Benjamin Franklin

Let's return to the efficient frontier, the Modern Portfolio Theory introduced by Harry Markowitz. Conceptually, any individual asset has risk and any individual asset has return. In Modern Portfolio Theory, rather than plotting the risk and return of each asset individually, assets can be combined to create a frontier yielding the highest return for a unit of risk with combinations that are called efficient. This makes sense. Investing involves risk; some risks are high, and some are low. Investing involves returns; some returns are positive, and some are negative. The goal, of course, is to have the highest return possible with the least amount of risk.

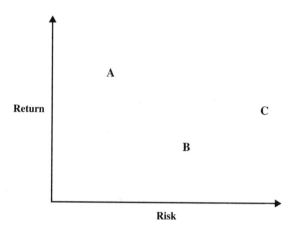

Figure 8.1   Chart of potential assets A/B/C.

Imagine if there were only three investments in the world and we could plot their risk and return in a single chart as shown in Figure 8.1.

In this simple example, investment A is the obvious choice because it is the most efficient portfolio. Investment A delivers the highest return for a unit of risk. There is no reason to choose investment B or investment C because they have much higher risk for less return.

Creating Money Under the Credit Theory of Money

Let's begin with some simple assumptions. The only holding in the world is investment A, which we will call the "risky" investment. We are also going to assume there is no inflation and there is absolute safety: no default, no creditor risk, and no theft. (The nice thing about economics is you get to start in a make-believe world and then apply real-world assumptions – we are going to do the same exercise here.)

People live in the world and can either have income from their job, which is paid in "units," or store their wealth in this "risky" investment. There is no place, other than this risky asset, where people can store money. "Money" must either be instantly spent or stored in something that goes up and down in value. The risky investment averages 10 percent per year, so society doesn't mind too much. But because it is risky, "average" is deceiving. It does not return 10 percent every year; its returns are volatile. In fact, they are determined by the throw of a single die on December 31 each year. If the die shows 1, the risky asset is down 30 percent. If the die shows 2, 3, 4, 5, or 6, the risky asset is up 15 percent.

Let's assume two people have all their money in this risky asset. One of them is very nervous about it; he wants more safety and stability. The other investor is not satisfied with the returns she is getting; she wants more than the risky asset is delivering. What could be the reasons for their completely different perceptions of the asset's value? Perhaps one of them is 70 years old and seeks safety and stability so he can retire. The 40-year-old wants more money and is willing to take more risk to get it.

Both investors determine that their risky assets are worth 1,000 units and decide to enter into a private transaction. In this agreement, the 70-year-old sells half of his risky assets to the 40-year-old. In exchange, the 40-year-old gives him a special form of IOU that she has backed with 100 percent of her assets. The IOU is a collateralized loan backed by her holdings in the risky assets. Further, it is a demand IOU. Any day, at any time, the 70-year-old can demand repayment as measured in units. If the 40-year-old does not have the units on hand, she would have to sell assets to somebody to get them.

Day One

Immediately after the transaction, the two have the following holdings:

40-year-old	70-year-old
Owns 1,500 units worth of risky assets	Owns 500 units worth of risky assets
Owes 500 units to the 70-year-old	Is owed 500 units from the 40-year-old
Net worth (owns − owes): 1,000 units	Net worth (owns an asset + owns a debt, somebody owes them money): 1,000 units

Two years pass, and they are both "good years" in which the risky asset increases in value by 15 percent.

40-year-old	70-year-old
Owns 2,000 units of risky assets	Owns 650 units of risky assets
Owes 500 units to the 70-year-old	Is owed 500 units of risky assets from the 40-year-old
Net worth: 1,500 units	Net worth: 1,150 units

Both individuals are happy. The 70-year-old is secured by more assets and has had appreciation. The 40-year-old had a significant increase in her net worth.

What about bad years? Two years pass, and the risky asset falls by 30 percent twice.

40-year-old	70-year-old
Owns 735 units of risky assets	Owns 245 units of risky assets
Owes 500 units to the 70-year-old	Is owed 500 units of risky assets from the 40-year-old
Net worth: 235 units	Net worth: 745 units

The 70-year-old is no longer comfortable with the level of safety and presents the note for repayment. This is a part of the terms to which the two parties agreed. The 40-year-old either sells her assets to somebody else or gives 500 units of risky assets back to the 70-year-old.

40-year-old	70-year-old
Owns 235 units of risky assets	Owns 745 units of risky assets
Net worth: 235 units	Net worth: 745 units

Remember, there is a constant demand for the risky asset because it is the only place where people can store their money. But let's say for some reason the 70-year-old could not sell the risky asset and instead repossessed it, much like a car loan or a home loan. He could then find a different 40-year-old, or perhaps a group of 40-year-olds, and repeat the transaction, constantly seeking a store of value.

Creating a Medium of Exchange

Let's assume things are going well and both parties are happy with their holdings and their agreement. However, the 70-year-old wants to enjoy his retirement, and he wants to buy some things. Because he is retiring and no longer has income, he either has to sell his risky asset or redeem his loan from the 40-year-old.

The 70-year-old determines he doesn't want to sell his risky asset, so he takes his initial 500-unit note and breaks it into 500 separate pieces of paper. Each piece of paper is redeemable for one risky unit. When people buy a loaf of bread for 1 unit, they provide the shop-keeper with a 1-unit note, which is also redeemable at any point in time. These pieces of paper then become a currency as a store of value and a medium of exchange. These individuals have created a private currency – money – that is independent of any government and fully collateralized.

Now, let's take a moment to compare this to the original dollar, a bearer bond that was redeemable for gold or silver. It is the same structure, yet through a privately managed transaction. This world, then, looks much like the United States in the 1920s. Recall our dollar bills said "will pay to the bearer on demand" and were certificates for an asset that was held in safe keeping.

A gold-standard 1928 dollar bill was identified as a "United States Note" rather than a "Federal Reserve Note." The words "will pay to the bearer on demand" do not appear on today's currency.

A gold standard 1928 US one-dollar bill.
Source: Public Domain; https://commons.wikimedia.org/wiki/File:One_
dollar_1928.jpg

US five-dollar banknote, silver certificate, series of 1923 (Fr. Ref#282),
depicting Abraham Lincoln.
Source: National Numismatic Collection at the Smithsonian Institution. https://
commons.wikimedia.org/wiki/File:US-$5-SC-1923-Fr.282.jpg

Here we have a note that is similarly backed by an asset. While the asset is not silver, it is an asset that is constantly marked to a value, a unit in which income is earned and purchases can be made. This asset is better than silver, because it is marked to market, based on a societal valuation at any and every point in time. Unless the value of an asset falls to whatever is determined to be the margin of safety, and before the asset falls to less than the value of the claim on the asset, the claim is always known to be valued by that society. If the claim is risk-free, the asset is risk-free.

FIND BALANCE

The key building block is understanding that a risk-free asset can be created by having a claim on a risky asset – by borrowing against a risky asset. The concept is not that all loans are risk-free, nor is it that all risky assets are created equal, and the construct as outlined still has risk – in particular there are gaps in trust, valuation, what triggers a break in the agreement, and knowing that the claim can be redeemed as well as knowing its valuation. At this point you may, and should, have more questions than answers, and we will explore those questions as we move through the concept. The important point to remember, the foundational building block, is that two parties can agree to a loan at zero cost simply to shift risk-and-return outcomes, and that loan can be broken apart into a form of private and secured money.

Summary of Pillar 2

In a world of risky assets, some investors have an incentive to seek a risk-free asset. The risk-free asset doesn't currently exist, but it could. It is possible via the combination of a market of people willing to buy the risky asset, a private transaction between parties, and a claim against risky assets (a loan). As long as the value of the risky assets is *always*, no matter what, greater than the value of the claim, and assuming no risk of loss or default, a claim on the asset can be risk-free.

This claim can be separated into units. These units, because they are redeemable always, at a constant and known store of value, can be subdivided into units that have limited supply and known economic value.

Chapter 9

Pillar 3 – Solving the Trust Gap = Blockchain

"Trust, but verify."

– Ronald Reagan

W hen the Nixon administration decided to yank the United States off the gold standard in 1971, there really wasn't a lot anyone could do about it. Citizens of the United States – and the world – had little choice but to accept that the words "redeemable in lawful money at the United States Treasury or at any Federal Reserve Bank" were no longer printed on the dollars they used. Instead, they were told to simply trust that the US government would uphold its promise of backing its "legal tender" with its "full faith and credit." As the US Treasury explains: "Federal Reserve notes are not redeemable in gold, silver, or any other commodity, and receive no backing by anything. ... The notes have no value for themselves, but for what they will buy. In another sense, because they are legal tender, Federal Reserve notes are 'backed' by all the goods and services in the economy."[1]

By untethering itself from the gold standard, the US government was in effect implying that it wanted to compete with any issuer of privately created money in a full faith and credit society. The government lost control of money and opened the way for Friedrich Hayek's vision. We could have denationalized money! Anyone could create a bank, issue ducats, and post balance sheets in the newspapers so consumers could judge whether they were more creditworthy than the government. This was something! But as we discussed in Chapter 5, Hayek's dream was severely handicapped by the trust gap. Why would people trust banks and newspapers to accurately report about financials when the incentive to lie is so very high? Well, Hayek might say, that's why we have auditors. But we don't have a lot of faith in them after corporate accounting scandals like the ones at Enron and WorldCom cost people billions of dollars. Enron and WorldCom had auditors.

Hayek had brilliant ideas, and his vision holds a lot of promise. But the trust gap is a huge issue, as we've discussed, and implementing his ideas is problematic in today's massively centralized financial system dominated globally by about 30 banks classified as systemically important financial institutions (SIFI) or "too big to fail."[2] I don't know about you, but the fact that we even have to have an acronym like SIFI – indicating that the demise of one single institution could take down the entire system – doesn't actually give me a lot of faith in the system's stability. And we're so entrenched in this way of doing things that it's hard to see how we can make our way out.

Let's look again at agriculture's massively decentralized system of inputs, which operates in a completely opposite manner than the financial system does. Our food system is made up of many farmers across the country (and the world) growing commodities (corn, soybeans, cows, pigs, you name it) to common standards. These commodities are sorted, segmented, and grouped extremely efficiently, with no dependence on any central producer. Though dominant producers such as Conagra and ADM could shake up the system if they failed, and increasingly centralized meat production is without question a moral and environmental disaster, there's no need to designate SIPs (systematically important producers) or SIFs (systematically important farmers). If a dairy farmer in Wisconsin – even a huge industrial one – goes bankrupt, no one worries about whether they'll have milk the next day.

Yet when Lehman Brothers collapsed in 2008, it very nearly brought down the entire global financial system and triggered a potentially catastrophic cash and credit crisis (in addition to losing the average American $70,000 in lifetime income).[3] Because I had many different client relationships in the industry at the time, I got something of an insider's look at what was going down – and it was way more frightening than most people know. Many retailers, losing faith in banks and credit card companies, were considering putting up signs saying, "Cash Only." They did not trust that the financial intermediaries they relied on to pay them for plastic transactions were not about to fail. Small businesses were forced to shutter when their access to capital was vaporized. At one point, a senior executive at a large bank told me to go to the ATM and take out all the cash I possibly could. He was that frightened.

What 2008 revealed about our financial system is that it's a helicopter rather than an airplane, and much more vulnerable. Airplanes have backup systems, redundancies, and most importantly, wings, that allow them to keep flying even if one system fails. On a helicopter, if the blades stop working, you are unequivocally screwed. You can't glide or coast to an emergency landing. You crash to the ground. That's the system we built and the system Hayek and others opposed, and the pillar holding it up – the helicopter blades – is trust. Blind trust. When you wave your phone and Apple pays for your Starbucks, you never think about how the system works, but you trust that Visa will pay Starbucks and Visa trusts that you will pay your credit card bill. There are a lot of people trusting each other in this system, and that has kept the helicopter blades spinning. Had the US government not intervened in 2008, however, the financial system would have dropped to the ground like a rock.

SUPERHERO TO THE RESCUE!

The issues plaguing our financial system are deep, murky, and seemingly impenetrable, until you consider blockchain. The technology is like a superhero shining a light that can break through the muck and zap out everything that makes decentralized money impossible. You want to create a ducat transparently, *Mr. Hayek? Kapow!* How about a fully decentralized peer-to-peer money market? Blockchain can provide asset registration, identity management, fraud prevention, and compliance as well as facilitate decentralized community management; automation and enforcement of all contracts and agreements (including payment upon delivery); all in a distributed, secure, permissioned, immutable environment. But we need to first understand the *what* and the *how* of this new core technology as another one of our key foundational building blocks.

It All Started with the Cloud

When I was growing up in the 1980s, my family had a standalone desktop computer in the kitchen that I would tinker on, writing papers and printing them on a connected printer. If I wanted to share files with someone else, I had to copy them onto a floppy disk. Our computer wasn't able to communicate with other computers, though the desktops at my dad's office were networked together through a central server so they could e-mail and share information. This centralized server/network model was a precursor to the internet, which had been invented in the 1980s but was being used by only 1.4 percent of adults in the United States.[4]

The RAND Corporation, one of America's foremost Cold War think tanks, created the internet as a solution to the problem of how US authorities could successfully communicate after a nuclear war. In 1964, RAND engineer Paul Banan envisioned a network with no central authority that "would be designed from the get-go to transcend its own reliability." A distributed network could keep working through alternative channels even if it were hit in multiple places, Banan theorized. Then, he broke up messages into discrete pieces that could be sent and reassembled at the end point to build more reliability and use communication lines more efficiently.[5] Internet usage didn't really begin to take off among the public until after 1990, when the first search engine was developed, and 1991, when Tim Berners-Lee published the code for the World Wide Web. As Berners-Lee later explained, the web changed everything. "It's like the difference between the brain and the mind ... Explore the internet, and you find cables and computers. Explore the web, and you find information."[6]

The next big breakthrough technology was cloud computing, or computing as a utility, which probably had a bigger impact on the Internet than the Internet itself. Cloud computing is a computing environment where one party can outsource its computing needs to another and access databases and e-mails via the Internet.[7] The ideology, which John McCarthy had floated in the 1960s when he predicted future calculations would be carried out through public utilities, began to take hold in 2007 as communication channels were being rapidly developed and businesses' and individuals' needs for information systems was increasing.[8] In his 2008 book, *Cloud Computing: Web-Based Applications That Change the Way You Work and Collaborate Online,* Michael Miller wrote that cloud computing was a major change in how we store information and run applications. "Instead of running programs and data on an individual desktop computer, everything is hosted in the 'cloud' – a nebulous assemblage of computers and servers accessed via the internet," he explained. "Cloud computing lets you access all your applications and documents from anywhere in the world, freeing you from the confines of the desktop and making it easier for group members in different locations to collaborate." Miller likened cloud computing to the electricity revolution, when farms and businesses could shut down their generators and buy electricity from the utilities for much less.[9] In a 2009 *Multimedia & Internet@Schools* article, Mary Ann Bell described it this way: "In the cloud, you can plug in to all that the internet has to offer from your computer and also from your smartphone, PDA, or other gizmos. Thus, the internet will be your computer!"[10]

I'll admit, when I first heard about cloud computing, I didn't understand how it related to me, what problem it would solve in my life. I soon found out. I'm a huge music junkie, and I used to travel around in my car with a CD folder holding more than 100 CDs. I worried every time I parked that someone would steal my CDs, and I never seemed to have the CD I wanted to play with me. (They were among the hundreds more stored on shelves at home.) I remember thinking when I was in high school that it would be so cool if I could just play any song I wanted at any time on demand. I was dreaming about cloud computing, though I never would have seen cloud-based services like Spotify, Netflix, and Google coming. Now I have access to multiple thousands of songs through my Spotify account, and I'm not worried about anyone stealing my CDs. Even if I lose or someone steals my phone, I'll still have access to my music. Cloud computing means I can have virtually anything I want, anytime, anywhere, with no risk of loss or theft. That's pretty awesome when you think about it.

What, Exactly, Is Blockchain?

The concept of "cloud computing" was hard for me to initially understand because I was overthinking it. If I focused on *what* it could do for me rather than *how* it could do it, I would have better understood it. The cloud enabled remote storage accessible on demand, which enabled me to get all my music anytime, anywhere, securely. That is such a powerful idea. It is so powerful that of course you have to be curious about *how* that works, but once it is in practice, much like our cellphone or antilock brakes, we use technology without a care in the world about *how* it works. We mostly care about *what* it does.

Applying a similar framework to blockchain, I would suggest beginning by not overthinking it. Blockchain is a simple concept that solves perhaps the biggest problem humans encounter when they transact: the trust gap. Today, most of our infrastructure, our legal system, our communications, and our economy are based on the fact that we don't trust each other, and we have good reasons not to. But with blockchain, we can have infinite trust. That is it: blockchain facilitates trust.

Part of the magic of the "what" is in the "how," which is nuanced but incredibly powerful. Blockchain facilitates trust because it is decentralized. When you have a centralized authority, there are incentives for that authority to violate the trust of those around it. This central authority could be ancient shopkeepers issuing more scripts than assets they had on hand, kings and emperors melting down and diluting the quality of their gold, governments issuing more in "bearer certificates" redeemable for silver than they had on hand, the list goes on. Central authorities have often abused their powerful role. With blockchain, there is no central authority, which is partly how the trust bond is created.

An added benefit of this decentralization is that there is no need for an intermediary, which creates the possibility of not only increasing speed, but also reducing systemic costs and frictions. Efficiency can be much higher. So, blockchain creates the possibility of *more trust* and *more efficiency*.

What problems could be solved with more trust?

- Problem: My tomato says it is organic, and I think my shoes were made ethically, but I don't really know. (I don't trust the farmer, grocer, shoe company.) Imagine 100 percent trust and visibility into the supply chain of all components of all products.
- Problem: My credit card (bank account) data gets hacked. Imagine a world where your ID is secure. You are you, and everybody knows it with 100 percent trust.
- Problem: Voter turnout is low, and voter fraud occurs. Each person's vote would count, and the system cannot be manipulated.
- Problem: There's no way to know if a buyer or seller actually owns the underlying asset they are buying or selling (house/car/ investments) in a paper-based system managed by central authorities (custodians, title companies). Blockchain can provide a clear, transparent view into asset ownership.
- Problem: I want all my healthcare data with me, at all times, but only want access granted with permission and upon a need. Blockchain allows this while enforcing HIPAA laws.
- Problem: I don't trust my family to be responsible when I die, and I don't know whom to trust as a trustee. Blockchain can execute your desires with 100 percent confidence that the outcome you desire is the outcome that will transpire.
- Problem: I want the dog walker – and only the dog walker – to access my house, only during certain hours. Imagine a 100 percent secure key where you can grant 100 percent secure access and control access rights.
- Problem: I want to share data sometimes, but only when it is good for me, and I want to control and know who sees what when. Blockchain lets you control secure and anonymous data sharing.

- Problem: I want to send money to my children, and I want to know it goes only to them and that only they can access it. *Presto!*

Blockchain bypasses certain government functions and enhances others. For example, the government does not trust you to provide all of your information for your taxes. Imagine, instead, that every one of your transactions was transparently reported to the government, 100 percent tied to you, and stored in an immutable record. The government has to trust you, because there's no way you could cheat.

Solving the trust gap is a powerful idea. Marc Andreessen, co-creator of Netscape, the first commercial web browser, exulted when he learned what blockchain could do in 2008. "He solved all the problems," he said of Satoshi Nakamoto, the pseudonym for blockchain's inventor. "Whoever he is should get the Nobel Prize – he's a genius. This is the thing! This is the distributed trust network that the internet always needed and never had."[11]

"'Trustless' means – for the first time in history – exchanges for value over a computer network can be verified, monitored, and enforced without the presence of a trusted third party or central institution," Trevor I. Kiviat explained in *Duke Law Journal*. "Because the blockchain is an authentication and verification technology, it can enable more efficient little transfers and ownership verification. Because it is programmable, it can enable conditional 'smart' contracts. Because it is borderless and frictionless, it can provide a cheaper, faster infrastructure for exchanging units of value."[12] Calling blockchain "the Internet of individuals," Melanie Swan wrote in *Blockchain: Blueprint for a New Economy* that it could be "the enabling currency of the machine economy."[13]

"Some of the key tenets of a disruptive technology are that it allows people and businesses within a certain industry (or industries) to do things cheaper, faster, and better than before by a significant, if not revolutionary, margin."

– Zerohedge.com

Why Should We Care?

In the book *Mastering Bitcoin: Unlocking Digital Cryptocurrencies*, Andreas M. Antonopoulos explains that bitcoin is not simply a digital currency, but a network of trust that could provide the basis for much more than currencies.[14] Don and Alex Tapscott predict in their book, *Blockchain Revolution: How the Technology Behind Bitcoin Is Changing Money, Business, and the World,* that blockchain will eliminate the need for executives to swear their companies' accounts are in order as well as any human errors or fraud (so long, accountants and auditors). Anyone – shareholders, regulatory agencies, citizens – will be able to examine the books, updated on the blockchain every 10 minutes, at any time, and people will be able to reliably establish one another's identities and trust one another so they can transact and exchange money without third-party validation, allowing us to keep our valuable data to ourselves rather than allowing banks, governments, and validation companies to "invade our privacy for commercial gain and national security."[15] The authors welcome this disruption with utopian zeal. "We can each own our identities and our personal data. We can do transactions, creating and exchanging value without powerful intermediaries acting as the arbiters of money and information," they write. "Billions of excluded people can soon enter the global economy. … We can change the way wealth is distributed – how it is created in the first place, as people everywhere from farmers to musicians can share more fully, a priori, in the wealth they create."[16]

Blockchain promises to disrupt the disrupters, taking the place of centralized platforms like Airbnb and Uber, with applications for everything from asset registry to inventory and exchange, to every area of finance, economics, and money, physical property, and intangible assets such as votes, reputation, and health data.[17] It allows shoppers to see products' entire histories before purchasing, and it can automate all contracts and agreements, including payment upon delivery, associated with that transaction.

How Does Blockchain Work?

At the simplest level, imagine your diary being encrypted and a copy of it being kept on thousands of computers. Every time you make a new entry, a copy of it is made and sent to all of the computers. It is always kept in order. New entries are verified and added to the blockchain, and the network continuously verifies that old entries aren't changed by comparing them to the copies. Blockchain simply creates multiple copies with multiple points of verification and encryption.

If you're looking to go deep, you can explore the Resource Guide at the back of this book. Here we will do a slightly deeper dive with an excellent description from a *Cointelegraph* article, "How Blockchain Technology Works: A Guide for Beginners":

- A blockchain is a type of diary or spreadsheet containing information about transactions.
- Each transaction generates a hash.
- A hash is a string of numbers and letters.
- Transactions are entered in the order in which they occur. Order is very important.
- The hash depends not only on the transaction but the previous transaction's hash.
- Even a small change in a transaction creates a completely new hash.
- The nodes check to make sure a transaction has not been changed by inspecting the hash.
- If a transaction is approved by a majority of the nodes, it is written into a block.
- Each block refers to the previous block and together make the blockchain.
- A blockchain is effective as it is spread over many computers, each of which has a copy of the blockchain.
- These computers are called nodes.
- The blockchain automatically updates itself every 10 minutes.[18]

I would add a few comments to this summary to further enhance understanding.

- A hash is a code – it looks like gibberish. A sample hash is: 219711e62645a21f2742ada2c6f2a900.
- A "node" is a computer on a network – anything that has an IP address can be a node.
- Nodes (computers) can store information.

- Nodes can be arranged into groups that are called tree structures because they look like trees when graphed.
- Similarly, the data in these nodes (computers) can be hashes, which can also be arranged into similar tree type structures (called Merkel trees after Ralph Merkle, the guy who invented them in 1979).
- Because the data is spread across many computers, these trees can be used as a form of check and balance to make sure data is pure.
- These thousands of computers (nodes), spread all over the world, come together to work together (collaborate or conspire, depending on view) to verify all new activity on the network (new blocks) and confirm the integrity of the old transactions (old blocks).
- New activity (a transaction) is verified through a two-step competitive process called proof-of-work. The winner of the competition gets a reward.
  - Step 1: A node has to solve a difficult problem/puzzle.
  - Step 2: The solution is verified by the other nodes on the network.

THE WEAKNESS: DEPENDENCIES AND CONSENSUS ATTACKS

Blockchain has dependencies and weaknesses. Much like the grain elevator needs the railroad and cloud computing needs Internet speed and bandwidth, there are certain aspects of the technology that are still being developed and are heavily dependent on the existing technology ecosystem. Imagine building a giant grain elevator far away from any roads, ports, or railroads – it would be of little value. Imagine having every movie ever made available on demand, but through a dial-up modem on a black-and-white TV. Then there's the havoc technological advancement can wreak on an ecosystem, ironically resulting in the demise of the initial technology (the VCR gave way to the LaserDisc, which gave way to the DVD, which gave way to on-demand streaming ...). Similarly, blockchain is not unassailable. In the short term, it is dependent on ecosystem advancements, and in the long term, advancements in supercomputing could weaken the underlying way that trust is protected.

One of the greatest challenges with blockchain comes from one of its greatest strengths. The problem/solution/verification approach takes place via a decentralized voting process. When everyone agrees, there is a consensus. To override the votes, someone would have to control the majority of the voting rights. This process is a dramatic strength and a potential weakness in how blockchain works, particularly for smaller, less developed projects. If an entry is changed (fraud), the nodes will recognize it as such and reject the change. However, if somebody controls 51 percent of the network (the votes), they can create results that are not what the other network participants intended. This is a particular challenge to anyone looking to create a new blockchain. The chain strength is a function of the network's size and reach.

This weakness is a known challenge, and many different solutions have been floated, including (1) building very, very large networks; (2) proof-of-stake (random groups on the network, rather than the majority, determine the outcome); (3) using other networks on large, established blockchains; and (4) cross-referencing blockchains (also called notarizing).

For the purposes of our discussion, this weakness isn't really relevant. We're not interested in creating a new blockchain, but in leveraging blockchain technology. For our discussion, let's assume the strength of the underlying blockchain technology is equal to the strength of the strongest blockchain in society at any given point in time. To change that underlying record, you would need to control approximately 51 percent of all the computing power on Earth.

Why Would Anybody Do This?

A natural next question is *why* people would dedicate time and computing power for the good of others. The key piece in the blockchain structure is the "reward" for solving the puzzles. The network offers some form of incentive for completing the calculations and verifications. In the case of bitcoin, for example, if you calculate the activity, you receive a coin. This process is called "mining."

Networks can also be maintained without mining through a consensus of network participants when a currency's supply is already known. Participants who verify transactions receive the underlying currency as payment for participating in the network. If network participants believe their currency is likely to hold its value, or even appreciate, they will come together to do the work. Because their activity does not create new coins, technically they are not "mining." Conceptually, it is very similar, and importantly, both systems create the possibility of a valuable reward to network participants.

SPECULATORS VS. MINERS

The relationship between speculators and those who actually do the work of mining is, well, complicated. Speculators are people who own a currency and have never done any work in the network. They do this because they believe the price is likely to rise over time. The more people who own (demand) the currency, the greater the price. The higher the price, the more a different set of people will be willing to do the underlying work. However, if the speculative cost gets too high, the cost of the underlying transactions can get too high. This phenomenon creates synergies and challenges in both extreme upside and extreme downside scenarios. It is because of this push–pull and underlying volatility that any token or coin cannot be a risk-free store of value. They can still be valuable, and some could be very valuable, but to be a risk-free store of value, the risk-free asset must be separated from the activities of speculators.

Who Maintains the Network?

If there is an incentive for doing something – a payment – and that payment is considered to have a value globally, then people around the world will spool up computers with the sole purpose of "mining." I know people who are in the business of selling equipment (hardware and software) so that you, in your own living room (or hopefully spare bedroom), can have a computer set up, plugged in, and dedicated to nothing more than verifying transactions on the blockchain – all with the premise that you will receive various forms of "coins" or "tokens" in return for your equipment and energy costs and effort in supporting the mining process. If the energy cost is low relative to the value received, then mining can be a great form of passive income for anybody anywhere on the planet who is connected to the Internet.

Blockchain is constantly looking at all data and all records to make sure they're secure and nobody is tampering with them. Imagine being protected by 1,000 soldiers, 1,000 secret service agents, 1,000 guard dogs, 1,000 accountants, and so on, all looking out all the time, to make sure your things are safe.

The network is also verifying *new* activity: transactions. For a new transaction to be posted to a block, it has to go through an extra special process, kind of like getting into college, joining a club, getting into a co-op, being brought into a fraternity – pick your own complicated process – but, once you are in, you are in for life. The process is driven by solving a math problem that essentially asks, Does this transaction belong on the block? Once that problem is solved, it must be verified – blessed if you will – by the other members of the network. Figuring out if something belongs is difficult; once admitted, it is easy (easier) to verify that it is in. It's like having soldiers, guard dogs, and secret service agents all verifying your student ID.

Finally, blockchain *can automate all contracts and agreements, including payment upon delivery, associated with any transaction.* Not only can you tell the soldiers, guard dogs, and secret service agents and accountants to protect your diary, but you can also tell them to monitor new activity (let the good guys in and keep the bad guys out) and give them orders, generally written in a format such as, "If this happens, then do this." For example: "Guard dogs, if a bad guy jumps the fence, hold him in place until the soldiers arrest him." In blockchain, an example would be, "When I die, give my kids this amount of money when they turn these ages."

Blockchain Components and Ecosystem

So far, we've looked at blockchain as though it were a single "thing" or phenomenon that occurs when a group of computers come together.

In reality, it is comprised of components, much like the Internet. Now that we know more about blockchain, we can look at its components to better understand the ecosystem.

Private and Public Blockchains

Don't think of blockchain as though there is just one of them. You may have heard the terms *intranet* and *Internet*. These two things can be built with the same underlying technologies and have the same look and feel and same core concepts. The primary difference is who has access. Only members of an intranet network can access intranet-hosted sites. The Internet can be accessed by virtually anyone, anywhere in the world, via a web browser. There are pros and cons to each structure, depending on your objectives and intended audience and use. This is similar to private and public blockchains.

Use Existing Infrastructure or Build Your Own?

There are some pretty major logistical challenges to building your own blockchain. Let's say you wanted to simply automate a contract for when you die. Rather than building your own private blockchain for this sole purpose, you could rent a blockchain, or better said, build upon an existing blockchain.

In Chapter 5, we discussed the difference between utility coins and utility tokens. We referred to Ethereum, which enables smart contracts or applications that, according to its website, "run exactly as programmed without any chance of fraud, censorship, or third-party interference." One of the features we saw was the ability to "create a tradable digital token that can be used as a currency, a representation of an asset, a virtual share, a proof of membership, or anything at all."[19]

Ethereum is a protocol. Think of it as the base layer. Many technologies have a base layer, including TCP/IP for the Internet, SMTP for e-mail, and VOIP for voice-over-Internet. With Ethereum, instead of making your own automated contract, you can run it on someone else's base layer, or blockchain. When you build a contract on Ethereum, you are creating an application of the underlying protocol. There are multiple blockchains that serve as protocols, or a base upon which decentralized applications can be built.

Think of it like a car and highway. The car runs on highways. Without the car, the highway has a pretty limited purpose and isn't very exciting. Without the highway, the car can't do as much, either. Another way to look at it is that Instagram is an application that runs on the Internet. Instagram chose to focus on building software, an application, on a public Internet. The company did not have to build the Internet to build its application. Just as anybody can build an application on the web today, anybody can access a variety of protocols to build their own applications on a public blockchain. Many people believe that outsourcing protocol development means less technical risk, less business risk, and less execution risk.

Proprietary or Open Sourced?

Let's say you wanted to build a car. You need an exterior, interior, engine and transmission, wheels, electronics, and other parts. You could start from the ground up and build your own exterior, interior, engine and transmission, and wheels. Each of those components has multiple subcomponents, so you would have to start by having a farm to grow the cow to make the leather. This isn't how most things are built in the physical or digital world. In the physical world, you might choose tires built by one company, interior built by another company, and perhaps build and design your own exterior.

In software, many people around the world collaborate on components to create a library of "greatest hits," arguing that this open-sourced software works better and is free. However, free is misleading. If all the components to your car were available for free and you could pick off the shelf everything you wanted to assemble it, curation would still require skill and would not be free.

Centralized or Decentralized?

When building a car, a central authority like Toyota, Ford, or BMW hires a design team to determine the best combination of components and an assembly team to put the components together on the manufacturing line. Similarly, central authorities like CNN and Fox filter, curate, edit, and post content to a user interface (a TV program or website).

An alternate approach would be something like Wikipedia, a "free encyclopedia, written collaboratively by the people who use it."[20] According to Wikipedia's website, "anyone can edit almost every page – and we are encouraged to **be bold**." This concept is frightening to some and incredibly powerful to others, Wikipedia is a great example of a decentralized process, a decentralized application.

How do we know it won't all be destroyed, that people won't put bad words out there and say malicious things? How will it maintain quality and integrity? Wikipedia has rules that govern the community. From the website: "Find something that can be improved and make it better – for example, spelling, grammar, rewriting for readability, adding content, or removing non-constructive edits. If you wish to add new facts, please try to provide references so they may be *verified*, or suggest them on the article's discussion page. Changes to controversial topics and Wikipedia's main pages should usually be discussed first."

Like Wikipedia, many communities are coming together to build decentralized projects, governed by rules, around a common vision and idea. Typically, these operate like design and assembly teams, pulling together different pieces of open-sourced code to create a decentralized application called a DApp (two syllables, not one – say the "D").

While the definition of a decentralized application is still under development and subject to debate, typical definitions include the following attributes:

- The code is open-source and autonomously managed.
- Records and data are stored using blockchain, providing trustless interaction and avoiding any single point of failure.
- Cryptographic tokens are used as a medium of exchange to reward users validating transactions or providing services on the network, etc.
- Tokens generated through a cryptographic algorithm.

There are three types of decentralized applications:

- Type I has its own blockchain, such as bitcoin.
- Type II has decentralized applications that use a Type I blockchain but are protocols and need tokens to function, such as the bitcoin omni layer, a digital currency and communications protocol built on the bitcoin blockchain.

- Type III has decentralized applications that use the protocol of a type II and are additionally protocols that have tokens necessary for their function, such as the SAFE Network that uses the omni protocol to issue safecoins.

HYPERLEDGER: OPEN-SOURCE BLOCKCHAINS

A group of large firms and entities from technology, financial services, business software, and consulting firms such as the Linux Foundation, IBM, Intel, SAP, JPMorgan, Wells Fargo, Accenture, and many others have come together under an umbrella project to support the collaborative development of open-source blockchains and related tools. This consortium calls the effort the Hyperledger or the Hyperledger Project.[21]

IBM describes the project this way: "The Hyperledger community is focused on the development, deployment, and use of open, transparent, reliable, and interoperable enterprise blockchains. That's why IBM has chosen Hyperledger Fabric as the foundation for the IBM Blockchain Platform. We're building additional value on an open-source blockchain protocol, so businesses can hit the ground running on their blockchain journeys."[22] IBM goes on to say that 250 companies are a part of the consortium and have contributed over 3.6 million lines of code.[23]

Protocol Tokens and App Coins/Tokens: Working Together

When we create kevincoin on Ethereum, we have a system in which two different coins/tokens are working together. Because the terms "coin" and "token" can become confusing, we will differentiate between the two by calling one the protocol token and the other the application token.

Kevincoin can simply be an application token built on the base protocol Ethereum, which uses its own protocol token. The way this coin exists and the way in which transactions are recorded, logged, and edited depends on the existence of the protocol token, Ethereum, the underlying blockchain.

Imagine 100 different kevincoins, all built upon one protocol. The value of the protocol is high, because many users are demanding the service of creating something, and the value of kevincoin is worthless. There is no demand, no underlying economic value. However, if we created a security or investment token affiliated with kevincoin, we could assign the rights to 25 percent of the company's profits to kevincoin holders. Now the dynamic has changed, and kevincoin is not only potentially valuable, it is potentially as valuable as any other investment in the world. The value is tied to the value of the underlying company.

What if we wanted to create a utility token on top of another protocol? We could create a virtual world in which kevincoin is considered a valuable currency (our virtual club example) and is perhaps an access right or a privilege in a game – it has no direct tangible economic rights or value. In this way, kevincoin can become an application protocol that sits on top of a base protocol.

Our system can move to three layers:

1. Application
2. Application protocol
3. Base protocol

Under this framework, application users may access or benefit from a blockchain-based application without needing to do the work associated with the underlying application protocol. Similarly, "workers" and/or speculators can invest in, or affiliate with, or do the work associated with a network based on the value they perceive they will receive over time – independent of whether they are users of the underlying application. This work can be different from the work required to maintain the underlying base blockchain protocol. You can have different users, accessing different platforms, with different benefits and the underlying work being done by different individuals with different incentives, all coming together at the top of the stack in a common user experience.

The Other Layers

On a cell phone, you can quickly download and connect different applications. Many applications come together for your benefit through a common device: your phone. These applications sometimes stand alone (the simple calculator that is included with the phone), and some may be standalone but pull in data from many different sources (your weather application). Finally, the application may be integrated with other applications.

Instagram works well because it integrates with your phone's camera application. Instagram did not need to create the underlying hardware (the camera), nor did it have to create the software that powers it (the camera application) or the storage library for all your photos (a separate application such as iPhoto). It is important that these different applications can interface or talk to each other. Different applications interface through what are called application programing interfaces or APIs, rules that let hardware, software, operating systems, and web-based systems talk to each other and share data.

A lot of these interfaces are standardized because they are common. For example, Instagram is not the only application that pulls in photos, so rather than reinvent the wheel, many of these bridges and connections can be created using a combination of open-sourced or custom software and/or standardized or custom application interfaces. The subset is that there is a universe of standardized communication protocols and many of these interact with open-sourced software.

Some bridges are needed for one-time, specific use. Let's say I want to upload a picture to Instagram and post it. I might post another picture in the future, but until I do, I don't necessarily need that bridge. Other bridges are more dynamic. For example, budgeting software such as Mint.com pulls data from many sources (your bank, your credit card, your retirement plan) every day. This data all converges into an interface that processes the information and provides the user up-to-the minute updates on their personal financial pictures. The process of Mint receiving information from your bank or Instagram receiving a photo is referred to as a "call." Mint "calls" your bank, and your bank answers. Instagram calls your photo library, and your library answers. Calls can be transactional, daily, or real time, and as such, data can be updated the same way (transactional, daily, or real time). This connectivity enhances the functionality and benefits of blockchain protocols. Connections can help with enhanced verification, trust, and security and enhance collaboration across users and systems.

The next time you question whether you should trust someone or something, imagine you could spool up infinite resources to check, verify, or be sure. If your answer is yes, with infinite resources you would feel secure, chances are blockchain could be the solution to the trust challenge you are facing. If you still would not feel confident in solving a trust gap with infinite resources, chances are there is a different underlying issue.

Summary of Pillar 3

Blockchain solves the trust gap. It makes sure data is secure, controls who has access rights, and can be used to enforce contracts. Blockchain can automate all contracts and agreements, including payment upon delivery, associated with a transaction. If parties to a transaction agree to terms, and it is coded on the network, the network will execute the orders as the parties outlined. Blockchain can make contract enforcement a predetermined reality. It works because it rewards participants in the network – the enforcers – for participating. It doesn't use a single enforcer; that would introduce risk and incentive conflicts. Instead, it spools up thousands of enforcers, creating rewards for the primary enforcer and smaller rewards for those who check and verify that the enforcer is doing what they are supposed to do. If the value of the reward exceeds the cost of executing the orders, there is always a market in enforcement.

IBM, one of the world's oldest multinational information technology companies, has this to say about blockchain on its website: "Blockchain can do for business what the internet did for communication. Blockchain provides a way to execute many transactions in a much better way. This is because 1) it is distributed, 2) it is permissioned, and 3) it is immutable – even a system administrator cannot delete a transaction."[24]

Blockchain technology can be as aggregated or deconstructed as you like. It can be a protocol and an application, built from the ground up, as a custom intranet for a select group of users. On the other hand, 100 percent can be outsourced to other providers in the ecosystem and/or whatever needs to be customized within the application can be decentralized and open sourced, interfacing with virtually infinite other systems via standard or custom application programming interfaces. This ability to share information across different applications means blockchain applications and tokens have the ability to specialize within a particular niche. One application might specialize in payments, another in identity verification, another in securely storing holdings (digital wallets and vaults), another in asset ownership, another in asset tokenization, etc. One application does not have to do everything. While this is quite clear on the web and on your phone, this simple idea doesn't appear to be clear to many newcomers to blockchain, who approach it as though everything has to be invented and created. Nothing could be further from the truth.

This, along with blockchain's ability to leverage decentralized, open-sourced structure, specialize within a niche, and create different permissions and uses within a vertical stack, mean blockchain should be able to scale with unprecedented speed, and as a result, dramatically disrupt traditional ways of interacting and doing business. But while blockchain is very powerful, it can't solve everything. Blockchain can only solve trust gaps on data within the network. Data outside the blockchain remains subject to the traditional process of verification.

Chapter 10

Pillar 4 – Capital Markets as a "Technology"

"In our view, derivatives are financial weapons of mass destruction carrying dangers that, while latent, are potentially lethal."

– Warren Buffett

We have covered three of the four pillars: the concept of a risk-free rate, money creation under the Credit Theory of Money as a secured claim on another's assets, and blockchain solving the trust gap. Our fourth pillar is the construct and advancement of modern capital markets.

Technologies are not just physical devices. They include intellectual property, business processes, and new ways of doing things. For example, what is the assembly line? It is a new process, a new technology, a new way of doing things. While there are many problems with our financial system, it is an incredible microcosm of advanced technology and new ways of doing things – advanced business processes. These processes enable you to be virtually cashless in your home country and travel the world with a single credit card. They enable a stunningly high percentage of the population to have access to credit for general liquidity, education, homes, and businesses at what are generally remarkably low rates. While it is easy to see advancements in technology (screens get bigger, speeds get faster, more features are added, and prices go lower), advancements in financial services are more nuanced and subtle, but perhaps even more significant in the long term. What do I mean? Very few things are the same today in capital markets as they were in 1920, let alone in 1820.

While some of these advancements could potentially be "financial weapons of mass destruction," we have to separate the tool from how the tool could be used. A knife, for example, is an amazing technology that can be used for cooking and day-to-day living. It can also be used for terrible acts. As we look at these technologies and advancements, we have to assess and isolate their underlying capabilities and possibilities from the actions of the actors who can and do use the tools the wrong way.

What Are Capital Markets?

Investopedia defines capital markets as "activities that gather funds from some entities and make them available to other entities needing funds. The core function of such a market is to improve the efficiency of transactions so that each individual entity doesn't need to do search and analysis, create legal agreements, and complete funds transfer."[1]

This is a good description, and I would build on it to frame the following core ideas.

Capital markets match those who have money with those who need money.

- Capital markets improve the overall efficiency of transactions.
- Central authorities oversee capital markets to protect against fraud, amongst other things.

- Capital markets are hosted on computer-based electronic trading systems.
- Capital markets are supported by many thousands of such systems.

Capital markets have many subcomponents. For the purposes of understanding money without boundaries, we will focus on a big-picture understanding of the esoteric world of money market funds and their primary ingredients: commercial paper and repurchase agreements. We also have to understand securitization – what it is, how it works, and the good, the bad, and the ugly it can create.

What Are Money Market Accounts?

When you deposit money (be it your paycheck or birthday money from your grandmother) at a bank or financial institution, you probably don't expect that your specific bills will be held in cash in a vault in your name. In fact, in the case of a check or paycheck, there never is any physical cash, but a transfer of "units" from one record to another. In the United States, these units are likely to be "dollars" from your employer to you. These dollars are not a claim on anything and can't be redeemed for anything. They are just units that are considered valuable to the people because they are a currency, a money: a medium of exchange (others will take my units), a unit of exchange (I understand what it means if something costs $1 or $1,000 and can relate it to me), and a store of value (I can keep my money in digital or physical units and buy something that costs those number of units).

The vast majority of these units (dollars) transfer via an electronic process such as "direct deposit" to your bank account and out, via transfer, to pay your mortgage, utilities, and other bills. These transfers can take place over a wire, in real time, or more commonly through an electronic funds transfer system via an automated clearing house (called "ETF" and "ACH" for short) in a batch process that takes place once daily. These transfers, in and out, are reconciled to an account, such as your bank account.

My wife is 10 years younger than me, and it has come to my attention that many younger people are not familiar with money markets. This is because the industry has undergone a significant change since the financial crisis of 2008. As such, we need to look at two distinct periods in the history of money markets: pre-2008 and post-2008.

Pre-2008

The problem with many bank accounts is that they pay a relatively low level of interest, sometimes zero. So, before 2008, my personal banking account for about 10 years was in a money market fund. This was the account from which I did all of my day-to-day transactions. I wrote checks, accessed money from an ATM, paid bills online, and used web bill pay. All of my electronic funds transferred in, and all of my electronic funds transferred out – you name it, and you can do it from a money market fund. My money market was a bit unique in that it wasn't as restricted as others that required $1,000 minimum checks and didn't facilitate as much daily activity. This isn't because they can't, technologically speaking, but because many generally prefer not to affiliate with the noise and activity around payments.

I was happy to be in my money market account because I earned a higher rate of interest than I would have in a traditional checking account. Until 2008, money market funds – with an objective of earning interest while maintaining a net asset value of $1 per share – were considered as safe and risk-free as bank savings accounts, delivering banking-like features with a higher interest rate. That is, until 2008.

Post-2008

On September 17, 2008, managers of the multibillion-dollar Reserve Fund, whose founder had helped invent money market funds more than 30 years earlier, announced they had "broken the buck," or reported that a share's value was less than a dollar. Investors would lose money. "We're really in uncharted territory here," Peter Crane, president of fund industry newsletter *Crane Data* told the *New York Times*.[2] Alarmed, the US Treasury offered insurance to money market funds under a one-year temporary guarantee program to prevent more money markets from following in the Reserve Fund's footsteps.

Something that had been solid for 30 years was suddenly not solid. Breaking the buck is a big deal. It means your cash, the paycheck you just deposited that you thought was worth $5,000, is now worth something less, say $4,850 (the net asset value of the Reserve Fund fell to 97 cents on the dollar). This wasn't the first time a fund had broken the buck; it happened in 1994 when Community Bankers Government Money Market became worth 94 cents. Imagine that you trusted something to be safe, and now it wasn't. How did this happen?

MONEY MARKET ACCOUNT OR MONEY MARKET FUND?

There are money market funds and money market accounts. Money market accounts are typically insured by the government, and most money market funds are not. Funds are a lot like mutual funds, but rather than changing the value or share price of the holding, they keep it constant, pegged at $1. As a result, any income generated is first used to pay expenses, and then the balance is distributed to fund holders as a higher interest (or dividend) payment. Operationally, as far as checks, deposits, banking features, and benefits go, both work in much the same way and have a lot in common. For our purposes, we'll focus on money market funds.

What's in a Money Market Fund?

Money market funds are comprised of loans. These loans are typically highly rated, which means the borrower is deemed by some central authority or rating agency to be safe. In the current environment, one central authority, the US government, deems investing in their debt – a claim backed by nothing – to be "risk free." (The irony is incredible.) Rating agencies are another form of central authority that assess credit quality. They may deem that a short-term loan (think overnight) to a large well-established institution is either risk free or nearly risk free.

Commercial Paper

Short-term loans to large companies are called commercial paper. Typically, commercial paper is not backed by any collateral specifically, but is a general unsecured claim on a company. As Investopedia explains: "An example of commercial paper is when a retail firm is looking for short-term funding to finance some new inventory for an upcoming holiday season. The firm needs $10 million, and it offers investors $10.1 million in face value of commercial paper in exchange for $10 million in cash, according to prevailing interest rates. In effect, there would be a $0.1 million interest payment upon maturity of the commercial paper in exchange for the $10 million in cash, equating to an interest rate of 1 percent. This interest rate can be adjusted for time, contingent on the number of days the commercial paper is outstanding."[3]

The point here is that the lender is not backed by any item of inventory in particular, or even a specific claim against the inventory being purchased, but a general claim against the entity making the purchase, like Macy's buying inventory for Christmas or a large car dealer financing inventory on its lot.

Repurchase Agreements

Another common holding in a money market fund is a repurchase agreement, a process in which somebody sells something at the end of the day and agrees to buy it back the next day. This is done to raise money. For example, imagine selling your car tonight when you go to bed and buying it back in the morning before you have to drive to work, or selling it before you go on vacation and buying it back when you return. You would have instant cash in your bank account, and you could do whatever you want with that cash. The purchaser owns your car.

To be clear, the collateral is not typically your car, but something like a highly liquid government bond. While technically there is a purchase and sale, because repurchase agreements are so short term, they are considered to be a form of loan. However, because they are technically a purchase, they are also considered to be very secure.

While having money overnight is helpful, sometimes people want money for longer. In this case, there is what is called an open repurchase agreement. As Investopedia explains: "An open repurchase agreement (also known as on-demand repo) works the same way as a term repo except that the dealer and the counterparty agree to the transaction without setting the maturity date. Rather, the trade can be terminated by either party by giving notice to the other party prior to an agreed-upon daily deadline. If an open repo is not terminated, it automatically rolls over each day. Interest is paid monthly, and the interest rate is periodically repriced by mutual agreement. ... An open repo is used to invest cash or finance assets when the parties do not know how long they will need to do so."

Repurchase agreements are basically a form of on-demand, secured, collateralized debt. According to the Securities Industry and Financial Markets Association, "With a national amount outstanding of $2.2 trillion, the repurchase agreement (repo) market is a vital, yet not always well understood, part of the US financial system. The repo market represents a liquid, efficient, tested, and safe way for firms to participate in a short-term financing arrangement, providing funding for their day-to-day business operations. Repurchase agreements are a sale of financial assets combined with a promise to repurchase those assets in the future (in many cases, the repurchase is agreed for the following business day). These arrangements have the economic characteristics of a secured loan – cash vs. collateral – and are used by short-term institutional cash investors as a secured money market instrument and by dealers to finance long positions in securities."[4] While $2.2 trillion is a large figure, it is just a piece of the pie. There are large markets for repurchase agreements throughout North America, Europe, Asia, Australia, and some parts of Africa and South America.

How Efficient Is the Repurchase Market?

Interest rates are normally positive, meaning people typically pay to borrow money. When you get a car loan, a home loan, or a student loan, you typically pay the bank for the privilege and ability to use the money.

As of February 1, 2019, the Repo Funds Rate in Europe was as follows:[5]

- Euro: −0.43%
- Belgium: −0.461%

- France: −0.438%
- Germany: −0.553%
- Italy: −0.398%
- Netherlands: −0.489%
- Spain: −0.435%

Yes, these are negative interest rates. A negative interest rate means the lender is paying the borrower to borrow money. Why on earth would somebody pay somebody to borrow money? Participants are *paying for safety*. While it may seem like a crazy idea on the surface, paying for safety is one of the oldest ideas related to money and valuables. Throughout time, people have paid various central authorities (banks, governments) to store their goods. If you aren't familiar with safe deposit boxes, you can pay a bank to rent a specific section of its safe. You get the benefit of the bank's extremely secure vault infrastructure, guards, and security system, yet you only have to pay a fraction of the price and, equally important, you only have to pay for the space you need. Gold, of course, has no interest rate. If you pay a bank to store your gold, you are experiencing a negative interest rate. Obviously, the market perceives that the construct is exceptionally safe – safer than, for example, leaving the money in a bank deposit program where it could be exposed to the bank's risks.

Our first pillar was the notion of the concept of the risk-free rate. Our second pillar was the concept that the risk-free rate, and money, can be created via borrowing and the Credit Theory of Money. Recall that a repurchase agreement is fulfilling the needs of both parties: liquidity for one, safety for the other. Theory and reality are converging. We are seeing this phenomenon today in the repurchase market in Europe, where the construct of absolute safety and liquidity is being accomplished via borrowing. A similar phenomenon is being seen in commercial paper markets and, as a result, rolls up to money market funds.

How Does This Relate to Our Third Pillar, Blockchain?

To understand how blockchain enters the picture, we need to understand some of the "how" of repurchase agreements. According to Investopedia, "The most common type is a third-party repo (also known as a tri-party repo). In this arrangement, a clearing agent or bank conducts the transactions between the buyer and seller and protects the interests of each. It holds the securities and ensures that the seller receives cash at the onset of the agreement and that the buyer transfers funds for the benefit of the seller and delivers the securities at maturation."[6] The article goes on to explain that in addition to acting as the neutral third party, these clearing firms follow the pre-set rules for market participants and settle transactions. Importantly, the third parties don't match borrowers and lenders. They simply make sure the rules are followed. Investopedia estimates that 90 percent of the repo market clears this way.

Now, let's think back to blockchain's ability to decentralize, fill trust gaps, and automate contracts. For now, let's let the soldiers, guard dogs, secret service agents, and accountants stand by while we dive just a little deeper into capital markets.

What Is Securitization, and Why the Prejudice Against It?

Securitization is the practice of dividing a single loan between several lenders in order to share the risk. Securitization has gotten a bad rap because many people blame mortgage securitization for the 2008 financial crisis. The media and academics have debated this ever since the housing and stock markets crashed, and all of them are able to find plenty of data to back up their theories. The fact is, though, securitization itself is neither inherently good nor bad. Yes, 2008 got ugly – really, really ugly – and mortgage securitization played a role. But imagine a terrible accident in which a drunk driver kills a person – it isn't the car's fault; it is the driver's. Securitization is itself a long and widely held practice in every aspect of the financial industry, from student loans to mortgages, and it, like the vehicle in the drunk driving accident, is not to blame. The problem leading up to 2008 was all about reckless drivers of the vehicles, not the vehicles themselves.

In 2011, while the country was still smarting, Robert J. Samuelson pointed out in a *Wilson Quarterly* article titled "Rethinking the Great Recession" that Americans "turn every major crisis into a morality tale in which the good guys and the bad guys are identified and praised or vilified accordingly." Because politicians, journalists, and intellectuals feel compelled to find and publicly humiliate the perpetrators, Samuelson wrote, there was "an outpouring of books, articles, and studies that describe what happened: the making of the housing bubble, the explosion of complex mortgage-backed securities, the ethical and legal shortcuts used to justify dubious but profitable behavior." That crime-and-punishment story is missing the point, Samuelson wrote, because the Great Recession was really about boom and bust. When inflation began to subside in the late 1980s after insane runaway inflation in the early 1980s, it triggered "corrupting overconfidence, the catalyst for the reckless borrowing, overspending, financial speculation, and regulatory lapses that caused the bust."[7]

The fact is, securitization is responsible for a lot of good things. Sharing risk allows interest rates to be lower than they would otherwise so students can get loans to go to college, then buy their first cars, and then their first houses. Without securitization, none of these things would be possible for a segment of the population. For the vast majority of people who borrow money at some point in their life to start families and businesses, securitization lowers the cost. By providing access to more capital at lower cost, securitization is a core piece of people's entire financial lives, and it certainly doesn't deserve the vilification it has received. At its core, securitization is a completely neutral concept. Like we do with many things in life, we humans tend to corrupt it when we put it into practice.

How Securitization Works

To get an idea of how securitization works, let's say there is a young person and an older person who are both fabulously wealthy. The young person has $20 million to invest, and the older person has $80 million to invest. A bank has packaged a group of 500 home loans with borrowers paying 5 percent interest on loans with a face value of $100 million. The two decide to take all of their money, partner together, and buy these loans from the bank.

If the interest rate is 5 percent, and the partners equally divide and distribute their shares, the younger investor would earn $1 million and the older investor would earn $4 million in interest on their investments. The partners also agree to split any additional gains or losses, 80 percent to the older partner and 20 percent to the younger partner. This is a simple structure, but perhaps not optimal for either of the two of them. Perhaps the younger investor wants more return, and the older investor wants more safety.

An alternative framework could be that the younger investor determines she wants to earn a 10 percent rate of return on the $20 million she's investing. There is only so much pie to be divided, so if the younger investor receives $2 million per year, there would only be $3 million left for the older investor. The older investor says she is willing to take $3 million of interest, but in exchange, risk and reward will no longer be shared equally. The older investor will not take a dime of loss until the younger investor loses all of her money. The older investor is paying for safety. While there isn't a direct cost, she is making $1 million less per year but adding what is more or less a $20 million insurance policy against any form of loss. The partners materially changed their risk characteristics with a slight change to their reward characteristics.

What about the younger investor? This potentially is a good trade for her as well. She looks at the underlying loans and sees that they are backed by homes worth $125 million. If the borrowers stop paying, the investors have the right to foreclose, a process in which the sheriff kicks out the homeowner and the investor can sell the home. Assuming these houses were well-appraised, the younger investor believes it would be difficult to lose money and accepts the trade. The younger investor is incentivized to do her homework about the asset, and the older investor can, to some degree, rely on the younger investor's efforts.

Times are good, and the rate of return jumps from 5 percent to 10 percent, a 100 percent increase. And now, my favorite question: *What could possibly go wrong?*

We all see this coming. What if housing prices fell 20 percent and the assets the younger investor thought were worth $125 million fell to $100 million? Arguably, both the younger investor and the older investor are fine – nervous, but fine. At this point, nobody has taken a loss, and both investors are still getting income.

What if prices fell by 30 percent and the homes that were worth $125 million are now worth $87.5 million? The younger investor guaranteed against a loss on the first $20 million, so she loses $12.5 million of her $20 million investment. The value of her investment would fall by 62.5 percent. The older investor is perhaps nervous, but she hasn't lost any money.

What if home values fell by 37 percent? At this point, the $125 million is worth $78.75 million. The older investor, who considered herself bulletproof, has lost $1.25 million, or 1.5 percent of her investment. The younger investor was, of course, wiped out. If this were a money market fund, the buck would have been broken.

This scenario is why securitization has been vilified, but it is again an example of how securitization is put into practice, not the practice itself. One of the many problems that contributed to the 2008 financial crisis was the overall lack of transparency and investors' inability to clearly see into the value of underlying assets in multiple slices (tranches) of securitized pools of loans. Incentives were also a problem, as people pushed boundaries because they were incentivized to do so. If a money market competes on rate, rather than on safety and security, then the portfolio manager's incentive is to deliver the highest return rather than the safest product. These incentive conflicts happened at virtually every level of the system: homeowner, mortgage broker, appraiser, bank, capital markets, and investors. It created a toxic, explosive combination, but the problem wasn't securitization as a structure. It's important to look at how we can get the good from this process and filter out the bad, something blockchain can help facilitate.

How Subordination Works

When you get a loan, typically originated by a bank, that bank often holds your loan for a little while and then combines it with a number of similar other loans. They then package this group of loans into a security, an investment, and sell it to a group of investors. Those investors then expect borrowers to continue repaying the loans. This process of efficiently matching borrowers and lenders and converting loans into securities is a regular part of the daily functioning of capital markets. Investors can decide how they want to divvy up and share that risk as well as the investment's rewards.

Shouldn't everyone want an equal share of both risk and reward? Usually not. It's a lot like our example of the 80-year-old and the 40-year-old. Some investors strive for safety; some strive for a higher return. Just as these objectives can be accomplished in a two-party lending transaction, they can also be accomplished in an investment security where risk and reward can be shared differently. This happens through a practice called subordination, in which one investor, or group of investors, takes losses first in exchange for a higher return. Often it is not until they have lost all their money that the rest of the investors start to lose their money. Through this process, a group of loans can be grouped into a variety of securities, each with different degrees of risk and reward.

Now, let's turn this around, and instead of the $20 million investor taking the risk, the $80 million investor acts as the buffer for the $20 million "safe" piece, with $125 million worth of property backing the loans in front of them. For the $20million investor to lose money, the value of the underlying homes would have to fall by 84 percent, and the safe investor would still get 100 cents on the dollar back. This is because the $20 million loan is protected by $125 million of assets; $20 million divided by $125 million equals 16%, meaning that the other 84 percent would first have a 100 loss before there was any loss to the first 16 percent. While this has never happened before in the United States, housing prices, of course, could fall by 84 percent. One way to manage the risk would be to increase the number of homes in and the geographic distribution of the pool. For example, rather than one $125 million mega mansion, the pool could be comprised of 250 homes worth $500,000 each, or $125 million worth of homes. If this isn't safe enough, the system can keep iterating for infinity.

Slicing and Dicing Our Way to Risk-Free

So, let's say a group of 4,000 people, each with $5,000 ($20 million total), pooled together around a common objective of achieving a 10 percent return on their money. Similarly, a group of 16,000 individuals could seek out a safe store of value for their $5,000 ($80 million total).

Importantly, there is no reason the participants have to invest the same amount. One person could invest $1, another $100,000, and another $1 million. Nothing restricts the number of pools people can invest in, creating another layer of potential customization. The system offers infinite flexibility to break down to any unit.

Securitization enables infinite slicing and dicing. You could have three groups, with one group taking the first 5 percent of the pool and the first 5 percent of the loss, looking for a 20 percent return; another group could take the next 40 percent of the pool and 49 percent of the loss for a 10 percent return; yet another group could take the final $50 million at a rate of 0 percent because they consider it to be risk-free.

Still not safe enough? You can add additional layers of subordination or more collateral, make the underlying loans more diverse, change the terms to an overnight loan, wrap it with insurance – you can keep iterating until you determine it is risk-free.

Worried that you won't be able to determine whether something is risk-free? This is where the decentralized market comes into play. I don't contribute to Wikipedia, but I read it all the time. The global contributors to Wikipedia make it an amazing encyclopedia – not perfect, but the best I've found. The same concept applies here. Every market participant who is lower in the stack than you has higher incentives than you to get it right. Everyone in the same section of the stack has exactly the same incentives as you. If the price is set to zero, the market has found an equilibrium and structure it believes is risk-free. That doesn't mean it is risk-free, but market actions, where money is on the line, matter more than relying on a central authority, such as a government or a rating agency.

Summary of Pillar 4

Capital markets leverage a complex system of technologies to match those who have capital with those who need capital. Capital markets have led to dramatic advancements in the way many financing activities are done, including the creation of money market funds and their key components, commercial paper and repurchase agreements. It is technically possible for money market funds to work exactly like a typical bank account with checks, ATM, debit card, funds transfer, and all other banking services as you know them, and some money market funds work that way today.

Money market funds are typically comprised of loans to governments, companies, or people or entities that hold assets. Sometimes these loans are secured, and sometimes they are not, but in either case the loans are considered extremely safe. Often a central authority such as a regulatory body or government determines what is eligible to be in a money market. This is the Credit Theory of Money in practice as a loan becomes money, a store of value – and this happens today, proving the theory is indeed a reality.

Certain segments of capital markets are very efficient – so efficient that no one is worried about a loss and people in fact pay for the safety of these transactions. This is represented in negative interest rates, in which people are paid to borrow – a situation that exists in many places around the world today – because the loans are considered so secure that they're risk-free. This shows that the risk-free rate can be created by borrowing against assets, and even unsecured claims for short-term loans against very secure borrowers have rates at and below 0 percent. This also happens today.

Securitization is the process of pooling multiple loans and converting them from individual loans into a security or investment. Different investors are then able to share in the risk and reward in a virtually infinite combination of sorting, segmenting, and grouping loans, cash flows, and payment prioritization.

Blockchain can play many important roles in this ecosystem. It can automate and enforce contracts following rules set by market participants to settle transactions, take out the middlemen, fill in trust gaps, and decentralize the process. Blockchain can do this through utility tokens operating on a protocol dedicated to the task. It can also create investment tokens or participation rights to different participants in a securitization. Finally, blockchain can make the whole process – each layer, every piece of collateral, and all of the data – secure and transparent.

Part Three

THE CONCEPT

Chapter 11

Transcending Space and Time

"The most dangerous weapon in the galaxy is money, Captain."
– Duchess Satine Dryze in *Star Wars: The Clone Wars*

L et's say I zoomed up to Mars in SpaceX, and after a long, somewhat harrowing flight, I wanted a drink. If I walked into the first bar I saw and plunked down a dollar bill, a twenty-dollar bill, my Visa, or even flashed my bitcoin wallet (if I had one), I'm pretty sure the bartender would laugh at me. I could tell him all day long that this was legal tender where I'm from and highly respected by all countries on Earth, but why would he trust me, an alien from a far-off planet he knows nothing about? How could he verify that he would ever actually get paid through his planet's system, whatever it might be? Because this universe doesn't have a system in place for people to make transactions that transcend space and time, I would end up thirsty.

If money is so valuable, shouldn't we be able to easily, quickly, and clearly communicate its value to anyone, anywhere–even on Mars or in deep space?

It's a historic problem as well as a futuristic one, as civilizations on planet Earth made contact and had to figure out how to transact with each other. The point of this exercise is not that I believe there will be a near-term interaction with people from other planets; it is that I believe there is value exploring how we would communicate a common store of value that we would both trust.

From *Star Trek* to the Death Star

Money, or the question of how cultures completely alien to each other make financial transactions, has been a continuing theme – and puzzle – in science fiction since the genre was born. One of the earliest and most abiding sci-fi television franchises, *Star Trek,* "made clear and emphasized several times in the course of the show that the Federation does not have money," *Trekonomics* author Manu Saadia said in *Wired.*[1] In the twenty-fourth century, when *Star Trek* was set, humans have unified as a species following a nuclear third world war, and Vulcan aliens have welcomed them into a galactic federation and given them replicator technology that abolishes scarcity. "A lot has changed in the past 300 years," Captain Jean-Luc Picard tells a cryogenically unfrozen twentieth-century businessman in *Star Trek: The Next Generation.* "People are no longer obsessed with the accumulation of things. We've eliminated hunger, want, the need for possessions. We've grown out of our infancy."[2]

Legend has it that screenwriter and producer Gene Roddenberry, who aired the first *Star Trek* television episode in 1966, was very specific about money in the twenty-fourth century. He said in addition to the concept that people were no longer interested in accumulating wealth, there would also be no currency.[3] "One of the things that's interesting about *Star Trek* is that it does try to imagine a post-scarcity economy where there's no money," Annalee Newitz, the editor of *Gawker*'s io9 blog said during a New York Comic Con panel on *Star Trek* economics. "People don't work for it. People don't work because they have to but because they want to."[4] Or as Saadia explained in *Wired,* cultivating talent and intellect is really the only way to gain status in a world without material wealth. "What is not abundant in *Star Trek*'s universe is the captain's chair," he said.[5]

This is all very utopian and lovely, but in my mind, Roddenberry simply found an elegant way to avoid the topic of money altogether. Yes, replicators could make the need to purchase things unnecessary, but what about payment for services—a huge chunk of any economy? Plus, Vulcans often had to find and use money to transact with planets that still had currencies. The whole concept of a world without any money is challenging, and it inevitably ends up in a whole lot of thirsty galactic travelers with no means of getting a drink.

In *Star Wars,* the sci-fi franchise that emerged in the 1970s, people clearly do use money. As Investopedia explains it, thousands of currencies are used on individual planets, but both the Republic and the Empire support galactic credits that are useful on inner-rim planets closer to trade hubs but worthless in wilder outer-rim planets.[6] According to the *Star Wars* wiki, the *wupiupi* is a currency used exclusively in the outer-rim territories, and various commodities were used as makeshift currencies in some areas. The rare nova crystal is used so often in barter that it is considered a de facto currency.[7] In *Star Wars: The Force Awakens*, Rey junks parts and sells them for food on the outer-rim planet Jakku, *Investopedia* points out, "because the only thing that matters on a planet with so little development is eating enough to stay alive."[8]

In *Star Wars: Episode 1 – The Phantom Menace,* when Qui Gon Jinn and Watto, Anakin's owner, are bartering over the cost of a ship, Watto refuses to take Republic credits, saying he needs something "more real." Just as libertarians and cryptocurrency fans distrust the "full faith and credit" US dollar, citizens of the planet Tatooine don't trust the Republic's fiat currency. With control of the banks, Emperor Palpatine is able to print his own money, and according to Washington University of St. Louis assistant professor Zachary Feinstein, he will spend $419 quintillion (that's $419,000,000,000,000,000,000) to build the Death Star, a moon-sized space station that can destroy entire planets, and fund its fleet.[9] If this sounds hauntingly familiar, that might be what the production team at Lucasfilm intended.

"Copper, Beads, and Such Like Trash" as Money

Earth is certainly a microcosm of the entire universe—which is what makes science fiction so much fun—and we've had our own challenges and conflicts over money, as we saw in Chapter 1. When Christopher Columbus set out to discover and conquer European countries' "first frontier" (worlds away from the "final frontier" in *Star Trek*), it was the first encounter between civilizations that had never before commingled — like humans meeting the Vulcans. Each of these civilizations had some form of money, whether a barter system or otherwise. There's no shortage of historical references to how Columbus and his fellow explorers, as well as the European settlers, knew how to take advantage of that. In 1524, a navigator from Florence named Giovanni de Verrazano wrote that the natives at Narragansett Bay prized "bells, azure crystals, and other toys to hang in their ears and about their necks." In Virginia, Captain John Smith noted the natives were "generally covetous of copper, beads & such like trash." For a pound or two of blue beads, Smith received 200 or 300 bushels of corn—and parted good friends with his trading partner.[10]

Were the Native Americans being taken advantage of? You could argue that if they took the trinkets home and were loved and admired for bringing home a cool, shiny object no one had ever seen before, the trades were completely worth it. The beads, Stephen Donnelly explains in *Historical Journal of Massachusetts*, "were a medium of exchange for the Native Americans of no less intrinsic value as gold was to the settlers, and therefore seemingly a bargain when traded for surplus pelts."[11] And while pelts could be considered a medium of exchange during the most heated days of fur trading in the United States and Canada in the fourteenth through seventeenth centuries, the Hudson Bay Company did set an official standard, the *made beaver,* that was essentially a monetary unit. Though no coins were ever minted, the standard served as a common unit of account for measuring goods such as kettles, blankets, beads, and lace, and furs such as fox, martin, lynx, and wolf.[12]

Encouraged by the fur traders, Native Americans ignored their own instincts and slaughtered the beavers, foxes, buffalo, and other animals that had sustained them. In essence, everyone involved killed their own trade, illustrating what Donnelly calls "the folly of unregulated market capitalism operating in the realm of renewable resources." This led to fabulous wealth for a select few, men like German-American businessman John Jacob Astor, the first multi-millionaire in the United States, and limited wealth for a limited time for relatively few more – and in the end, led to "extinction of the animals and therefore the trade."[13]

From the beginning here on planet Earth, it seems, we've struggled to get this money thing right – and this is where our superhero, blockchain, could step in to revolutionize "money." By providing verification at the first, weakest bridge into a node, blockchain eliminates the need to just trust. Native Americans would understand that gold was valuable to Columbus, who would be aware that headdresses were valuable to them. Columbus could say, "Hey, no worries. If we take advantage of each other, I get your headdress, and you get my boat." Putting a claim against an asset far and above the value of what they're trading provides the perfect store of value. The claim on an asset becomes money, and if we're able to deal in fractional claims on those assets, Columbus will behave — because if he doesn't, he'll lose his ship. If he's pledging everything of value to him for, say, a beaver pelt, the Native American doesn't have to worry about getting repaid because Columbus is not going to lose everything over something small. The Native American can verify this by looking into his network through blockchain.

BITCOIN'S MASSIVE ENERGY CONSUMPTION

Money, commerce, and the impact on the environment is both an old and a new topic. The energy consumption used to power the servers that run bitcoin's software in 2017 was estimated to be equal to the annual energy consumption of all of Ireland,[14] and a new study estimates that could nearly quadruple in the next few years.[15] Estimates about how much money bitcoin mining actually uses range wildly. One study estimates that bitcoin mining consumes the equivalent of 20 European countries, and another estimates it consumes more energy than 159 individual countries.[16] Annual costs are estimated to be over $1.5 billion – excluding the environmental impact –all to create something with limited supply and no underlying economic value. It is important to know that all uses of blockchain technology do not need to consume as much energy. Surely, there is a better way.

A Store of Value that Transcends Space and Time

Whether here on planet Earth or in a galaxy far, far away, once-independent nodes learn to interact with very little communication as bridges are built between societies. Cheyenne Indians living in the middle of the United States had vastly different cultural values from people living in London in the fourteenth century because the two worlds had never been connected. When Christopher Columbus first interacted with the native people he encountered during his journeys, he needed to quickly figure out what those cultures valued in order to dominate them in trade. Lacking that understanding results in a high probability that one party will get screwed.

When we have information asymmetry in which I don't know what's dear to you, we end up with a problem of verification and trust. What we really need at that point is the ability to do a Vulcan mind meld, a technique in which Vulcans merge their minds with the essence of someone else's mind through their fingers. I need perfect information directly from your head about how you perceive things to directly connect my node to your node, because I know the incentive for anyone in a transaction to lie is very high. Imagine if I could connect through your portal and see into the civilization in which you live, understand what your people value and exactly what they consider assets, and know exactly what they're worth on a proportional and relative basis — with full verification from every member of your community. Further, imagine I knew and understood my ability to look through to secured claims on those assets. As long as I trust my connection into your network, which would be possible with multiple points of verification, receiving information from your entire node dramatically lowers the odds that you can take advantage of me.

For the Native Americans, this would mean that instead of having to trust one man, Columbus, on his word, they could take the word of the one million people living in Spain—and beyond—because someone in Spain has done business with someone in France, who's done business with someone in England, Italy, and Egypt. Once the Native Americans build their bridge into Spain, they'll understand the store of value across the European continent. As the different nodes in the network overlap, their ability to verify increases at a logarithmic pace. Over time, this network is fortified so it's almost infinitely strong.

Chapter 12

Bringing the Building Blocks Together

"It is technically possible to control the quantity of any kind of token money so that its value will behave in a desired manner, and that it will for this reason retain its acceptability and its value."

– F.A. Hayek, *The Denationalization of Money*

During Part 1, we laid our foundation by looking at money throughout time and the fundamentals of money and banking. We explored theories around money and banking and examined the rise of cryptocurrency and the role model system. From there, we established four pillars or building blocks to put together a new framework around money.

Pillar 1: There should be a risk-free asset.

Pillar 2: Money is credit, and credit is money. Money always has been an asset or a claim on an asset. This is the Credit Theory of Money. Money can be created by borrowing against an otherwise risky asset.

Pillar 3: Problems around trust can be solved via blockchain.

Pillar 4: Advancements in capital markets technology like money markets, securitization, commercial paper, and repurchase agreements enable virtually infinite combinations of sorting, segmenting, grouping, and managing risk.

We can reframe these pillars as steps toward a goal.

1. The goal is to create a risk-free asset, a safe store of value.
2. The risk-free asset can be created via borrowing. This process creates money. This is the Credit Theory of Money in practice.
3. The multiple trust gaps associated with this solution can be managed and solved via blockchain and decentralized community management.
4. This community can be managed via a structure that looks and feels like a money market fund, built upon a foundation of secured loans with unprecedented security and transparency.
5. Direct and decentralized connections result in secondary benefits to network participants.

The fundamental idea is really quite simple. The future of money is fully decentralized, community-managed direct money markets managed and facilitated by blockchain technology. Within these money markets will be a variety of solutions and therefore a variety of rates. One solution, the epicenter, is the creation of the risk-free asset.

Much like money markets today, these money markets will serve as a medium of exchange. And, much like money markets today, these money markets will be able to exist in any unit of value, including their own. The difference is that these decentralized money markets will be a superior store of value because, unlike today's money markets that peg to a currency, such as the dollar, they will peg to being risk-free, offering a zero rate of real return but a nominal rate of return equal to inflation in every market. Lenders' purchasing power will be protected. Borrowers will be able to borrow at a rate equal to inflation.

While the whole process can happen within the community, by the community, for the community, there are also a series of steps through which the evolution can take place, with the baton being handed gradually from the physical to virtual world.

A Known Store of Value:
The Blockchain Revolution

We are trying to create a transparent and certain store of value. We are not trying to create a store of value because somebody says it is a store of value: we are seeking a known store of value. How do we know something is valuable? Because the market tells us so and adjusts every day to all conditions.

Fiat money (paper money) is intrinsically worthless and only deemed to have value because a central authority says it does. Commodity money is tied to a commodity, such as gold or silver. But under the Credit Theory of Money, money is credit, and credit is money. As Innes puts it: "The Credit Theory is this: that a sale and purchase is the exchange of a commodity for credit. From this main theory springs the sub-theory that the value of credit or money does not depend on the value of any metal or metals, but on the right which the creditor acquires to 'payment,' that is to say, to satisfaction for the credit, and on the obligation of the debtor to 'pay' his debt and conversely on the right of the debtor to release himself from his debt by the tender of an equivalent debt owed by the creditor, and the obligation of the creditor to accept this tender in satisfaction of his credit."[1]

Blockchain makes Friedrich Hayek's idea that banks could post their financials in daily newspapers possible – but in 5G – and it actually begins to make his dream of denationalizing money possible on a much more granular scale through a completely decentralized process.

In the financial world, blockchain will allow us to have decentralized, transparent money market accounts, and we could actually know what we own, unlike today's securitized, sliced-and-diced accounts. People will have unprecedented granular ability to sort, segment, and group transactions and data across infinite nodes without any intermediaries.

This is the holy grail the Nobel laureates have been chasing since the Great Depression, the fulfillment of Hayek's dream of denationalized money. For the first time ever, we can lower uncertainty in peer-to-peer transactions without any intervention from political and economic institutions – with technology alone. With blockchain, we can create trust and limited supply *and* tie it to things we know have underlying economic value. Rather than being tethered to a limited supply of 21 million like bitcoin, you are tethered to zero risk, a dynamic – a concept – that transcends time and space.

A Different Objective: Zero Risk

In theory, staying pegged to the dollar, as money market funds do, is a great idea, and they've historically been well regarded because of this discipline. But as we've seen, any time you have a central authority such as the Reserve Fund, you have incentive conflict. Investors want higher rates of return, so they incentivize money market managers to take more risk by moving their assets to the fund delivering the highest return. This makes sense on the surface. If I offer you a money market fund paying 1 percent or a money market fund paying 2 percent, which one would you like? Most investors seek the higher yield.

But what if we inverted the objective? What if we had a system that instead of striving for the highest amount of risk it can "get away with" seeks absolute safety with zero return? "Zero" could, of course, be the objective of a money market fund.

Weight, Mass, and the "Risk-Free Rate"

How much do you weigh? A simple question, unless you're in the time/space continuum. Mass and weight are separate and distinct concepts. According to Wikipedia, "In common usage, the mass of an object is often referred to as its weight, though these are in fact different concepts and quantities. In scientific contexts, mass is the amount of 'matter' in an object (though 'matter' may be difficult to define), whereas weight is the force exerted on an object by gravity. In other words, an object with a mass of 1 kilogram will weigh approximately 9.81 newtons on the surface of the Earth (its mass multiplied by the gravitational field strength), since the newton is a unit of force while the kilogram is a unit of mass. The object's weight will be less on Mars (where gravity is weaker), more on Saturn, and negligible in space when far from any significant source of gravity, but it will always have the same mass."[2]

Similarly, we must separate the concept of a risk-free asset into a concept like the kilogram, a measure of mass, from the forces that are exerted upon it, like the newtons of gravitational force around it – a measure that can exist with consistency in any environment.

The Kilogram and the Specimen

For a long time the kilogram was determined by a specimen known as the International Prototype of the Kilogram, which Reuters called a "shiny lump of platinum-iridium kept in a special glass case" at the International Bureau of Weights and Measures (French acronym BIPM). But the specimen can pick up microparticles of dirt and be affected by the atmosphere, meaning its weight could vary. In 2018, the BIPM decided to redefine the kilograms in terms of the Planck constant. "It is arguably the most significant redefinition of an SI unit since the second was recalculated in 1967, a decision that helped ease communication across the world via technologies like GPS and the internet," Reuters noted.[3] This is just another example of how scientists have been working to redefine nearly every unit of measurement into one that transcends the space-time continuum.

We can take a similar approach to defining risk-free, starting with the framework used in weights and measures: a specimen. Long-term, the specimen is defined simply as zero. Zero is the fulcrum, or the balance point, the point at which you can store money with what the market is pricing as safe, but get no return. Zero also does not mean the absolute safest in the world. As we have seen for almost a decade since the global financial crisis, many people are willing to pay for safety, with trillions of dollars exposed to negative interest rates. At this zero, you don't pay for safety and you don't receive a return on your asset. It is simply zero, determined by the market at any given point in time. As such, the conditions that drive zero can change and evolve based on the forces around it. Zero is constant, like Plank's constant; everything else around it changes.

Let's take a look at what an optimal "specimen" could look like. Doing so requires isolating risks into categories related to credit, operations, and interest rates.

Credit Criteria Risks

1. The loan must be secured (backed by an asset).
2. There must be a clear ability for the lender to claim the asset and sell it at a price higher than the amount of the underlying loan.
3. The lender must never end up with the actual asset and must be able to liquidate the asset to recover costs, fees, and the time value of their money in any liquidation process. In the ideal specimen, the asset could be liquidated within a day.
4. The loan must be exceptionally short term. This could be 30 days. For this specimen, the loan is reset daily.
5. The lending criteria must have no observed historic loss. Any observed historic loss – including the Great Recession, the Great Depression, and all other global crises – means it is not risk-free. The loan to value must have enough cushion to protect the lender so that if the value of the underlying asset decreases, the asset is still valuable relative to the claim on the asset.
6. The loan must have a margin of safety relative to any other historic event. Records are broken. Chances are low that the crises we have witnessed so far are the largest we will ever witness in the time/space continuum. Therefore, there must be a margin of safety relative to any historic loss.

Items that fit these criteria:

– An overnight loan secured by a gold ring for 50 percent of the liquidation value of the ring.
– An overnight loan to a college secured 2:1 by the college endowment's diversified portfolio of stocks and bonds.

These are claims, a currency no different than paper currency issued by a country with a convertible claim on tangible assets – like the initial dollar (which of course has nothing in common with the current dollar).

Operational and Regulatory Risks

Operational risk is related to the ability to enforce the underlying contracts and terms of these financial agreements. With blockchain, this could be completely managed by the community, for the community, in a nonprofit, fully decentralized structure through private agreements. The community, much like a credit union or other not-for-profit, would be aligned around a common objective: the ability to borrow and lend at the risk-free rate. It is in the best interest of the community to enforce the community's rules.

Because the rules are programmed, set criteria, they can be managed automatically. The community records the contract and the rules. For example, when a borrower pledges one gold ring and receives funds, the rules are that if the loan is not repaid, the lender will sell the ring to repay the loan. There can be no discrimination or cases of people of different races or sexual orientation receiving different rates in this completely rules-based level playing field for all.

For now, lenders and borrowers must follow laws, rules, and regulations, particularly with respect to the process of originating, servicing, and collecting on loans. Failure to comply with a law or regulation could make a contract unenforceable, which would certainly not make it risk-free. Therefore, in the near term there is likely a role for a servicer (a bank or nonbank entity) to handle the process of extending credit, servicing loans, and collecting on credit during delinquencies.

Until there is confidence in the operational capabilities of a virtual decentralized platform, there is operational risk that orders or contracts may not be executed. Service providers can indemnify, insure, and protect against operational risks, just as they do in virtually every form of lending today, with an ecosystem of firms specializing in the origination, servicing, and collection of credit.

NOMINAL VS. REAL RETURNS

Nominal versus real returns is an important concept here. Nominal is the face amount that you pay or receive. Real is the rate of return you receive (or pay) after inflation. So, the nominal rate less inflation = the real rate. They may seem the same, but it is a lot like weight and mass. You may weigh a different amount on the moon instead of Earth, but you have the same mass. A similar concept exists with rates, where nominal would be like weight and real would be like mass. To understand this, let's assume you deposit money in a checking account at 2 percent. Your nominal return is 2 percent.

- If inflation is 0 percent, you have a real return of 2 percent.
- If inflation is 4 percent, you have a real return of −2 percent.
- If inflation is 2 percent, you have a real return of 0 percent.

Like a constant mass, with zero as the center, currency can stabilize across every market (Japan, US, Europe, Brazil … you name it) to adjust for local inflation. This creates a common store of value that transcends local currencies and policies.

Interest Rate Risk

When the interest rate is zero in real terms, it is not zero for all loans, but only for the market-determined specimen, which is organic and changes in various conditions driven by the market rather than a central authority. This ensures that the value of the currency doesn't suffer because of inflation for the people who hold and transact in it.

People who transact exclusively in the currency as a unit of value, a store of value, and a medium of exchange never experience inflation, and their price for borrowing, lending, and storing money is zero. This reduces vast systemic inefficiencies in today's market.

A segment of the global population is likely to choose to transact in other currencies, such as the yen, euro, or dollar, either by force or by choice. In these cases, the cost of borrowing is simply tied to the rate of inflation for the other currency. For example, an individual who lives and works in the United States could pledge qualifying assets under an approved operational framework, and their cost of borrowing would be zero + the rate of inflation in the United States. In the framework of the specimen, the inflation rate would be adjusted daily, protecting the people who store money from the government's inflationary policies and episodes of hyperinflation. Borrowers who have income or assets that appreciate with inflation are protected. Borrowers who do not will need to understand and manage this risk.

An Elastic Definition of the Specimen

Like all commodities, the currency must conform to a model designating quality levels. Quality criteria, such as "prime" or "choice," are first established then the price of a good meeting those standards fluctuates. This approach defines the price and lets the market establish the criteria for the specimen, creating balance and counteracting forces. The definition is dynamic.

LET'S CALL THIS CURRENCY THE PLANCK

Max Planck discovered that atoms can only take certain specific values. His discovery, known as "Planck's constant," is the basis for quantum mechanics. Planck's constant changed physics by introducing the question of whether anything was constant while getting as close as possible to it by iterating a decimal point with thirty-six zeroes in front of it. Planck's constant is used across science, including how we define mass.

Let's call our currency the planck in honor of this groundbreaking scientist's discovery of a universal constant.

A Money Gyroscope Stabilized Around Safety

In Chicago, where I live, I see natural opposing forces at work every day. For 100 years, Chicago's massive drawbridges have been opening and closing to let ships and people pass with a fairly simple mechanical process based on counterbalance.

My city claims to be the Drawbridge Capital of the World, and it was a hotbed for innovation in the technology in the twentieth century as engineers found new and better ways to move foot and automobile traffic across the Y-shaped Chicago River while allowing ships to use it as a harbor and waterway. Chicago-type drawbridges, also known as *bascule* bridges after the French word for "seesaw," are based on the principle that balancing with a counterweight makes them easier to open and close.[4] Every time I watch the double-deck Michigan Avenue Bridge open so a ship can pass through the river's main channel, I'm witnessing the same physics that Leonardo da Vinci used when he built the first bascule bridge in the fifteenth century.[5]

Chicago's drawbridges work because they're brilliantly engineered. Counterbalancing a limited number of people can be a lot messier. Let's say I, an adult male, want to play on a teeter-totter with my eight-year-old son. If we both get on and sit in the same position on either side of the board, I would launch my much-lighter son into space (never a good parenting move). This doesn't mean that Reid and I can never seesaw together, however. It just means that I have to move out on the board while he moves in until we find the natural opposing balance that makes the teeter-totter sit flat. We can make it work, though it takes some effort because having just two inputs is limiting. We'll never get the board's full range of motion, and it can only withstand so much weight imbalance. I certainly wouldn't want to try teeter-tottering with an elephant.

Consider, on the other hand, a gyroscope – essential to making everything from bicycles and fidget spinners to space shuttle navigation and the Hubble Space Telescope work – in which an infinite number of inputs can move on a spinning center kept constant by natural opposing forces. This powerful model is what we should be modeling our financial system after, so we have a constant, stabilizing core no matter what is happening in the world. (In theory, this is what the Federal Reserve is supposed to be doing.) A money gyroscope would never be thrown off kilter, whether by world wars or hurricanes, because it would also consider balancing forces like technological breakthroughs that could create peace and prosperity.

This takes us back to the planck. In a money gyroscope, forces counterbalance to keep the core constant at zero, making it the perfect risk-free store of value. Zero becomes the tether. Money is safe; no one pays or is paid to hold it. The market, not the Federal Reserve, controls the supply and price of money.

This is not a new idea. In 1912, Ludwiig von Mises wrote in *The Theory of Money and Credit*: "A variation in the objective exchange-value of money can arise only when a force is exerted in one direction that is not cancelled by a counteracting force in the opposite direction. If the causes that alter the ratio between the stock of money and the demand for it from the point of view of an individual consist merely in accidental and personal factors that concern that particular individual only, then, according to the law of large numbers, it is likely that the forces arising from this cause, and acting in both directions in the market, will counterbalance each other."[6]

A Sample Specimen

Trying to define an elastic specimen is like trying to predict the price of oil two years from now. It is impossible to do because oil prices are constantly changing and market-driven. We can, with some confidence, predict that oil will be more than $20 a barrel, a level it has not dipped below for over 50 years, and we can establish a similar approach to defining a sample specimen.[7] The network builds consensus around a common idea of what is risk-free, which can happen in person, via remote voting, or, as we discussed earlier, in a process blockchain can facilitate. This universe begins with all loans in existence across all borrowers (governments, companies, and people) on planet Earth. The ability to do infinite sorting, segmenting, and grouping of loans or segments of loans makes this a universe of infinite choice.

Today, all physical cash and many if not most cash deposits, savings accounts, checking accounts, and short-term money markets deliver less than a 0 percent real return. In the United States today, it is not uncommon for people to have a checking account at less than 0.5 percent while inflation is running at close to 2 percent. These investors are receiving a negative real return. Investors who hold these assets are all taking risk relative to inflation. So, what *would* make it through this zero-risk – meaning zero-real-return – filter?

For the purposes of this discussion, let's assume there is no operational risk so we can focus on what the borrower and loan would look like. (Operational risk can be solved in the near term with well-established third parties and in the long term with blockchain solving the trust gap and executing contracts and orders on behalf of the network.) Imagine that 1,000 millionaires each pledge $5 million in cash and investments in exchange for 1,000 $1 million loans. All of their portfolios are fully diversified, completely liquid, and valued daily, creating $5 billion in diversified and liquid collateral to secure $1 billion in loans. This creates a win/win scenario in which high-net-worth individuals can borrow at the rate of inflation, a risk they can easily protect against. In this decentralized money market – a form of full-reserve banking – people receive a superior store of value. If 200,000 people each stored $5,000 in it, they would get a higher level of income and a money market backed by tangible assets.

What about people who are not as affluent? Imagine 1 million of these people each pledged $5,000 of assets to secure 1 million $1,000 loans. This would result in a similar scenario in which $5 billion of assets secures $1 billion in loans. Borrowers borrow at a real cost of zero. Savers receive a superior store of value. The democratization works for people of all net worth and creates value equally for all people, whether they're borrowers or lenders.

Borrowing, lending, and money then become a commodity. High-net-worth borrowers and low-net-worth borrowers are treated the same – as a function of risk rather than a function of net worth. High-net-worth savers have access to the same rates as lower-net-worth savers. We are combining the best of agriculture (decentralized commoditized inputs) and banking (securitization) and solving the trust gap that made Hayek's dream of private, independent money impossible.

Re-centering around zero as the tether reframes supply, demand, prices, inflation, and monetary stability. Items quoted in planck are price constant, and supply is determined by the market. It is the universal core – the center – and all other prices and currencies move around it. As market conditions change, supply changes. Perhaps most importantly, zero is the fulcrum point – but it is not the only point. *There are supply and demand forces on either side of zero.* Understanding this is key to understanding the market and its efficiency and operation. Zero as a starting point lowers the cost for borrowers and increases the return for savers, creating a win-win outcome.

HOW STABLE HAVE PRICES BEEN?

Student Loan Hero took a look and found that Americans' wages have increased 67 percent since 1970, but that hasn't been enough to keep up with inflation. Rent, home prices, and college costs have all risen faster than incomes. The study found some shocking examples of price increases.

1 Gallon Regular Unleaded Gas
>   1976: $.060
>   2016: $1.96

1 Movie Ticket
>   1976: $2.13
>   2016: $8.65

1 Pint of Beer
>   1976: $1.12
>   2016: $3.99

1 Yankees Ticket
>   1976: $ 5.50
>   2016: $245.00

Rent
>   1960: $ 71.00
>   2000: $602.00

Home Value
>   1960: $ 11,900.00
>   2000: $119,600.00

Private College
>   1987–88: $15,160
>   2017–18: $34,740

Public College
>   1987–88: $1,486
>   2017–18: $9,970

Source: https://www.cnbc.com/2018/04/17/how-much-more-expensive-life-is-today-than-it-was-in-1960.html

Convergence Checklist

Let's revisit the pillars in a different order. Pillar 4 is that loans can be sorted, segmented, and grouped into virtually infinite components of risk. In Pillar 1 we also established that loans today are pooled into money markets that enable people to transact as they would with any other checking account and that credit is money and money is credit. We established with Pillar 1 that there should be a risk-free rate and that borrowers and lenders should be able to borrow at this rate, based not on net worth but on democratized access to common rates. We further established that in order for this rate to be risk-free, it needs to also be protected from inflation. We created a currency, the planck, with zero real return as its core and objective. This is simply a criteria through which loans are sorted segmented and grouped. It is possible today and does not require blockchain.

Blockchain takes everything to a completely new level because it enables tokenization of money markets, a completely digital world of cash and payments – a safe, secure way to store and access money. This could arguably happen without the help of blockchain, but the technology facilitates much more efficient operations than we have ever experienced, including fully decentralized community management; unprecedented opportunities to include more assets, more types of assets, with more information, more securely; incredible granular functionality; the ability to quickly and easily enforce contracts; and the ability to minimize and potentially eliminate various transaction costs.

Perhaps most importantly – and most revolutionary – when these pillars combine with blockchain technology, we can eliminate switching costs. Everyone can quickly, easily, and even automatically move from one product to the next, creating the possibility of a neural network that will change just about everything you know about modern finance. Today's financial world will look like an operator-assisted call in the age of the smart phone.

Chapter 13

A Neural Network Begins

"Whatever you are studying right now, if you are not getting up to speed on deep learning, neural networks, etc., you lose. We are going through the process where software will automate software, automation will automate automation."

– Mark Cuban

Y ou're probably familiar with the term network (a group or system of interconnected people or things), but you may not have heard about neural networks, frameworks where many different processes can work together toward optimization. In many ways, a team of people trying to problem solve their way out of an escape room is a neural network because everyone benefits from the collective knowledge and "computing power" of the other team members.

More participants drive more perspective. (When my kids and I participated in an escape room experience, we solved a critical problem because something that was intuitive to my daughter was not at all easy for the adults to see or recognize.) One can argue that markets – from bazaars in Morocco to high-frequency options traders – are another form of neural network. In technology, the term "neural network" is a process where constantly changing inputs are optimized to the best result. It is a form of autopilot technology, utilizing multiple information systems to optimize to the best course from a set of multiple possible courses, all in a common system. This optimization happens by passing data through multiple layers. These layers act like a screen, filtering inputs to get to an optimized output.

In this chapter we will explore the convergence of multiple powerful forces:

1. A market in money with supply and demand forces.
2. Zero as the epicenter or the market in money: a risk-free store of value, with a market existing on either side of zero with its own supply and demand forces.
3. The ability to price risk at the margin, dynamically.
4. The ability to make direct connections.
5. No switching costs – the ability to quickly and easily change solutions.
6. The ability to infinitely sort, segment, and group loans or segments of loans.
7. Decentralized enforcement of the market rules and conditions.
8. A network filter/overlay that optimizes connections based on changes in inputs.

A Perspective on a Decentralized Market in Money

Though we may not have a universal currency accepted at every bar on every planet – yet – we do know that one important key to making nearly everything in the universe work, from airplanes and automobiles to bridges and arches, is the law of natural opposing forces. The stability created by the push–pull of opposing forces is the very foundation of physics, and this law is rampant in nature as well as in markets. This is what Adam Smith's 1776 magnum opus *The Wealth of Nations* was all about, as he believed opposing forces within markets – people and businesses acting in their own self-interest – gave markets natural stability and the ability to regulate themselves without oversight from a central authority.

In Chapter 6, we looked at how efficiently this works in the relatively decentralized food industry in which farmers, not the government, choose how much corn they will grow and milk they will produce every year. Congress is not responsible for these decisions – a blessing for all of us – and we never worry about whether we will have enough corn or milk because natural opposing forces are at work. When farmers grow too much corn and the price drops, they decide to grow soybeans. The second the farmers make this decision, scarcity pushes corn prices back up, and they'll grow it again. Farmers working in their own self-interest naturally keep commodity markets from overflowing and underachieving.

As we've also seen, this is not how money and banking works today. Our financial system, controlled as it is by the US Federal Reserve, has limited natural opposing forces within it. From a data persepective, the primary motive of the central authority that controls our monetary system is full employment over price stability. Throughout this book, we've been laying the foundation for a better way.

Milton Friedman was never shy about sharing his (often salty) opinions, and he garnered his fair share of critics over the years. Perhaps nothing peeved him more, however, than people who did not understand the basis of his ideas and philosophies. In 1992, Friedman wrote a letter to the *Wall Street Journal* expressing his frustration that the media consistently referred to him as well as his friend and colleague Friedrich Hayek as conservatives. "We are liberals," Friedman stated, "in the classical sense of a belief in individual freedom, not in the modern depraved sense. On another level, we are radicals in the etymological sense of seeking to get at the root of our problems."[1]

Friedman's favorite line, which he repeated over and over again in his essays and in interviews, was that "money is much too important to be left to central bankers" – and that is the fundamental tenet of a philosophy he called monetarism.[2] As monetarist Henry Calvert Simons explained in 1935, "No liberal can contemplate with equanimity the prospect of an economy in which every investment and business venture is largely a speculation in the future actions of the Federal Reserve board."[3]

Monetarists believed government should fight inflation by controlling the money supply and allow interest rates to adjust in unrestricted free markets. In his 1953 essay, "The Case for Flexible Exchange Rates," Friedman called for foreign exchange rates to be determined daily by the forces of demand and supply and without government restrictions rather than the International Monetary Fund's "adjustable peg" system, in which countries commit to acting as residual buyers or sellers of their currencies in order to maintain their foreign values within a narrow margin of a fixed par value. In a 1972 *Newsweek* column, Friedman explained, "A monetary rule would insulate monetary policy from both the arbitrary power of a small group of men not subject to control by the electorate and from the short-run pressures of partisan politics."[4]

The keystone of monetarism is the distinction between the nominal quantity of money (number of dollars held as money) determined by a central authority and the real quantity of money (the volume of goods and services those dollars will buy) determined by money holders.[5] In Friedman's ideal world, as he laid it out in a 2002 interview, the central bank would be abolished and a computer would grind out a 5 percent per year increase in high-powered money.[6] He wrote in his introduction to Hayek's book *Road to Serfdom* that "central direction is also a road to poverty for the ordinary man; voluntary cooperation, a road to plenty."[7]

Friedman disagreed with the "elitist political philosophy" set forth by the most famous economist of the day, John Maynard Keynes, who believed monetary authorities could be trusted to manage money and exchange rates.[8] He gravitated instead toward Adam Smith's "invisible hand" philosophy. "We all know the key insight that Adam Smith brought to this subject, which underlies the possibility of markets operating to coordinate economic activity," Friedman wrote. "That key insight is that if exchange is voluntary – if two people engage in any exchange on a voluntary basis – the exchange will occur only if both sides benefit."[9]

In 1963, Friedman and Anna Schwartz published an influential study, *Monetary History of the United States,* showing that the only times when there was an absolute fall in the money stock corresponded with six periods of economic contraction between 1867 and 1960. Friedman and Schwartz believed monetary changes caused major recessions and argued that the Federal Reserve's failure to prevent a major decline in the money stock turned what could have been a relatively mild depression into the Great Depression. "In consequence Friedman argued that the money supply should be allowed to grow at a fixed rate in line with the underlying growth of output to ensure long-term price stability," Brian Snowdon and Howard R. Vane explained in *A Macroeconomics Reader.*[10]

In a speech he gave while accepting the Nobel Prize in Economics in 1976, Friedman made no bones about how he felt. "As some of you may know, my monetary studies have led me to the conclusion that central banks could profitably be replaced by computers geared to provide a steady rate of growth in the quantity of money," he told the crowd. "Fortunately, for me personally, and for a select group of economists, that conclusion has had no practical impact – else there would have been no Central Bank of Sweden to have established the award I am honored to receive."[11]

The Other Sides of Zero

Zero is an outcome of the planck, the point at which a transaction is taking place at zero real cost to the borrower and lender. However, this is just *a point in an infinite series of points*. It is the infinite series of points around it that create a dynamic, self-adjusting network.

When they fill up their gas tanks, some people prefer premium gas and some prefer regular gas. The same is true in investing, and the same is true with money. Some investors/savers are comfortable with a zero as a real return, some individuals want a higher return, and some want a lower return.

The reason for wanting a lower real return is that not everyone will agree with the market determination (consensus) of what is risk-free.

Participants or groups of participants who find the market clearing price of what is risk-free still too risky could bid a negative real rate for a safer group, segment, or portion of a loan or many loans. Investors receive an even safer store of value, and borrowers get paid to borrow. (This phenomenon already occurs in the world today, as we've seen with negative nominal rates.)

Some investors will want a real return higher than zero percent. In that case, the market can sort, segment, and group to where investors receive 1 percent and borrowers pay 1 percent in real terms – an elastic, market-driven specimen. Once we recognize a different specimen for 1 percent, the same framework applies to investors who want 2 percent, 3 percent, 4 percent, and so on. More importantly, these can be sections or subsections of loans.

What we begin to see is an infinite world of specimens surrounding zero – some above zero and some below zero. Loans and segments of loans are sorted, segmented, and grouped into pools via a decentralized community where operational roles, responsibilities, and tasks are either managed by the community, for the community, within the community, or outsourced to a third party. Blockchain helps facilitate the management of this process through decentralized community management and unprecedented transparency, solving trust gaps and enabling people to transact directly and securely.

The Paradigm Begins to Shift

Once we embrace democratized borrowing and lending, we can envision the beginning of a paradigm shift. Let's accept that, absent servicing, administrative, or other costs, a $1,000 loan secured by a $5,000 asset is the same loan to value as a $1 million loan secured by a $5 million asset (1,000 / 5,000 = 20% and 1 million / 5 million = 20%).

Let's assume the market specimen puts loans up to 30 percent loan to value at a zero percent rate of return. The cost of borrowing and lending is exactly equal to inflation. In this case, borrowers could borrow more at zero cost, and lenders would be willing to lend more at zero cost.

It could turn out the market is more efficient and comprised of building blocks. The zero percent level could be derived by the following subcomponents:

- The first 10% was bid at a real cost of −1%.
- The next 10% was bid at a real cost of 0%.
- The next 10% was bid at a real cost of 1%.

In this scenario, the market is bidding a different price for each incremental unit of risk added or taken on by the borrower. Imagine the risk bidding continues:

- $0\% - 10\% = -1\%$
- $11\% - 20\% = 0\%$
- $21\% - 30\% = 1\%$
- $31\% - 40\% = 2\%$
- $41\% - 50\% = 3\%$
- $51\% - 60\% = 4\%$
- $61\% - 70\% = 5\%$
- $71\% - 80\% = 10\%$
- $81\% - 90\% = 15\%$
- $91\% - 100\% = 20\%$

Borrowers begin to have higher and higher units of marginal cost as a function of the risk. They can access more capital, but at higher rates. If they either increase their assets or their overall quality as a borrower, they receive a lower rate. For example, imagine an individual has a $1,000 loan and $5,000 of assets. The next year they have the same $1,000 loan but have saved and have $10,000 of assets. Their condition has improved, and the market price on the quality of their "money" – their loan – has fallen. The opposite is true as well. If somebody has $1,000 borrowed against $5,000 of assets and their assets deteriorate to $2,000, the cost of their borrowing will increase. Obviously, there are two types of market participants: borrowers likely to benefit from this type of a structure and those who will not. Borrowers who are more likely to be disadvantaged by market-based risk pricing of their loans will either have to insure against risks or, better yet (from the network's perspective), opt out of the network. All of this takes place through a single blended cost of the underlying loan, all based on risk.

Borrowers know how much credit they have access to every day, at every price. If they pay down their debt, they receive a rate of return equal to their highest marginal cost of debt. More importantly, they know how the price of their credit changes depending on how they use their funds. Incremental borrowing is priced at the margin, and marginal pricing can occur across secured and unsecured loans. Unsecured loans can also have a variety of rates ranging from negative to positive. Loans and pools of loans can be looked at independently or grouped across secured and unsecured. For example, the market may say that a 10 percent loan-to-value loan to an individual that is secured by assets that can instantly be sold is less risky than an unsecured loan to a large company, or the market may say the two have the exact same level of risk, and therefore price. The point is the ability to create infinite pools around infinite characteristics with prices set by the market on a daily elastic basis.

The Paradigm Shifts: One Loan

Blockchain enables the ability to make direct connections with 100 percent trust. Blockchain also enables the decentralized enforcement of market rules, conditions, and terms. Securitization enables the ability to infinitely sort, segment, and group loans or segments of loans. As these technologies converge, what we have is the pure and transparent securitization of the individual, at the individual level, with the marginal pricing of risk. But how exactly does this structure take place? It could be that one has a car loan, a home loan, and a student loan, but this system is inefficient. In today's world, we sort, segment, and group at the loan level, rather than the borrower level. Imagine, instead, a single, integrated lending solution. All assets, all income, all information reported to a single lending facility. The pieces of this single facility are sorted, segmented, grouped, and sold to different investors in sections, or tranches, based on market conditions of supply and demand.

One loan instead of many loans, begins the catalyst to a world of optimization. With one loan as a single solution, switching costs – the cost of refinancing a loan or moving to a better deposit account – move to zero. In this shift there is a nuanced but important evolution in the world of consumer lending. There is a movement to available credit and a store of value. At the epicenter of this world, the cost of borrowing is exactly equal to the cost of lending. There is no penalty for holding "cash" and "debt" as long as both are in planck, because the cost of borrowing is equal to the return on storing money.

This is fundamentally different from today's atomized lending world. Today when you want a car, you get a car loan. When you want a house, you get a home loan. The rate of your car loan is generally the same whether you borrow 95 percent of the value or 20 percent of the value. Your home loan has a rate that is generally the same whether you borrow 50 percent of the value or 80 percent of the value. Behind the scenes, your home loan and car loan are sliced and diced and sold to many different investors, at many different rates. In the event of bankruptcy, the administrator of your car loan must fight with the administrator of your home loan to determine who gets what as your assets are liquidated. Imagine having one loan secured by both assets, with terms and conditions managed by the community, for the community and a rate determined by your risk and the overall amount you borrow. Terms and conditions are known and transparent to all. Bankruptcy becomes a straightforward process for the borrower and lender.

WHAT ABOUT CASH AND DAY-TO-DAY TRANSACTIONS?

In the world of democratized money, there is no cash, or certainly no need for cash. As we discussed in the foundational part of this book, this is not unlike how most people live today, with very little physical cash, primarily transacting in a world of digital available credit. Transactions take place either from available credit (how a credit card works today), or from a store of value (how money markets operate today). More likely, for those who hold planck, transactions would take place via the blockchain tokenization of these money market(s), much how stable coins transact today.

These tokens can be stored in decentralized block chain–based wallets or with "central authorities," such as a bank, depending

(*Continued*)

on the individual consumer preference and view on safety. While these transactions could take place as they do in the United States and Europe, what is more likely is how they take place in China, via QR codes. Dollars, euros, and yen may or may not exist, but from an individual perspective, they are generally unnecessary. To the extent they are, one can access them quickly and easily from an ATM, just how one does today. This is simply a conversion from planck to another currency at the conversion rate that exists at the time of conversion.

The central theme is that day-to-day there is little required change with how one approaches their current activity around payments. It is what is taking place behind the scenes that is much more exciting.

The Neural Network is Born

What we have is a market with borrowers on one side of the market and lenders on the other side of the market. In the middle is a direct connection, full trust, and the ability to infinitely sort, segment, and group. Surrounding this connection are market forces of supply and demand for both borrowers and lenders. Borrowers place "bids" at the level they are willing to borrow. Investors place bids at the rate they are willing to fund loans, or segments of loans. At the center of these bids is zero, the price at which one can borrow and lend at zero in real terms.

Because zero is the fixed center, the price is set, the market is elastic with respect to quality, not price. *Therefore, the market is incentivized to create quality.* The higher the degree of confidence the network has in your financial path, the lower the overall rate will be for borrowers and the better the store of value for savers and investors. This incentivizes users to upload as much information as possible, which can be kept secure and anonymous through blockchain. As information is uploaded, the network can act as a filter and leverage the information surrounding it to make predictive, market-based suggestions. Borrowers get nudged to make decisions to optimize their cost of debt. Savers get a world of infinite choice, and all inefficiencies in the middle are eliminated.

Chapter 14

Conclusion

"I'm inclined to think that there's no field so rife with cranks as currency and money."

– Milton Friedman

At the conclusion of *The Denationalization of Money*, Hayek presents 10 questions for discussion. These questions provide a fitting way to evaluate money without boundaries, the planck, and the creation of a decentralized self-stabilizing currency, the risk-free rate.

1. "Examine the long-held view that there should be only one currency in a country and that it should be controlled by government. Illustrate your discussion with examples from remote and recent history."[1]

   • There is not one currency in most any country today. You can live in Europe and store your money in dollars or live in America and keep your net worth in yen, but most citizens place their precious savings in trust to their home government's central bank, either in cash or bank deposits. Why citizens do this is a mystery. Since the tether of the gold standard has been removed, governments have been terrible at maintaining price stability. While citizens have a choice – and should opt for a different system, with a different objective – the most plausible reason why they tolerate the destruction of their wealth is the lack of a credible, easy, secure, and transparent alternative.

2. "What are the origins of legal tender? Argue for and against it as the necessary basis of a monetary system."[2]

   • "Legal tender" is not a necessary basis of a monetary system.

3. "Define money. How is it distinguished from non-money? Argue for and against the concept of a 'quantity' of money. Apply the argument to the 'quantity' theory of money."[3]

   • Money is a unit of value, a medium of exchange, and a store of value. Society tolerates hundreds of units of value. Credit works as well as a medium of exchange as cash – and is becoming the preferred medium of exchange as society moves toward cashless. Money then should be defined as a store of value – and that is it. A store of value is risk-free, including from the risk of inflation. The quantity of the supply of this store of value can be set only by the market rather than by a central authority.

4. "'It is desirable for government to control money so that it can vary its supply according to the needs of the economy.' 'People have been losing confidence in money because it has been controlled by government.' Discuss."[4]

   • Why complain about money, interest rates, or the government? It is perfectly possible to vote with our feet and opt into an alternative system. While governments can control a form of money – theirs – they do not have a practical way to control all stores of value. Governments are unlikely to convert to another form of money unless they have a compelling reason or incentive to do so. Why would they? It has been too long, and this horse is out of the barn. Governments will, however, have to compete on equal footing with other stores of value – namely, people – who may in many cases be a superior store of value.

5. "History shows that there has sometimes been lack of confidence in 'legal tender' paper currencies. How could a régime of competing paper currencies maintain the confidence of the public?"[5]

- Simple: communicate what specifically makes it a store of value. What protects it? What backs it? What enforces it? Does it depend on a central authority? What is the incentive? What will make it immune from the risk of inflation? With solid answers to these important questions, governments are well positioned to compete and maintain confidence in their currency. Absent solid answers, society may choose an alternative store of value.

6. "'To be trusted, paper money must be convertible into valuable goods or precious metals.' Do you agree? Discuss the condition in which convertibility is and is not essential."[6]

- Partially agree. If money is able to be converted into something valuable, then it is, by definition, a store of value. As long as the asset to which it converts is valued by any section of society and can quickly and easily be liquidated for a greater value, then the "money" is valuable. The irony is that if it is able to be converted, it is unlikely to be converted. Rather than be redeemed, it is instead likely to be sold to the next market participant and/or adjusted as market conditions dictate. This is what forms the market and the quality of the Credit Theory of Money.

7. "Discuss the view that inflation and deflation would be difficult or impossible if the quantity of money were not controlled by the government. Illustrate your answer from the 1929–1932 Great Depression and the 1972–1975 Great Inflation."[7]

- Inflation and deflation would be difficult or impossible if the market stabilized around a market-based determination of zero, the risk-free rate. Zero is the center of the monetary gyroscope – big swings on one side are offset by counter-swings. These swings are instant and range from microscopic to large structural changes.

8. "Boom and slump are associated with 'capitalism.' Are they found in non-capitalist economies? Are they the result of capitalism or other causes?"[8]

- Time has provided more insight on this question as well. It is clear that boom and bust have been associated with virtually every form of government, in virtually every country, over the past 50 years.

9. "It is politically impossible for a monetary authority subject or
exposed to severe sectional pressures to avoid increasing the quantity
of money to increase employment, thus creating inflation. The gold
standard, fixed exchange rates, and other restraints in the way of
monetary expansion have been found inadequate. Discuss."[9]

- It would be hard to disagree, particularly after 2008. But so long as
both the state and the individual have the freedom of choice, the
goal of the individual and the goal of the state do not necessarily
have to be aligned.

The final question triggers a broader set of questions for us to
consider.

10. "How would you remove the power of national government to control the international movement of currency? Would international
agreement suffice? How could competition in currency be more
effective?"[10]

Here we have a deeper question about what the government can
and cannot control. New technologies clearly enable more competition in currency. This is true with respect to capital market technologies
(business processes) and digital technologies, such as blockchain. People
can, and do today, bypass the use of government currency for many, if
not most, of their daily transactions. Credit is a currency that is difficult
to control, but it would be foolish to think governments won't try. Better to reframe the question to look at how markets could adapt to the
obstacles governments might place upon the system.

Right now, governments control the process of extending credit.
Lending is one of the most regulated sections of the economy in most
markets. Governments can require high switching costs and make credit
extension difficult. Though governments could simply restrict the
extension of credit, at any price, economies stop growing without smooth
operating credit markets, creating even bigger burdens for overleveraged
governments that need a combination of growth, inflation, and devaluation to solve their underlying problems. Restricting a decentralized
market is likely to hurt the government as much as, if not more than,
the market.

The other thing the government can control is taxes. Imagine that
inflation in the United States is 3 percent and an investor in the United

States receives a real rate of return of 3 percent in planck. If the government chooses to tax that return at, say, 50 percent, the investor is receiving a real return of only 1.5 percent, less than the required 3 percent. The investor here has two options: seek a higher rate of return, say 6 percent, or hold less cash.

Currently, most investors – most people – hold very little cash. A large segment has negative cash; they owe more than they have. High-net-worth investors tend to hold assets other than cash. Those who do not hold much cash are barely impacted by changes in taxation policy (insomuch as the policy is related to taxation of cash-like holdings). High taxes on money incentivize people to hold less of it. Others might follow suit, pushing toward small amounts of negative cash, knowing they have plenty of available credit at a series of prices.

I'd like to present a few more elegant alternatives. The first is a construct in which plancks are held as a fund with gains either subject to capital gains or, perhaps more likely, made available to be borrowed against at zero cost. In this way, capital is accessed through borrowing without taxes. This leads to the most likely construct in which the planck exists simply as a currency, like any other. As transactions clear in the currency itself, the currency begins a process of appreciation relative to other currencies that pursue inflationary policies. As long as transactions settle in the currency, there is no need to convert, and therefore no tax.

These blocks can build in their own infinite series of combinations. If it's difficult to extend credit in the United States and easy in Australia, Australians could create a store of value that is used and digitized by Americans as their daily "money market." Any 10-foot wall can be approached with an 11-foot ladder. Governments should be encouraged to protect the core: low-cost lending solutions and access to low-cost credit for as many people as possible combined with the freedom of choice around a stable store of value.

WINNERS AND LOSERS?

Who wins and who loses in this world of democratized money? This is like asking who won the Industrial Revolution, the Green Revolution, or the modern technology revolution.

Society wins, and as such, it is not at all apparent that there need to be any "losers." Clearly there are some entities that exist today extracting a high economic rent from current market inefficiencies, lack of choice, high switching costs, and general consumer ignorance. In these cases, these rents will fall. However, much as cereal mills benefited from being able to transact in bulk, banks benefit from an unprecedented ability to get direct, transparent exposure at an unprecedented granular level. Further, it isn't clear that banks are rewarded for balance sheet risk as much as they are for servicing fees and income. There is in fact a considerable ability for them to evolve their business model to, on one hand, get laser-precision access, transparency, and the ability to manage their credit risk and, on the other hand, capture a non-credit risk, recurring revenue, in the form of servicing fees. This is because absent significant regulatory reform, for the foreseeable future banks and nonbank lenders will likely have a role as intermediaries facilitating the extension and servicing of credit.

Securitizing Individuals at an Individual Level with Blockchain

Safety is a valuable commodity because people are risk-averse. Creating a direct, secure, transparent, anonymous connection between lenders and borrowers based on their desired risk level, then, results in a market-based, self-stabilizing, neutral currency: the risk-free asset. In this marketplace, participants acting in their own self-interest through a decentralized, open-sourced, mathematically driven network can create a mutually beneficial stable financial ecosystem that leverages the collective knowledge, products, and solutions available in society via our superhero, blockchain.

As loans are efficiently sorted, segmented, and grouped across common characteristics, both borrowers and lenders benefit from economies of scale when lending is commoditized. Just as the farmer and the cereal mill both benefited from farm mechanization and the ability to transact relatively anonymously and in bulk, consumers will benefit by having the ability to quickly and easily seek the lowest possible rate on loans and the highest possible rate on deposits. With a completely free market in the production, distribution, and management of these assets, units of risk can be infinitely broken down into smaller and smaller units with common characteristics that can be aggregated and sold in bulk. Lenders then bid for the units across multiple categories to affect their desired risk/return profile in aggregate. Credit is money.

This process eliminates structural inefficiencies that hinder both borrowers and lenders in today's financial system. Idiosyncratic risk is eliminated as borrowers optimize real-time information about risk, return, and access to credit and serve as infinite currency issuers that can be broken into infinite transparent risk categories with dynamic market-based pricing, then rolled up and held by lenders.

When you get a bank loan today, you create a liability for yourself and an asset for the bank. You receive the money in your checking account and consider it an asset. The bank is set back whatever it loaned you but will enter the loan as an asset on its balance sheet because it expects to be repaid with interest. (This is how we create money.) There's inherent risk in this system; the bank has no guarantees you won't default on the loan. In a decentralized system of commoditized credit, that risk would be segmented, sorted, and grouped through blockchain nodes into independently valued units with common characteristics, then aggregated and sold in bulk.

With blockchain, whether lenders own an entire loan or part of one, they have full visibility into borrowers' assets and income while borrowers remain anonymous. Lenders can trust that, just as we trust the cloud will store our music today. They can base their willingness to lend, and at what rate, on real-time information about borrowers' assets and income, and they'll be willing to lend some amount at zero because these loans are safer than gold, safer than bitcoin, safer than the US government, safer than Switzerland – and if that's not safe enough, blockchain can keep iterating until the market says it's willing to lend at zero.

Blockchain makes securitization of individuals possible at an individual level. It paves the way for decentralized peer-to-peer money markets where all people can borrow some level of money at zero cost. Any other borrowing is priced at the margin and in the middle; all inefficiencies are eliminated.

Welcome to a Whole New World, Mr. Keynes

Friedman died in 2006, just before the global financial meltdown that surely would have had him shaking his head and saying he told us so. Hayek died in 1992, just before the digital revolution that would make his dreams of denationalized money possible. It's a shame neither of these scholars could be here today as the seeds are being planted for their visions to come true. Even Adam Smith would have a hard time arguing for the superiority of a centrally planned monetary system now that blockchain has solved the trust gap problem and brought life to his "invisible hand."

To Keynes, who died in 1946, I would say, "Welcome to a whole new world, Mr. Keynes." I would explain that this new world doesn't have a centrally planned economy, and the government doesn't set interest rates. All governments are forced to compete on equal footing with creditors around the world, and all of them can be infinitely sorted, segmented, and grouped so that interest rates can be set based on risk level, not on central planning. The government won't be able to just wake up one day and declare the federal funds rate is 2 percent, then make that happen by moving levers – buying and selling money – until it's there. "You will control your own cost of borrowing based on your expenditures, Mr. Keynes," I would explain. "And if your theories are correct, everybody should be empowered to live and die by their own swords."

As for Hayek, I can imagine he might say, "I already wrote this book. It's called *The Denationalization of Money*." To which I would reply that his vision would have remained a utopian dream until our superhero blockchain came along to solve that pesky trust gap problem. Mr. Hayek, your vision is now possible with the technology that exists in the world. Instead of banks issuing ducats, all investors will be able to issue credit with the same access to borrowers who are segmented, sorted, and grouped every millisecond.

When it comes down to it, I'm pretty certain of a few things:

1. Everything herein is possible and conforms to the leading economic theories.
2. Private currencies will win the currency war and facilitate the denationalization of money.
3. Society will be more peaceful and prosperous as a result of having a decentralized, stable form of value.

I'm also confident this theory isn't perfect. I'm guaranteed to laugh, and to cry, when I look at it with the benefit of hindsight. But I'm not worried; the goal is an inversion of the way in which we approach the problem. Today we look at money as a system out of our control, managed by central authorities. In the future, money and credit will be democratized and decentralized – an idea that is bigger than governments and an idea that has no boundaries.

Appendix A

The Future of Money – A Credit-Based Society

Money always has been, and always will be, credit or a claim on an asset. In the future, there will be no "money;" we will have a credit-based society or the complete denationalization of money that Friedrich Hayek foresaw. Unlike Hayek's vision of banks issuing competing currencies, the denationalization of money will take place via the transparent securitization of an individual, at the individual level. New technologies will facilitate his vision.

Each person and entity is a unique issuer of currency. Each currency has infinite subunits, each with its own value, creating a world with infinite currencies. Money serves as a store of value, a medium of exchange, and a unit of value. For the infinite creators and purchasers of money, these roles are best served through complete decentralization. Debt is the creation of credit, which is the creation of money. The decentralization and commoditization of credit creation becomes the basis of currency: one facility, infinitely broken down into units of risk, dynamically market priced, and sold to the market in groups.

Economic Theory

1. Market participants, acting in their own self-interest, make a market more efficient.
2. Investors are risk averse.
3. Markets reflect all available information.
4. One can borrow and lend at the risk-free rate.
5. Investors hold cash for investment and transaction reasons.
6. One should be a borrower or a lender, not both.
7. The relevance of capital structure is a function of exogenous events to the firm and a function of need for the individual.
8. It is far simpler to establish one constant and to let the multitude of conditions change around that core constant.
9. There can be a complete free market in the production, distribution, and management of money.

Proofs

1. Assets are assets: a store of value with a price.
2. Money is a medium of exchange, yet there is no binding constraint on the potential number of currencies; it is infinite.
3. The creator of a liability (a borrower) receives assets (money) from the purchaser (lender).
4. The purchaser of a liability (lender) is the holder of an asset.
5. Liabilities constitute risk to the entity that created the liability.
6. Units of risk can be infinitely broken down into smaller and smaller units.
7. These units can be independently valued by the market.
8. Units with common characteristics can be aggregated and sold in bulk.
9. Credit is money, and money is credit.

Construct: The separation and creation of pure credit (money) and pure assets

Borrower (Entity or Individual) with:

Assets of A
Income of B (current and potential)
Obligations of C (current and potential)
Market determined credit capacity of Z

Credit capacity ranges from negative to infinity. Negative credit capacity and infinite capacity are both corrected by market forces until an equilibrium whole positive number of Available Credit Capacity is created: Z_a.

Z_a is broken into infinite individual units with individual characteristics of risk and return. These units are Dutch auctioned, as individual units, with the lowest price being the winner. Prices are not aggregated across units and, therefore, when assessing Z_a, pricing is cumulative to the borrower.

When a borrower accesses their credit capacity (borrows), an asset is created. The market-determined credit capacity, Z, is then divided into two categories, Accessed Capacity Z_x and Available Capacity Z_{a1}.

Z_x is distributed across the infinite subunits that were bid by the lender(s) in stack order, filling the units from lowest cost (negative interest rates, if any) through highest cost (positive interest rates, if any). The sum of balances of units multiplied by the interest rate of each unit determines the weighted average cost of capital to the borrower. The weighted average cost is the cost paid by the borrower, but does not represent the price received by any individual unit holder.

The lender(s) hold an asset(s). As asset value A and income level B and obligations C change, the prices of the units comprising Z_a and Z_x change. The volatility of price (interest rate) is highest for the highest-priced unit of Z_a and price volatility is lowest for the lowest-priced unit Z_x. This process creates a transparent distribution of risk with individual units (both Accessed and Available) receiving dynamic market-based prices of risk.

Units are grouped into common characteristics. Lenders then bid for units in bulk, across multiple categories of units to affect their desired risk/return profile in aggregate.

Structural Superiority

This process eliminates all structural inefficiencies for both borrowers and lenders. Lenders can optimize their exact desired risk/return characteristics. Idiosyncratic risk is eliminated for both the borrower and the lender. Borrowers can hedge risks (such as a desire for a committed facility or a fixed rate) through private contracts available across all individual infinite units. Borrowers know their exact costs of transacting: the direct and opportunity costs of paying down or accessing credit. Real-time information creates an informed view on risk, return, and access to credit. This information is optimized against a market view on risk and return where price becomes an indication of probability of success, creating positive feedback loops that create mutually reinforcing, market-based incentives.

Result: infinite issuers of currency (borrowers), broken into infinite transparent categories of risk, with dynamic market-based pricing on each unit, rolled up and held by society (lenders), with no idiosyncratic risk.

Illustration

Today

Borrower has many loans:

Loan 1 rate A	Loan 2 rate B	Loan... rate...	Cash / Currency rate < cost of loans

No relation between the cost of Loan 1, Loan 2, or cash and currency. Static. No optimization. Lenders have limited transparency, inefficient costs, and inefficient allocations.

Future

Borrower has one loan:

Last loss   First loss

Unit 1 rate A	Unit 2 rate B	Unit... rate...	Available Credit

Lowest rate   Highest rate

Structural incentives to include as much as possible (assets, income, information), but borrower may opt to include or exclude items and information of their choice. These choices and the perceived risks are reflected in market prices of interest.

Appendix B

A House of Cards

A s I was finishing up writing this book, the US government was in the throes of a record-setting government shutdown over President Donald Trump's demand that Congress allocate $5 billion to build a wall along the border with Mexico. I was at a dinner, and as it always does, whether you want it to or not, the conversation turned to this potentially volatile political topic. One bright individual, who is quite well-read on current events, was appalled that Trump would suggest spending so much money – $5 billion! – on the project. I was surprised.

"Do you think $5 billion is a lot of money?" I said. "Of course," they said, and everyone around the table – very smart, well-educated people – nodded in agreement.

I guess that makes sense. People think millions of dollars is a lot of money, so of course $5 billion seems like gobs of money – but when you put it in perspective, it's not. Not in the make believe money world we live in today. When you consider that in 2019 the US government would spend about $4.4 trillion and take in $3.4 trillion – creating a deficit of $985 billion[1] – $5 billion is chump change (everyone's feelings about the politics behind the wall aside, of course). It's like having household debt of $1 million, making $250,000, yet still putting $30,000 per year on a credit card, and arguing with your wife over the cost of toothpaste.

There are so many bigger issues that could shut down a household, and to get a divorce over toothpaste would be absurd. It's such a small thing, and as you learn in any healthy relationship, you have to learn to compromise on the small things.

But what I found out that night at the dinner table was that intelligent, informed citizens are blissfully unaware of how much our government spends – and just how deeply we're in debt. I asked, "Does anyone know our total federal debt?" They gamely made guesses ranging from $5 trillion to $100 trillion, but nobody guessed right. I asked, "Does anyone know how much the federal government is going to spend this year?" Stumped them again. In fact, I have learned that few people even understand the difference between debt and deficits or projections about how the mass of Baby Boomers who are about to retire and need entitlements and health care will affect the deficit – let alone concepts like how all of this may affect inflation and the value of the dollar.

The fact is, the US government uses a misleading accounting system in which it sorts spending into "discretionary" and "mandatory" segments. Discretionary includes things like education and infrastructure, while mandatory includes Social Security, Medicare, and Medicaid. It doesn't count "unfunded liabilities," debts like unfunded civilian and military pensions and retiree healthcare, additional underfunding for Social Security and Medicare, and other commitments and contingencies. When you factor those in, the US government is actually closer to $65 trillion in debt, according to former US comptroller general and former Government Accountability Office Chief David Walker.[2]

The debt in 2010 was around $10 trillion. Since then, it has more than doubled. As the *Chicago Tribune* pointed out, it took 200 years for the United States to rack up the first $10 trillion in debt and a mere decade to add another $10 trillion.[3] "Here's the key," Walker said in 2009, before the continued explosion of our debt. "The Congressional Budget Office projects it will be more than 100 percent of the nation's GDP by 2040 and continue to rise, a trend it also pointed out was unsustainable."[4] Walker believed the same factors that led to the mortgage-based subprime crisis are in place for the federal government's finances. "Therefore," he said, "we must take steps to avoid a super subprime crisis, which frankly would have much more disastrous effects, not only domestically but around the world."[5]

It's not always easy to explain to the average citizen why a strong financial foundation is so important. When everything's running along smoothly, people are too busy and too content to care much. When the economy tanks, everyone says, "Oh, well, it was obviously all a house of cards."

And a house of cards it is. Seventy-seven million Baby Boomers (defined as individuals born between 1946 and 1964) are hitting retirement age, AARP estimates 10,000 will turn 65 and become eligible to receive Social Security benefits every day well into the 2030s[6] – causing Social Security and Medicare trustees to project in their 2018 annual report that by 2034 the combined trust funds for Social Security will run dry and retirees will be able to receive only 79 percent of the benefits promised to them.[7] Add Medicare and Medicaid expenses – which are even larger than Social Security – and you can see how insanely fragile this house is.

A Debt-Fueled Illusion

Economists and politicians love to point to the robust economic growth we've seen in the United States in the past 20 years, but I don't believe we've actually had any. What we've had is a debt-fueled illusion.

GDP is calculated with this simple equation: GDP = consumption (C) + investment (I) + government (G) + (exports + imports). If the government is contributing approximately 3 percent to the economy by spending more than it takes in, reason would suggest the GDP would grow by at least 3 percent – yet GDP has grown by an average of 2.5 percent. Understanding this seemingly complex concept is actually quite simple: if G is at 3, and everything else is at zero, then the economy should grow by 3 percent. If GDP is growing at less than 3, we need to ask some tough questions. What we are experiencing is, mathematically, a debt-fueled illusion of growth.

This concept was extremely important in 2012, when Federal Reserve Chairman Ben Bernanke told the nation it was headed for a "massive fiscal cliff" when it would reach its debt ceiling, causing taxes to increase and financing for federal programs to be cut. This was a big deal because a decrease in government spending (G) and an increase in taxes would have led to a decrease in consumption (C), causing a significant recession during an already weak recovery. If the GDP was naturally growing at, say, 2 percent, and the contraction shaved 4 percent off of the economy, then all else being equal, 2 percent minus 4 percent equals minus 2 percent.

The debate centered around whether we should take steps to address our long-term financial issues now or "push through" this period and deal with change later. Unfortunately for my kids, we chose the wrong path. We've been kicking that ball down the road ever since, making the problem more and more difficult and the day of reckoning more and more severe.

Our Perspective Must Shift

From 1980 to 2018, interest rates and inflation have generally moved from high to low while government debt has moved from low to high. While I'm not saying interest rates cannot move lower, the economic phenomena of rates moving from the mid-teens to the 2 percent (and lower) range cannot repeat itself at a similar magnitude.

In the past 30 years, both consumer debt and government spending have moved from low to high. Government debt went from a relatively low nominal amount in 1980 to a massive figure today (on an absolute and relative basis). In the early 1980s, the Baby Boomer generation was just hitting its workplace stride and was fully employed; today, the same generation is well on its way to being fully retired. These data trends also cannot be repeated to the same degree in the next 30 years.

Where can we look, then, for models of where we might be headed? Japan, Argentina, and Europe illustrate some of the different challenges the United States could face.

- Japan experienced deflation from 1980 to 2000, roughly equivalent to the Dow Jones trading at about 7,000 and interest rates staying under 2 percent, resulting in the gradual collapse of the Japanese economy, often referred to as the Lost Decade.
- Argentina experienced inflation, hyperinflation, and devaluation between 1990 and 2000.
- The current European economic crisis, characterized by weak equities, higher interest rates, and contracting GDP in Spain, Greece, and Italy.

This is not a comprehensive list. France lost its status as a reserve currency because of its massive debts after World War I, and the same thing happened to England after World War II. A review of history suggests that once countries hit a significant debt issue, the problem is usually ultimately resolved through a combination of default, growth, inflation, and devaluation. Although it is unlikely the fate of the United States will be exactly like any of these case studies, it is also highly unlikely, if not impossible, for the next 30 years to look like the past 30 years. Our perspective must shift.

Let's start with some key assumptions made by the Congressional Budget Office, starting with the idea that our economy will have stable to moderately increasing interest rates (never going above 5 percent), decreasing unemployment, and consistent GDP growth (growing by approximately 62 percent over the next 10 years). The Federal Reserve, it is generally assumed, will keep inflation low and stable, and federal revenues will increase by approximately 100 percent over the next decade. These assumptions should be stress tested.

What if interest rates go up at a faster rate? Let's assume the government's average cost of borrowing moves from 2 percent to 6 percent on the $11.5 trillion of debt held by the public. Conceptually, the resulting increase in interest expense would be 4 percent multiplied by 11.5 trillion, resulting in an additional $460 billion per year in expense. With all else equal, this would lead to three economic possibilities: revenue must go up (tax increases), government spending would decrease, or the deficit would increase.

Over the long term, letting the federal debt continue to grow is like driving with the emergency brake on. As the debt-to-GDP ratio increases, debt holders could demand larger interest payments as compensation for an increasing risk they won't be repaid. Diminished demand for US Treasuries would further increase interest rates, slowing the economy and putting downward pressure on the dollar because the dollar's value is tied to the value of Treasury Securities. As the dollar declines, foreign holders get paid back in worthless currency, further decreasing demand.

So somehow, we need to cut $460 billion out of the budget – and that's a really big number. In fact, you could fire every federal employee, including all military service personnel, and still be running the same deficit and have the same debt. The questions, then, are where the cuts should be coming from and what the offsetting revenues are, and what would happen to GDP as a result. All else being equal, increasing taxes and decreasing government spending result in decreases in GDP. In a highly leveraged country like ours, that could mean rising interest rates and contracting GDP. Rolling it onto the deficit may end up having other adverse consequences. All of this could also have implications on inflation as well as on the value of our currency.

For a look at what could be our future, let's examine some of the threats Spain has faced in recent years. Increasing taxes are causing consumption (C) to decline, austerity measures have triggered a decrease in government spending (G), and investments (I) are falling because of a lack of confidence. This has, of course, led to a contraction in the nation's GDP. At the same time, global markets have expressed concern, and interest rates have gone up. Unemployment has trended up and housing prices down.

My point is, the possibility of a scenario in which a country experiences rising interest rates, contracting GDP, falling equity prices, rising unemployment, and falling housing prices has tremendous implications. The same is true for a period of extended deflation, inflation, or hyperinflation. There has perhaps never been a more important time for citizens around the world to seek and create a safe store of value.

WHO OWNS GOVERNMENT DEBT?

Public debt: 72%

Intra-governmental debt: 28%

Of the public debt:

- Foreign governments: 42%
- Federal Reserve, state and local governments: 23%
- Banks, insurance companies: 7%
- Mutual funds, private pension, savings bonds: 16%

Source: Kimberly Amadeo, "Who Owns the US National Debt?" *The Balance,* February 13, 2019, https://www.thebalance.com/who-owns-the-u-s-national-debt-3306124.

Glossary

adjustable peg system: Governments act as residual buyers or sellers of their currencies to maintain their foreign values within a narrow margin of a fixed par value.

asset-backed securities: Combining standardized asset classes into a pool that is divided and sold.

acid-based loan facility: A broad term representing all types of lines of credit secured by assets that are on deposit at financial institutions.

balance sheet: A statement of the assets, liabilities, and capital of an individual, business, or other organization at a particular point in time.

beta: Measure of a security's or portfolio's volatility, or systemic risk, compared with the entire marketplace or a benchmark.

bimetallism: Government recognizes fixed ratios of gold and silver as legal tender.

bitcoin: The first digital currency based on blockchain technology.

blockchain: Technology that digitally secures the ownership of an item and its full history.

break the buck: Money market fund shares' value falls below a dollar so investors will lose money.

Bretton Woods Agreement: Pegged all nations' currencies to the dollar following World War II.

broad money: Anything of value that resembles money.

capital allocation line: Graph investors use to measure assets' risks, with a slope known as the "reward-to-variability ratio."

Chicago Plan: Called for complete separation of money as a governmental function and loaning as a banking function.

cloud computing: Computing environment where one party can outsource its computing needs to another and access databases and e-mails via the Internet.

commoditization of lending: Decentralized lending in which everyone who produces a commodity of a certain quality receives the same rate.

commodity money: Money with value derived from the commodity it's made from.

credit: The ability to obtain goods or services before payment based on trust the payment will be made in the future.

Credit Theory: A sale and purchase is the exchange of a commodity for credit independent of the value of any metal and based only on the debtor's obligation to pay and the creditor's right to acquire payment and accept the tender.

cryptocurrency: Digital currency based on blockchain technology.

currency: A system of money in general use.

decentralized: Authority and accountability is distributed over a delegation of individuals or units rather than a central authority.

debt: Loan agreement that is a liability of the individual. An obligation to repay a specified amount at a particular time.

debt capacity: Ability to borrow. The amount an individual or firm can borrow.

depreciation: A non-cash expense reflecting the decreased value of an asset over its estimated useful life.

devaluation: Reduction or underestimation of the worth or importance of something.

digital coin: Asset that is native to its own blockchain.

digital token: Asset that requires a platform such as Ethereum or Omni to exist and operate.

discount rate: Rate used to calculate the present value of future cash flows.

dual mandate: The Federal Reserve System's simultaneous goals of price stability and maximum sustainable employment.

Federal Reserve System: Agency charged with meeting business and industry's liquidity needs to keep the financial system and the economy stable.

fiat currency: Legal tender whose value is backed by the government that issued it.

Fisher, Irving: Economist who formulated the quantity theory of money.

foreign exchange markets: Markets in which participants buy, sell, exchange, and speculate on currencies.

fractional reserve: Banks keep only a portion of deposits and loan out the rest.

Friedman, Milton: Economist who proposed foreign exchange rates be determined daily by the forces of demand and supply, without government restrictions.

Friedman Rule: Milton Friedman's proposal to set the nominal interest rate to zero so the marginal benefit to society of holding money would equal the marginal cost to society of producing it, setting the nominal interest rate at the real interest rate plus expected inflation.

"full faith and credit":   Full borrowing power of a government based on investors' assurance that expected interest and principal interest payments will be made no matter what.

full reserve banking: Banks are required to keep all deposits in cash, ready to be withdrawn on demand.

Glass–Steagall Act: Regulations put in place in response to financial crisis that triggered the Great Depression.

gold standard: Paper currency is backed by gold.

Gold Standard Act: 1900 law establishing gold as the only standard for redeeming paper money.

gold window: Informal name for two-tiered system of gold pricing in which central banks could buy and sell at the official price of $35 per ounce and a private market where gold was freely traded at market prices.

greenback: Incontrovertible currency used by the Union during the US Civil War.

gyroscope: Device in which an infinite number of inputs can move on a spinning center kept constant by natural opposing forces.

Hayek, Friedrich: Economist who wrote *The Denationalization of Money.*

International Monetary Fund: Established to promote financial stability and monetary cooperation.

hyperinflation: Prices spiral out of control by as much as 80 percent.

income: Earned income, wages, salaries, profits from stocks or real estate sales, stock dividends, interest payments, lottery or gambling winnings, the cash value of bartered items, and anything else defined by statute or case law by the IRS as income.

inflation: A fall in the buying power of a unit of currency.

inflation risk: The chance that a change in the interest rate will result in an adverse effect on the borrower.

Innes, A. Mitchell: Economist who wrote *The Credit Theory of Money.*

interest rate: The price paid for borrowing money.

invisible hand: Adam Smith's theory that people and businesses acting in their own self-interest give markets natural stability and ability to self-regulate.

junk bond: A speculative-grade bond.

liabilities: Debts of an individual or business.

liquidity: The ease and quickness of converting assets to cash. Also called marketability.

long-term debt: An obligation having a maturity of more than one year.

M1: Money that can be used immediately and does not need to be converted, such as cash and traveler's checks.

M2: M1 plus things that can easily be converted to M1, such as saving's accounts, money market funds, and CDs.

MM: Money multiplier: amount banks can "pyramid" new deposits on top of reserves.

medium of exchange: Intermediary instrument used to facilitate the sale, purchase, or trade of goods between parties, representing a standard of value accepted by all parties.

Mises, Ludwig von: Economist who proposed a "pure credit" economy.

Modern Monetary Theory: Recognition that governments have unlimited power to issue fiat currency and force people to use it through taxation.

Modern Portfolio Theory: Risk-averse investors can build portfolios for maximum expected reward based on a given level of market risk.

monetarism: Milton Friedman's Friedman Rule setting the nominal interest to zero.

money supply: Total supply of currency and other liquid investments in a country's economy.

municipal bonds: Bonds issued by a municipality such as a city or state.

Nakamoto, Satoshi: Pseudonym for author of whitepaper and code that launched bitcoin.

narrow money: Easily convertible into cash.

nominal interest rate: The interest rate before taking inflation into account.

Planck, Max: Discovered that atoms can only take certain specific values; "Planck's constant" is the basis for quantum mechanics.

prime interest rate: Rate the Federal Reserve charges banks for loans.

profit-and-loss statement: Financial statement that summarizes revenues, costs, and expenses incurred during a specific period.

proof of work: Algorithm used to confirm transactions and produce new blocks on a blockchain.

quantitative easing: Central banks buying securities to lower interest rates.

quantity theory of money: The general price level of goods and services is directly proportional to the amount of money in circulation, or money supply.

real rate of return: Annual percentage realized on an investment adjusted for inflation.

reserve ratio: Portion of reservable liabilities that financial institutions must hold onto rather than lend or invest.

risk: A peril or danger; in financial matters, the chance the return on your investment will become worthless or just worth less than it started out or than you expected it to be.

risk-free rate: A market-based, self-stabilizing global currency that can be measured in any unit of value and take place in any medium of exchange.

risk tolerance: The degree of variability in investment returns that an individual is willing to withstand; how much risk or potential loss of return or value an individual or couple is able to emotionally and psychologically tolerate in the pursuit of reward or return.

safe store of value: Standardized, fixed constant that can be measured in any unit of value and take place via any medium of exchange.

secured lending: Borrower pledges some asset as collateral for a loan, which then becomes a secured debt.

securities: Tradable financial investments such as stocks, bonds, and derivatives.

securitization: Dividing a single loan between several lenders to share the risk.

securities-based lending: Making loans using securities as collateral that can be used for almost any purpose.

Smith, Adam: Economist who advocated for private money issuance in the eighteenth century.

specie: Gold and silver.

systematically important financial institutions (SIFI): Banks considered "too big to fail."

trustless: Ability to verify and monitor exchanges for value over a computer network without a third party or central institution.

Troubled Asset Relief Program: 2008 bank bailout in response to financial crisis.

Resource Guide

This compilation of free online education videos from Khan Academy and Wikipedia content provides information that can help you better understand concepts in this book. With a mission "to provide a free, world-class education for anyone, anywhere," Khan Academy is a not-for-profit entity; there are no ads and no subscriptions. Wikipedia is a free online encyclopedia created and edited by volunteers around the world and hosted by the Wikipedia Foundation.

Inflation, Interest Rates, and Hyperinflation

Inflation Overview – Khan Academy
- https://www.khanacademy.org/economics-finance-domain/core-finance/inflation-tutorial/inflation-basics-tutorial/v/inflation-overview

What Is Inflation? Khan Academy
- https://www.khanacademy.org/economics-finance-domain/core-finance/inflation-tutorial/inflation-basics-tutorial/v/what-is-inflation

Inflation – Wikipedia
- https://en.wikipedia.org/wiki/Inflation

Real and Nominal Return – Khan Academy
- https://www.khanacademy.org/economics-finance-domain/core-finance/inflation-tutorial/real-nominal-return-tut/v/real-and-nominal-return

Relations Between Nominal and Real Returns and Inflation – Khan Academy
- https://www.khanacademy.org/economics-finance-domain/core-finance/inflation-tutorial/real-nominal-return-tut/v/relation-between-nominal-and-real-returns-and-inflation

Moderate Inflation in a Good Economy – Khan Academy
- https://www.khanacademy.org/economics-finance-domain/core-finance/inflation-tutorial/inflation-scenarios-tutorial/v/moderate-inflation-in-a-good-economy

Stagflation – Khan Academy
- https://www.khanacademy.org/economics-finance-domain/core-finance/inflation-tutorial/inflation-scenarios-tutorial/v/stagflation

Hyperinflation – Khan Academy
- https://www.khanacademy.org/economics-finance-domain/core-finance/inflation-tutorial/inflation-scenarios-tutorial/v/hyperinflation

Hyperinflation – Wikipedia
- https://en.wikipedia.org/wiki/Hyperinflation

Money

Money – Wikipedia
- https://en.wikipedia.org/wiki/Money

Functions of Money – Khan Academy
- https://www.khanacademy.org/economics-finance-domain/ap-macroeconomics/ap-financial-sector/definition-measurement-and-functions-of-money-ap/v/functions-of-money

Money Supply: M0, M1, and M2 – Khan Academy
- https://www.khanacademy.org/economics-finance-domain/ap-macroeconomics/ap-financial-sector/definition-measurement-and-functions-of-money-ap/v/money-supply-m0-m1-and-m2

When the Functions of Money Break Down: Hyperinflation – Khan Academy
- https://www.khanacademy.org/economics-finance-domain/ap-macroeconomics/ap-financial-sector/definition-measurement-and-functions-of-money-ap/v/when-the-functions-of-money-break-down-hyperinflation

Commodity Money vs. Fiat Money – Khan Academy
- https://www.khanacademy.org/economics-finance-domain/ap-macroeconomics/ap-financial-sector/definition-measurement-and-functions-of-money-ap/v/commodity-money-vs-fiat-money

Fiat Money – Wikipedia
- https://en.wikipedia.org/wiki/Fiat_money

Monetary Theory

Monetary Economics – Wikipedia
- https://en.wikipedia.org/wiki/Monetary_economics

Credit Theory of Money – Wikipedia
- https://en.wikipedia.org/wiki/Credit_theory_of_money

Quantity Theory of Money – Wikipedia
- https://en.wikipedia.org/wiki/Quantity_theory_of_money

Modern Monetary Theory – Wikipedia
- https://en.wikipedia.org/wiki/Modern_Monetary_Theory

Monetarism – Wikipedia
- https://en.wikipedia.org/wiki/Monetarism

Banking

Introduction – Khan Academy
- https://www.khanacademy.org/economics-finance-domain/core-finance/money-and-banking/modal/v/banking-1

A Bank's Income Statement – Khan Academy
- https://www.khanacademy.org/economics-finance-domain/
  core-finance/money-and-banking/modal/v/banking-2-a-
  bank-s-income-statement

Fractional Reserve Banking (Introduction to) – Khan Academy
- https://www.khanacademy.org/economics-finance-domain/
  core-finance/money-and-banking/modal/v/banking-3-
  fractional-reserve-banking

Multiplier Effect and The Money Supply – Khan Academy
- https://www.khanacademy.org/economics-finance-domain/
  core-finance/money-and-banking/modal/v/banking-4-
  multiplier-effect-and-the-money-supply

Introduction to Bank Notes – Khan Academy
- https://www.khanacademy.org/economics-finance-domain/
  core-finance/money-and-banking/modal/v/banking-5-
  introduction-to-bank-notes

Bank Notes and Checks – Khan Academy
- https://www.khanacademy.org/economics-finance-domain/
  core-finance/money-and-banking/modal/v/banking-6-bank-
  notes-and-checks

Giving Out Loans Without Giving Out Gold – Khan Academy
- https://www.khanacademy.org/economics-finance-domain/
  core-finance/money-and-banking/modal/v/banking-7-giving-
  out-loans-without-giving-out-gold

Reserve Ratios – Khan Academy
- https://www.khanacademy.org/economics-finance-domain/
  core-finance/money-and-banking/modal/v/banking-8-
  reserve-ratios

A Reserve Bank – Khan Academy
- https://www.khanacademy.org/economics-finance-domain/
  core-finance/money-and-banking/modal/v/banking-11-a-
  reserve-bank

The Federal Reserve (and the Dual Mandate) – Wikipedia
- https://en.wikipedia.org/wiki/Federal_Reserve

Treasuries – Khan Academy
- https://www.khanacademy.org/economics-finance-domain/
  core-finance/money-and-banking/modal/v/banking-12-
  treasuries-government-debt

Open Market Operations – Khan Academy
- https://www.khanacademy.org/economics-finance-domain/
  core-finance/money-and-banking/modal/v/banking-13-open-
  market-operations

Fed Funds Rate – Khan Academy
- https://www.khanacademy.org/economics-finance-domain/
  core-finance/money-and-banking/modal/v/banking-14-fed-
  funds-rate

Detail on Fed Funds Rate – Khan Academy
- https://www.khanacademy.org/economics-finance-domain/
  core-finance/money-and-banking/modal/v/banking-15-more-
  on-the-fed-funds-rate

Why Target Rates vs. Money Supply? – Khan Academy
- https://www.khanacademy.org/economics-finance-domain/
  core-finance/money-and-banking/modal/v/banking-16-why-
  target-rates-vs-money-supply

What Happened to the Gold? – Khan Academy
- https://www.khanacademy.org/economics-finance-domain/
  core-finance/money-and-banking/banking-and-money/v/
  banking-17-what-happened-to-the-gold

Federal Reserve Balance Sheet – Khan Academy
- https://www.khanacademy.org/economics-finance-domain/
  core-finance/money-and-banking/banking-and-money/v/
  federal-reserve-balance-sheet

The Discount Rate – Khan Academy
- https://www.khanacademy.org/economics-finance-domain/
  core-finance/money-and-banking/banking-and-money/v/the-
  discount-rate

LIBOR – Khan Academy
- https://www.khanacademy.org/economics-finance-domain/
  core-finance/money-and-banking/banking-and-money/v/libor

National Savings and Investment – Khan Academy
- https://www.khanacademy.org/economics-finance-domain/ap-macroeconomics/ap-financial-sector/the-market-for-loanable-funds/v/national-savings-and-investment-ap-macroeconomics-khan-academy

The Loanable Funds Market – Khan Academy
- https://www.khanacademy.org/economics-finance-domain/ap-macroeconomics/ap-financial-sector/the-market-for-loanable-funds/v/loanable-funds-market-ap-macroeconomics-khan-academy

Repurchase Agreements/Repo Transactions – Khan Academy
- https://www.khanacademy.org/economics-finance-domain/core-finance/money-and-banking/banking-and-money/v/repurchase-agreements-repo-transactions

Banking Systems

Fractional Reserve Banking – Wikipedia
- https://en.wikipedia.org/wiki/Fractional-reserve_banking

Full Reserve Banking – Wikipedia
- https://en.wikipedia.org/wiki/Full-reserve_banking

Full Reserve Banking – Khan Academy
- https://www.khanacademy.org/economics-finance-domain/macroeconomics/monetary-system-topic/macro-banking-and-the-expansion-of-the-money-supply/v/full-reserve-banking

Weakness of Fractional Reserve Banking – Khan Academy
- https://www.khanacademy.org/economics-finance-domain/macroeconomics/monetary-system-topic/macro-banking-and-the-expansion-of-the-money-supply/v/weaknesses-of-fractional-reserve-lending

Pros and Cons of Various Banking Systems – Khan Academy
- https://www.khanacademy.org/economics-finance-domain/core-finance/money-and-banking/banking-and-money/v/banking-18-big-picture-discussion

The Chicago Plan – Wikipedia
  • https://en.wikipedia.org/wiki/Chicago_plan
The Chicago Plan Revisited – Wikipedia
  • https://en.wikipedia.org/wiki/The_Chicago_Plan_Revisited

Nonprofit and Cooperative Banking

Credit Union
  • https://en.wikipedia.org/wiki/Credit_union
Cooperative
  • https://en.wikipedia.org/wiki/Cooperative
Cooperative Banking
  • https://en.wikipedia.org/wiki/Cooperative_banking

Fractional Reserve Banking – Expanded

Bank Balance Sheets in a Fractional Reserve System – Khan Academy
  • https://www.khanacademy.org/economics-finance-domain/
    ap-macroeconomics/ap-financial-sector/banking-and-the-
    expansion-of-the-money-supply-ap/v/bank-balance-sheets-in-
    a-fractional-reserve-system
Money Creation in a Fractional Reserve System – Khan Academy
  • https://www.khanacademy.org/economics-finance-domain/
    ap-macroeconomics/ap-financial-sector/banking-and-the-
    expansion-of-the-money-supply-ap/v/money-creation-in-a-
    fractional-reserve-system-ap-macroeconomics-khan-academy
Fractional Reserve Banking Commentary – Khan Academy
  • https://www.khanacademy.org/economics-finance-domain/
    core-finance/money-and-banking/banking-and-money/v/
    fractional-reserve-banking-commentary-1
Fractional Reserve Banking Commentary: Deposit Insurance – Khan
Academy
  • https://www.khanacademy.org/economics-finance-domain/
    core-finance/money-and-banking/banking-and-money/v/frb-
    commentary-2-deposit-insurance

Fractional Reserve Banking: Big Picture – Khan Academy
- https://www.khanacademy.org/economics-finance-domain/
  core-finance/money-and-banking/banking-and-money/v/frb-
  commentary-3-big-picture

The Relationship Between Money and Interest Rates

Money Market – Wikipedia
- https://en.wikipedia.org/wiki/Money_market

Money Market Fund – Wikipedia
- https://en.wikipedia.org/wiki/Money_market_fund

The Demand Curve for Money in the Money Market – Khan Academy
- https://www.khanacademy.org/economics-finance-domain/
  ap-macroeconomics/ap-financial-sector/the-money-market-
  apmacro/v/demand-curve-for-money-in-the-money-market-
  ap-macroeconomics-khan-academy

Equilibrium Interest Rates in the Money Market – Khan Academy
- https://www.khanacademy.org/economics-finance-domain/
  ap-macroeconomics/ap-financial-sector/the-money-market-
  apmacro/v/equilibrium-nominal-interest-rates-in-the-money-
  market-ap-macroeconomics-khan-academy

Monetary Policy Tools – Khan Academy
- https://www.khanacademy.org/economics-finance-domain/
  ap-macroeconomics/ap-financial-sector/monetary-policy-
  apmacro/v/monetary-policy-tools-ap-macroeconomics-khan-
  academy

Modern Portfolio Theory

Modern Portfolio Theory – Wikipedia
- https://en.wikipedia.org/wiki/Modern_portfolio_theory

Risk-Free Rate – Wikipedia
- https://en.wikipedia.org/wiki/Risk-free_interest_rate

Capital Asset Pricing Model – Wikipedia
- https://en.wikipedia.org/wiki/Capital_asset_pricing_model

Beta – Wikipedia
- https://en.wikipedia.org/wiki/Beta_(finance)

Efficient Frontier – Wikipedia
- https://en.wikipedia.org/wiki/Efficient_frontier

Capital Allocation Line – Wikipedia
- https://en.wikipedia.org/wiki/Capital_allocation_line

Capital Market Line – Wikipedia
- https://en.wikipedia.org/wiki/Capital_market_line

Securitization and Collateralized Pools of Loans

From Wikipedia:

Securitization
- https://en.wikipedia.org/wiki/Securitization

Asset-Based Lending
- https://en.wikipedia.org/wiki/Asset-based_lending

Asset-Backed Securities
- https://en.wikipedia.org/wiki/Asset-backed_security

Collateralized Debt Obligation
- https://en.wikipedia.org/wiki/Collateralized_debt_obligation

Collateralized Loan Obligation
- https://en.wikipedia.org/wiki/Collateralized_loan_obligation

From Khan Academy:

Collateralized Debt Obligation – Overview
- https://www.khanacademy.org/economics-finance-domain/
  core-finance/derivative-securities/cdo-tutorial/v/collateralized-
  debt-obligation-overview

Collateralized Debt Obligation
- https://www.khanacademy.org/economics-finance-domain/
  core-finance/derivative-securities/cdo-tutorial/v/collateralized-
  debt-obligation-cdo

Mortgage-Backed Security Overview

- https://www.khanacademy.org/economics-finance-domain/
  core-finance/derivative-securities/modal/v/mortgage-back-
  security-overview

Mortgage-Backed Securities

- https://www.khanacademy.org/economics-finance-domain/
  core-finance/derivative-securities/modal/v/mortgage-backed-
  securities-i
- https://www.khanacademy.org/economics-finance-domain/
  core-finance/derivative-securities/modal/v/mortgage-backed-
  securities-ii
- https://www.khanacademy.org/economics-finance-domain/
  core-finance/derivative-securities/modal/v/mortgage-backed-
  securities-iii

Bitcoin and Blockchain

Bitcoin: A Peer-to-Peer Electronic Cash System

The original paper by Satoshi Nakamoto: https://bitcoin.org/bitcoin.pdf

From Wikipedia:

Blockchain

- https://en.wikipedia.org/wiki/Blockchain

Cryptography

- https://en.wikipedia.org/wiki/Cryptography

Cryptographic Hash Function

- https://en.wikipedia.org/wiki/Cryptographic_hash_function

Distributed Ledger

- https://en.wikipedia.org/wiki/Distributed_ledger

Peer-to-Peer

- https://en.wikipedia.org/wiki/Peer-to-peer

Consensus

- https://en.wikipedia.org/wiki/Consensus_(computer_science)

Digital Currency

- https://en.wikipedia.org/wiki/Digital_currency

From Khan Academy:

What Is Bitcoin?
- https://www.khanacademy.org/economics-finance-domain/
  core-finance/money-and-banking/modal/v/bitcoin-what-is-it

Bitcoin Overview
- https://www.khanacademy.org/economics-finance-domain/
  core-finance/money-and-banking/modal/v/bitcoin-overview

Cryptographic Hash Functions
- https://www.khanacademy.org/economics-finance-domain/
  core-finance/money-and-banking/modal/v/bitcoin-cryptogra
  phic-hash-function

Digital Signatures
- https://www.khanacademy.org/economics-finance-domain/
  core-finance/money-and-banking/modal/v/bitcoin-digital-
  signatures

Bitcoin: Transaction Records
- https://www.khanacademy.org/economics-finance-domain/
  core-finance/money-and-banking/modal/v/bitcoin-transaction-
  records

Proof-of-Work
- https://www.khanacademy.org/economics-finance-domain/
  core-finance/money-and-banking/modal/v/bitcoin-proof-of-
  work

Transaction Blockchains
- https://www.khanacademy.org/economics-finance-domain/
  core-finance/money-and-banking/modal/v/bitcoin-transaction-
  block-chains

Bitcoin: Money Supply
- https://www.khanacademy.org/economics-finance-domain/
  core-finance/money-and-banking/modal/v/bitcoin-the-
  money-supply

The Security of Transaction Blockchains
- https://www.khanacademy.org/economics-finance-domain/
  core-finance/money-and-banking/modal/v/bitcoin-security-
  of-transaction-block-chains

Key Technologies and Terms

Decentralization
- https://en.wikipedia.org/wiki/Decentralization

Distributed Computing
- https://en.wikipedia.org/wiki/Distributed_computing

Cloud Computing
- https://en.wikipedia.org/wiki/Cloud_computing

Kubernetes
- https://en.wikipedia.org/wiki/Kubernetes

Key Theories and Phenomena

Freidman Rule
- https://en.wikipedia.org/wiki/Friedman_rule

Friedman's K-percent Rule
- https://en.wikipedia.org/wiki/Friedman™percnt;27s_k-percent_rule

Taylor Rule
- https://en.wikipedia.org/wiki/Taylor_rule

Phillips Curve
- https://en.wikipedia.org/wiki/Phillips_curve

Zero Interest Rate Policy
- https://en.wikipedia.org/wiki/Zero_interest-rate_policy

Negative Interest Rates
- https://en.wikipedia.org/wiki/Interest_rate#Negative_interest_rates

Key Historic Events, Panics, and Shocks of the Past 200 Years

Panic of 1825
- https://en.wikipedia.org/wiki/Panic_of_1825

Panic of 1837
- https://en.wikipedia.org/wiki/Panic_of_1837

Panic of 1857
- https://en.wikipedia.org/wiki/Panic_of_1857

Black Friday (1869)
- https://en.wikipedia.org/wiki/Black_Friday_(1869)

Panic of 1873
- https://en.wikipedia.org/wiki/Panic_of_1873

Panic of 1884
- https://en.wikipedia.org/wiki/Panic_of_1884

Panic of 1893
- https://en.wikipedia.org/wiki/Panic_of_1893

Panic of 1896
- https://en.wikipedia.org/wiki/Panic_of_1896

Panic of 1901
- https://en.wikipedia.org/wiki/Panic_of_1901

Panic of 1907
- https://en.wikipedia.org/wiki/Panic_of_1907

Wall Street Crash of 1929
- https://en.wikipedia.org/wiki/Wall_Street_Crash_of_1929

Great Depression
- https://en.wikipedia.org/wiki/Great_Depression

Bretton Woods (1944)
- https://en.wikipedia.org/wiki/Bretton_Woods_system

Nixon Shock (1971)
- https://en.wikipedia.org/wiki/Nixon_shock

1973 Oil Crisis
- https://en.wikipedia.org/wiki/1973_oil_crisis

Latin American Debt Crisis
- https://en.wikipedia.org/wiki/Latin_American_debt_crisis

Black Monday (1987)
- https://en.wikipedia.org/wiki/Black_Monday_(1987)

Savings and Loan Crisis
- https://en.wikipedia.org/wiki/Savings_and_loan_crisis

Japanese Asset Price Bubble
- https://en.wikipedia.org/wiki/Japanese_asset_price_bubble

Black Wednesday
- https://en.wikipedia.org/wiki/Black_Wednesday (1992)

Mexican Peso Crisis
- https://en.wikipedia.org/wiki/Mexican_peso_crisis

Argentine Great Depression
- https://en.wikipedia.org/wiki/1998%E2%80%932002_Argentine_great_depression

Asian Financial Crisis (1997)
- https://en.wikipedia.org/wiki/1997_Asian_financial_crisis

Russian Financial Crisis (1998)
- https://en.wikipedia.org/wiki/1998_Russian_financial_crisis

Dot-Com Bubble (2000)
- https://en.wikipedia.org/wiki/Dot-com_bubble

Global Financial Crisis
- https://en.wikipedia.org/wiki/Global_financial_crisis_in_2009

Notable Hyperinflations

Rome
- https://en.wikipedia.org/wiki/Hyperinflation#Rome

Austria
- https://en.wikipedia.org/wiki/Hyperinflation#Austria

China
- https://en.wikipedia.org/wiki/Hyperinflation#China

France
- https://en.wikipedia.org/wiki/Hyperinflation#France

Weimar Republic
- https://en.wikipedia.org/wiki/Hyperinflation_in_the_Weimar_Republic

Hungary
- https://en.wikipedia.org/wiki/Hungarian_peng%C5%91#Hyperinflation

Soviet Russia
- https://en.wikipedia.org/wiki/Hyperinflation_in_early_Soviet_Russia

Venezuela
- https://en.wikipedia.org/wiki/Crisis_in_Venezuela

Zimbabwe
- https://en.wikipedia.org/wiki/Hyperinflation_in_Zimbabwe

10 Most Severe Hyperinflations in World History

Highest Monthly Inflation Rates in History

Country	Currency name	Month with highest inflation rate	Highest monthly inflation rate	Equivalent daily inflation rate	Time required for prices to double	Highest denomination
Hungary	Hungarian pengő	July 1946	4.19×10^{16} %	207.19%	15.6 hours	100 Quintillion (10^{20})
Zimbabwe	Zimbabwe dollar	November 2008	7.96×10^{10} %	98.01%	24.7 hours	100 Trillion (10^{14})
Yugoslavia	Yugoslav dinar	January 1994	3.13×10^{8} %	64.63%	1.4 days	500 Billion (5×10^{11})
Republika Srpska	Republika Srpska dinar	January 1994	2.97×10^{8} %	64.3%	1.41 days	10 Billion (10×10^{10})
Germany (Weimar Republic)	German papiermark	October 1923	29,500%	20.87%	3.7 days	100 Trillion (10^{14})
Greece	Greek drachma	October 1944	13,800%	17.84%	4.3 days	100 Billion (10^{11})
China	Chinese yuan	April 1949	5,070%	14.1%	5.34 days	6 Billion
Armenia	Armenian dram and Russian ruble	November 1993	438%	5.77%	12.5 days	50,000 (ruble)
Turkmenistan	Turkmenistan manat	November 1993	429%	5.71%	12.7 days	500
Taiwan	Taiwanese yen	August 1945	399%	5.50%	13.1 days	1,000

Source: https://en.wikipedia.org/wiki/Hyperinflation; Steve H. Hanke and Nicholas Krus, "World Hyperinflations" (working paper, Cato Institute), August 15, 2012, cato.org; "The Worst Hyperinflation Situations of All Time," CNBC, https://www.cnbc.com/2011/02/14/The-Worst-Hyperinflation-Situations-of-All-Time.htm.

The Coming Crisis

Currency Wars: The Making of the Next Global Crisis by James Rickards

The Road to Ruin: The Global Elites' Secret Plan for the Next Financial Crisis by James Rickards

The Death of Money: The Coming Collapse of the International Monetary System by James Rickards

A History of Central Banking and the Enslavement of Mankind by Stephen Mitford Goodson

The Big Debt Crisis by Ray Dalio

The Dollar Crisis: Causes, Consequences, Cures by Richard Duncan

Aftershock: Protect Yourself and Profit in the Next Global Financial Meltdown by David Wiederner, Robert Wiederner, and Cindy Spitzer

America's Bubble Economy: Profit When It Pops by David Wiederner, Robert Wiederner, and Cindy Spitzer

The Real Crash: America's Coming Bankruptcy by Peter Schiff

Manias, Panics, Crashes by Charles Kindleberger and Robert Aliber

Why Nations Fail by Daron Acemoglu

This Time Is Different: Eight Centuries of Financial Folly by Carmen Reinhart and Kenneth Rogoff

Bibliography

Adam, Martin. "Remembering Nixon's Gold-Standard Gamble: Interrupting 'Bonanza.'" *The Atlantic*, August 15, 2011. https://www.theatlantic.com/politics/archive/2011/08/nixon-gold-standard-gamble-interrupting-bonanza/354136/.

Allen, William R. "Irving Fisher and the 100 Percent Reserve Proposal." *Journal of Law & Economics* 36, no. 2 (1993): 703–717. http://www.jstor.org/stable/725805.

Anderson, Thomas J. *The Value of Debt: How to Manage Both Sides of a Balance Sheet to Maximize Wealth*. Hoboken, NJ: John Wiley & Sons, 2013.

Anderson, Thomas J. *The Value of Debt in Building Wealth*. Hoboken, NJ: John Wiley & Sons, 2017.

Anikin, A. *Gold – The Yellow Devil*. New York: International Publishers, 1983.

Antonopoulos, Andreas M. *Mastering Bitcoin: Unlocking Digital Cryptocurrencies*. Sebastopol, CA: O'Reilly Media, 2015.

Arutyunov, V.V. "Cloud Computing: Its History of Development, Modern State, and Future Considerations." *Scientific and Technical Information Processing* 39, no. 3 (July 2012): 173–178. https://doi.org/10.3103/S0147688212030082.

Baron, Joshua; O'Mahony, Angela; Manheim, David; and Dion-Schwartz, Cynthia. "The Current State of Virtual Currencies." In *National Security Implications of Virtual Currency: Examining the Potential for Non-State Actor Deployment*. RAND Corp., 2015. https://www.jstor.org/stable/10.7249/j.ctt19rmd78.8.

Bell, Mary Ann. "Cloud Crowd: You Belong Whether You Know It or Not!" *Multimedia & Internat@Schools*, July–August 2009. http://www.questia.com/read/ 1G1-203230755/cloud-crowd-you-belong-whether-you-know-it-or-not.

Bellofiore, Riccardo. "Between Wicksell and Hayek: Mises' Theory of Money and Credit Revisited." *American Journal of Economics and Sociology* 57, no. 4, 1998. http://www.questia.com/read/1G1-53449312/between-wicksell-and-hayek-mises-theory-of-money.

Benes, Jaromir, and Kumhof, Michael. *The Chicago Plan Revisited*. International Monetary Fund, 2012. http://193.205.144.19/dipartimenti/distateq/garofalo /wp12202.pdf.

Bernanke, Ben S. "A Century of US Central Banking: Goals, Frameworks, Accountability." Journal of Economic Perspectives 27, no. 4 (Fall 2013): 3–16. https://www.jstor.org/stable/23560019.

Bernstein, Peter L. *The Power of Gold: The History of an Obsession*. Hoboken, NJ: Wiley, 2012.

Block, Fred L. *The Origins of International Economic Disorder: A Study of United States Monetary Policy from World War II to the Present*. Berkeley and Los Angeles: University of California Press, 1977.

Bodie, Ziv; Kane, Alex; and Marcus, Alan. *Investments*, 9th ed. New York: McGraw-Hill, 2011.

Bonamy, Price. "What Is Money?" *Fraser's Magazine*, no. 602, February 1880, 248–260. https://search.proquest.com/openview/069615c7110f1baa/1?pq-origsite=gscholar&cbl=1795.

Bordo, Michael D. "The Gold Standard and Other Monetary Regimes." *NBER Reporter*, 1992. http://www.questia.com/read/1G1-12730329/the-gold-standard-and-other-monetary-regimes.

Bordo, Michael D., and Rockoff, Hugh. "The Influence of Irving Fisher on Milton Friedmabn's Monetary Economics." *American Economic Association*, January 1, 2011. http://citeseerx.ist.psu.edu/viewdoc/download;jsessionid=CF3C959A D00B985D086474688AE41088?doi=10.1.1.364.5640&rep=rep1&type=pdf.

Bowles, Nellie. "Everyone Is Getting Hilariously Rich, and You'Re Not". *New York Times*, January 13, 2018. https://www.nytimes.com/2018/01/13/style/ bitcoin-millionaires.html?em_pos=large&emc=edit_li_20180113&nl=nyt-living&nlid=12940167&ref=headline&te=1&_r=0.

Browne, Ryan. "Digital Payments Expected to Hit 726 by 2020 – But Cash Isn't Going Anywhere Yet." *CNBC*, October 8, 2017. https://www.cnbc.com/ 2017/10/09/digital-payments-expected-to-hit-726-billion-by-2020-study-finds.html.

Carlos, Ann M., and Lewis, Frank D. *Commerce by a Frozen Sea: Native Americans and the European Fur Trade*. Philadelphia: University of Pennsylvania Press, 2010. http://www.questia.com/read/124342734/commcrce-by-a-frozen-sea-native-americans-and-the.

Carney, John. "The Size of the Bank Bailout: $29 Trillion." *CNBC*, December 14, 2011. https://www.cnbc.com/id/45674390

Catherwood, Hugh R. "The U.S. National Debt." *Government Accountants Journal* 49, no. 2 (2000). http://www.questia.com/read/1P3-55109496/the-u-s-national-debt.

Chang, Sue. "Here's All the Money in the World, in One Chart." MarketWatch, November 28, 2017. https://www.marketwatch.com/story/this-is-how-much-money-exists-in-the-entire-world-in-one-chart-2015-12-18.

Chennov, Adrian. "Much Ado About Bitcoin". *New York Times*, November 26, 2013.   https://www.nytimes.com/2013/11/27/opinion/much-ado-about-bitcoin.html?nl=opinion&emc=edit_ty_20131127&_r=0.

Collins, Mike. "The Big Bank Bailout." *Forbes*, July 14, 2015. https://www.forbes.com/sites/mikecollins/2015/07/14/the-big-bank-bailout/#5900bf202d83.

Collins, Tim. "The Rise of Bitcoin Was Predicted by Nobel Prize–Winning Economist Milton Friedman in an Interview Recorded 18 Years Ago, Footage Reveals." *Daily Mail*, October 20, 2017. https://www.dailymail.co.uk/sciencetech/article-5000260/Bitcoin-predicted-Milton-Friedman-18-years-ago.html.

"Conferees Agree on Currency Bill." *New York Times*, February 24, 1900a, 1–2. https://www.nytimes.com/1900/02/24/archives/conferrees-agree-on-currency-bill-it-declares-unqualifiedly-for-a.html.

Conrad, Edward. *Unintended Consequences: Why Everything You've Been Told about the Economy Is Wrong*. New York: Portfolio Penguin, 2012.

"Currency and Coin Services." *The Federal Reserve*. https://www.federalreserve.gov/paymentsystems/coin_currcircvolume.htm.

Dam, Kenneth W. "From the Gold Clause Cases to the Gold Commission: A Half Century of American Monetary Law." *University of Chicago Law Review* 50, no. 2 (Spring 1983): 504–532. https://www.jstor.org/stable/1599500?read-now=1&loggedin=true&seq=16#page_scan_tab_contents.

Davies, Antony. "Going for Broke: Deficits, Debt, and the Entitlement Crisis." *Independent Review* 20, no. 4 (2016). http://www.questia.com/read/1G1-449314256/going-for-broke-deficits-debt-and-the-entitlement.

Davies, Anthony. "Debt Myths, Debunked." *US News & World Report, December* 1, 2016. https://www.usnews.com/opinion/economic-intelligence/articles/2016-12-01/myths-and-facts-about-the-us-federal-debt.

Davis, S. "Greek and Roman Coins and Their Historical Interest." *Acta Classica* 3. https://www.jstor.org/stable/24591082.

Deleplace, Ghislain. "Problems and Paradoxes of Money." *UNESCO Courier*, January 1990. http://www.questia.com/read/1G1-8561011/problems-and-paradoxes-of-money.

Dellas, Harris, and Tavlas, George S. "Milton Friedman and the Case for Flexible Exchange Rates and Monetary Rules." *Bank of Greece*, October 2017. https://www.bankofgreece.gr/BogEkdoseis/Paper2017236.pdf.

Del Rowe, Sam. "Mobile Payment Technologies Set to Increase: Reports from Juniper and Forrester Indicate That Use of Mobile Payment Solutions Will Increase for Both Businesses and Consumers." *CRM Magazine*, April 2017, 17. http://www.questia.com/read/1G1-488193746/mobile-payment-technologies-set-to-increase-reports.

Doherty, Brian. "The Life and Times of Milton Friedman: Remembering the 20th Century's Most Influential Libertarian." *Reason*, March 2007. http://www.questia.com/read/1G1-159238152/the-life-and-times-of-milton-friedman-remembering.

Donnelly, Stephen. "Fur, Fortune, and Empire: The Epic History of the Fur Trade in America." *Historical Journal of Massachusetts* 39, no. 1/2 (2011). http://www.questia.com/read/1P3-2384275071/fur-fortune-and-empire-the-epic-history-of-the.

Durden, Tyler. "How Bitcoin Could Serve the Marijuana Industry (With Banks Still Nervous)." *ZeroHedge*, January 13, 2014. https://www.zerohedge.com/news/2014-01-13/how-bitcoin-could-serve-marijuana-industry-banks-still-nervous.

Eberhardt, Doug. "What Really Backs the U.S. Dollar?" *Seeking Alpha*, June 28, 2009. https://seekingalpha.com/article/145722-what-really-backs-the-u-s-dollar.

Eder, Elizabeth. "The Golden Solution." *Harvard International Review* 4, no. 3 (November 1981): 18–19. https://www.jstor.org/stable/42763896.

Eichengreen, Barry, and Temin, Peter. "The Gold Standard and the Great Depression." *Contemporary European History* 9, no. 2 (July 2000): 183–207. https://www.jstor.org/stable/20081742.

Eichengreen, Barry. "Financial Crisis: Revisiting the Banking Rules That Died by a Thousand Small Cuts." *Fortune*, January 16, 2015. http://fortune.com/2015/01/16/financial-crisis-bank-regulation/.

Ferguson, Niall. *The Ascent of Money: A Financial History of the World*. New York: The Penguin Press, 2008.

Fisher, Irving, and Brown, Harry G. *The Purchasing Power of Money: Its Determination and Relation to Credit Interest and Crises*. Norwood, MA: J.B. Cushing Co., 1911.

Frankel, Matthew. "How Many Cryptocurrencies Are There?" *The Motley Fool*, March 16, 2018. https://www.fool.com/investing/2018/03/16/how-many-cryptocurrencies-are-there.aspx.

Friedman, Milton. *Essays in Positive Economics*. University of Chicago Press, 1953.

Friedman, Milton. "The Counter-Revolution in Monetary Theory." *IEA Occasional Paper*, no. 3. Institute of Economic Affairs, 1970.

Friedman, Milton. "The Case for Monetary Rule." *Newsweek*, February 7, 1972, 67.

Friedman, Milton. "Monetary Policy: Theory and Practice." *Journal of Money, Credit, and Banking* 14 (February 1982): 98–118. https://miltonfriedman.hoover.org/friedman_images/Collections/2016c21/OSU_02_1982.pdf.

Friedman, Milton. "Defining Monetarism." *Newsweek*, July 12, 1982b, 64.

Friedman, Milton. "The Keynes Centenary: A Monetarist Reflects." *The Economist*, June 4, 1983, 17–19. https://miltonfriedman.hoover.org/friedman _images/Collections/2016c21/Economist_06_04_1983.pdf.

Friedman, Milton. "M1's Hot Streak Gave Keynsians a Bad Idea." *Wall Street Journal*, September 18, 1986. https://miltonfriedman.hoover.org/friedman_ images/Collections/2016c21/WSJ_09_18_1986.pdf.

Friedman, Milton. "Bimetallism Revisited." *Journal of Economic Perspectives* 4, no. 4 (Autumn 1990): 85–104. https://www.jstor.org/stable/1942723.

Friedman, Milton. "Letter to the Editor: Roots." *Wall Street Journal*, October 30, 1992. https://miltonfriedman.hoover.org/friedman_images/Collections/2016 c21/WSJ_10_30_1992.pdf.

Friedman, Milton. "The Quantity Theory of Money: A Restatement." Reprinted in *Studies in the Quantity Theory of Money*. Chicago: University of Chicago Press, 2005.

"FSB Publishes 2017 G-SIB List." *Financial Stability Board*, November 21, 2017. http://www.fsb.org/2017/11/fsb-publishes-2017-g-sib-list/.

Gittlitz, A.M. "'Make It So': 'Star Trek' and Its Debt to Revolutionary Social- ism." *New York Times*, July 24, 2017. https://www.nytimes.com/2017/07/24/ opinion/make-it-so-star-trek-and-its-debt-to-revolutionary-socialism.html.

Gjerding, Kristian. "The Cashless Economy: Why and Where It's Evolving and What Businesses Can Do Now to Prepare." *Forbes*, October 24, 2017. https://www.forbes.com/sites/forbesfinancecouncil/2017/10/24/the- cashless-economy-why-and-where-its-evolving-and-what-businesses-can- do-now-to-prepare/#731997d93e11.

"Gold Now the Standard." *New York Times*, March 15, 1900, 1. https://times machine.nytimes.com/timesmachine/1900/03/14/102500611.html?action= click&contentCollection=Archives&module=ArticleEndCTA&region=Arch iveBody&pgtype=article&pageNumber=1.

Graeber, David. *Debt: The First 5000 Years*. Brooklyn: Melville House, 2011.

Hankin, Aaron. "Winklevoss Twins' Gemini Trust Launches World's First Regu- lated Stablecoin." *Marketwatch*, September 10, 2018. https://www.marketwatch .com/story/winklevoss-twins-gemini-trust-launches-worlds-first-regulated- stablecoin-2018-09-10.

Harwick, Cameron. "Cryptocurrency and the Problem of Intermediation." *Independent Review* 20, no. 4 (Spring 2016): 569–588.

Harris, C. Lowell, ed. *Inflation: Long-Term Problems*. New York: Academy of Politi- cal Science, 1975. http://www.questia.com/read/101947454/inflation-long- term-problems.

Hayek, F. A. *Denationalisation of Money: The Argument Refined*, 3rd ed. London: Institute of Economic Affairs, 1990. https://nakamotoinstitute.org/static/ docs/denationalisation.pdf.

Hayek, F.A. *The Road to Serfdom*. Chicago: University of Chicago Press, 1994.

Hofstadter, Richard, and Hofstadter, Beatrice. *Great Issues in American History, Vol. III*. New York: Vintage Books, 1982.

Hoving, Thomas, and Gomez-Moreno, Carmen. "Gold." *The Metropolitan Museum of Art Bulletin* 31, no. 2 (new series) (Winter 1972–1973). https://www.jstor.org/stable/3258582.

"How the End of Bretton Woods Started Our Woes." *The Evening Standard*, August 15, 2011. http://www.questia.com/read/1G1-264293376/how-the-end-of-bretton-woods-started-our-woes.

"How Much Money Is There in the World?" (video), *World Economic Forum*. https://www.facebook.com/worldeconomicforum/videos/how-much-money-is-there-in-the-world/10154018639106479/.

Hurst, James Willard. "Alexander Hamilton, Law Maker." *Columbia Law Review* 78, no. 3 (April 1978): 483–547. https://www.jstor.org/stable/1122042.

Hvistendahl Mara. "You Are a Number." *Wired*, January 2018. http://www.questia.com/read/1P4-1984095355/you-are-a-number.

Ingham, Geoffrey. "Money Is a Social Relation." *Review of Social Economy* 54, no. 4, (1996). http://www.questia.com/read/1G1-19115414/money-is-a-social-relation.

Ingves, Stefan. "Going Cashless." *International Monetary Fund* 55, no. 2 (June 2018). https://www.imf.org/external/pubs/ft/fandd/2018/06/central-banks-and-digital-currencies/point.htm.

Innes, A. Mitchell. "What Is Money?" *Banking Law Journal* 30 (May 1913): 377–408. http://www.newmoneyhub.com/www/money/mitchell-innes/what-is-money.html.

Innes, Mitchell. "The Credit Theory of Money." *Banking Law Journal* 31 (December/January 1914). https://www.community-exchange.org/docs/The%20Credit%20Theoriy%20of%20Money.htm.

Ip, Greg, and Whitehouse, Mark. "How Milton Friedman Changed Economics, Policy and Markets." *Wall Street Journal*, November 17, 2006. https://www.wsj.com/articles/SB116369744597625238.

Jadeja, Yashpalsinh, and Modi, Kirit. "Cloud Computing—Concepts, Architecture and Challenges." *International Conference on Computing, Electronics and Electrical Technologies, March* 2012. https://ieeexplore.ieee.org/document/6203873.

Jeffries, Zay. "Gold." *Proceedings of the American Philosophical Society* 108, no. 5 (October 20, 1964). https://www.jstor.org/stable/985818.

Joffe, Marc. "Just How Ugly Is America's Balance Sheet?" *Fiscal Times*, July 24, 2017. https://www.thefiscaltimes.com/Columns/2017/07/24/Just-How-Ugly-Americas-Balance-Sheet.

Jones, J.H. "The Gold Standard." *Economic Journal* 43, no. 172 (December 1933): 554. https://www.jstor.org/stable/2224503.

Kestenbaum, David. "How Former Fed Chairman Paul Volcker Tamed Inflation – Maybe for Good." *NPR*, December 15, 2015. https://www.npr.org/

2015/12/15/459871005/how-former-fed-chairman-paul-volcker-tamed-inflation-maybe-for-good.

Kiviat, Trevor I. "Beyond Bitcoin: Issues in Regulating Blockchain Transactions." *Duke Law Journal* 65, no. 3 (2015). http://www.questia.com/read/1G1-439635382/beyond-bitcoin-issues-in-regulating-blockchain-transactions.

Klein, Aaron. "'Everyone' Is the Wrong Way to Define CU Members." *American Banker*, July 10, 2017. https://www.americanbanker.com/opinion/everyone-is-the-wrong-way-to-define-cu-members?feed=00000158-080c-dbde-abfc-3e7d1bf30000.

Koning, Hans. Columbus: *His Enterprise: Exploding the Myth*. New York: Monthly Review Press, 1991. http://www.questia.com/read/125248315/columbus-his-enterprise-exploding-the-myth.

League of Southeastern Credit Unions and Affiliates, "About Credit Unions." https://www.lscu.coop/about/about-credit-unions/.

Leonard, Robert A. "Money and Language." In *Money, Lure, Lore, and Literature*, ed. John Louis Digaetani. Westport, CT: Greenwood Press, 1994. http://www.questia.com/read/33826756/money-lure-lore-and-literature.

Luther, William J. "The Battle of Bretton Woods: John Maynard Keynes, Harry Dexter White, and the Making of a New World Order." *Independent Review* 18, no. 3 (2014). http://www.questia.com/read/1G1-353438637/the-battle-of-bretton-woods-john-maynard-keynes.

Luther, William J. "Friedman vs. Hayek on Currency Competition." *American Institute for Economic Research, August* 22, 2014. https://www.aier.org/article/sound-money-project/friedman-vs-hayek-currency-competition.

Luther, William J. "Bitcoin and the Future of Digital Payments." *Independent Review* 20, no. 3 (2016). http://www.questia.com/read/1P3-3922329951/bitcoin-and-the-future-of-digital-payments.

McCallum, Bennett T. "The Bitcoin Revolution." *Cato Journal* 35, no. 2 (2015). http://www.questia.com/read/1G1-419267235/the-bitcoin-revolution.

Malkeil, Burton. *A Random Walk Down Wall Street*, 9th ed. New York: W.W. Norton & Co., 2007.

Markowitz, H. "Portfolio Selection." *Journal of Finance* 7, no. 1 (March 1952): 77–91. http://links.jstor.org/sici?sici=0022-1082%28195203%297%3A1%3C77%3APS%3E2.0.CO%3B2-1.

Martin, Adam. "Remembering Nixon's Gold-Standard Gamble: Interrupting 'Bonanza.'" *The Atlantic*, August 15, 2011. https://www.theatlantic.com/politics/archive/2011/08/nixon-gold-standard-gamble-interrupting-bonanza/354136/.

Martin, Emmie. "Home Prices Have Risen 114% Since 1960 – Here's How Much More Expensive Life Is Today." *CNBC*, April 17, 2018. https://www.cnbc.com/2018/04/17/how-much-more-expensive-life-is-today-than-it-was-in-1960.html.

Mazonka, Oleg. "Blockchain: Simple Explanation." http://jrxv.net/x/16/block chain-gentle-introduction.pdf.

McBriarty, Patrick. "For Bridge Lovers, Chicago is the Greatest Show on Earth." *Chicago Architecture*, March 31, 2014. https://www.chicagoarchitecture.org/ 2014/03/31/for-bridge-lovers-chicago-is-the-greatest-show-on-earth/.

McCracken, Paul W. "Economic Policy in the Nixon Years." *Presidential Studies Quarterly* 26, no. 1 (Winter 1996): 165–177. https://www.jstor.org/stable/ 27551556.

McCraw, Thomas K. "The Strategic Vision of Alexander Hamilton." *American Scholar* 63, no. 1 (Winter 1994): 31–57. https://www.jstor.org/stable/412 12203.

McKinsey & Company. "Global Payments 2016: Strong Fundamentals Despite Uncertain Times." https://www.mckinsey.com/~/media/McKinsey/Indus tries/Financial%20Services/Our%20Insights/A%20mixed%202015%20for%20 the%20global%20payments%20industry/Global-Payments-2016.ashx.

McMurray, John. "Economist Milton Friedman Championed Free Markets and Individualism." *Investor's Business Daily*, November 10, 2016. https://www .investors.com/news/management/leaders-and-success/economist-milton-friedman-championed-free-markets-and-individualism/.

Miller, Adolph C. "Whence and Whither the Gold Standard?" *Proceedings of the Academy of Political Science* 17, no. 1 (May 1936): 83–93. https://www.jstor .org/stable/1172418.

Miller, Christopher L, and Hamell, George R. "A New Perspective on Indian–White Contact: Cultural Symbols of Colonial Trade." *Journal of American History* 73, no. 2 (1986).

Miller, Merton H. "Debt and Taxes." *Journal of Finance* 32, no. 2 (papers and proceedings of the Thirty-Fifth Annual Meeting of the American Finance Association, Atlantic City, NJ, September 16–18, 1976) (May 1977): 261–275. http://www.jstor.org/stable/2326758.

Miller, Michael. *Cloud Computing: Web-Based Applications That Change the Way You Work and Collaborate Online*. Indianapolis: Que Publishing, 2009.

"Milton Friedman Assesses the Monetarist Legacy and the Recent Performance of Central Banks." *Central Banking*, August 2002, 15–23.

Mitchell, Broadus. "Alexander Hamilton, Executive Power and the New Nation." *Presidential Studies Quarterly* 17, no. 2 (Spring 1987): 329–343. https://www .jstor.org/stable/40574455.

Mises, Ludwig von. *The Theory of Money and Credit*. New Haven: Yale University Press, 1953.

Modigliani, F., and Miller, M. "The Cost of Capital, Corporation Finance and the Theory of Investment." *American Economic Review* 48, no. 3 (1958): 261–297.

Modigliani, F., and Miller, M. "Corporate Income Taxes and the Cost of Capital: A Correction." *American Economic Review* 53, no. 3 (1963): 433–443.

"Money." *Wikipedia*. https://en.wikipedia.org/wiki/Money.

"Money Fights the Fear of Death." *BusinessTech*, June 7, 2013. https://businesstech
.co.za/news/general/39520/money-fights-the-fear-of-death/.

"Money Makes the World Go Round." *USA Today* (November 1995), 9.
http://www.questia.com/read/1G1-17606148/money-makes-the-world-
go-round.

"Money-Market Fund 'Breaks the Buck.'" *New York Times*, September 17,
2008. https://dealbook.nytimes.com/2008/09/17/money-market-fund-says-
customers-could-lose-money/.

Morgan, H. Wayne. "The Origins and Establishment of the First Bank of the
United States." *Business History Review* 30, no. 4 (December 1956): 472–492.
https://www.jstor.org/stable/3111717.

"Movable Bridges Types, Design and History." *History of Bridges*. http://www
.historyofbridges.com/facts-about-bridges/movable-bridge/.

Moyo, Jeffrey and Onishi, Norimitsu. "A Cashless Economy in Zimbabwe? With
Little Cash, There's Little Choice." *New York Times*, November 3, 2016.
https://www.nytimes.com/2016/11/04/world/africa/zimbabwe-robert-
mugabe-cash-debit-cards.html.

Mundell, R.A. "A Reconsideration of the Twentieth Century." *American Economic
Review* 90, no. 3 (June 2000). https://www.jstor.org/stable/11733.

Nakamoto, Satoshi. "Bitcoin: A Peer-to-Peer Electronic Cash System." *Satoshi
Nakamoto Institute*, October 31, 2008. https://nakamotoinstitute.org/bitcoin/.

Nelson, Edward, and Schwartz, Anna J. "The Impact of Milton Friedman on Modern Monetary Economics: Setting the Record Straight on Paul Krugman's
'Who Was Milton Friedman?'" *National Bureau of Economic Research* (October
2007). https://www.nber.org/papers/w13546.pdf.

Nousek, Debra L. "Turning Points in Roman History: The Case of Caesar's Elephant Denarius." *Phoenix* 62, no. 3/4 (Fall–Winter 2008). https://www.jstor
.org/stable/25651734.

"Number of Restaurants in the United States from 2011 to 2018." *Statista*. https://
www.statista.com/statistics/244616/number-of-qsr-fsr-chain-independent-
restaurants-in-the-us/.

Press, Gil. "A Very Short History of the Internet and the Web." *Forbes*, January
2, 2015. https://www.forbes.com/sites/gilpress/2015/01/02/a-very-short-
history-of-the-internet-and-the-web-2/#4bccfa967a4e.

Quiggin, H. *A Survey of Primitive Money: The Beginnings of Currency*. London:
Methuen & Co., 1949.

Quinn, Shannon. "What the 'Star Wars' Movies Can Tell Us About Our Finances."
MoneyWise, May 28, 2018. https://moneywise.com/a/the-not-so-far-far-
away-economics-of-the-star-wars-galaxy.

Reagan, Courtney. "What's Behind the Rush into the Low-Margin Grocery
Business." *CNBC*, June 6, 2013. https://www.cnbc.com/id/100794988.

Reinhart, Carmen M., and Kenneth S. Rogoff. *This Time Is Different: Eight
Centuries of Financial Folly*. Princeton, NJ: Princeton University Press, 2009.

Rice, Denis T. "The Past and Future of Bitcoins in Worldwide Commerce." *Business Law Today* 2013, 1–4. http://www.jstor.org/stable/businesslawtoday .2013.11.06.

Rickards, James. *Currency Wars: The Making of the Next Global Crisis.* New York: Portfolio Penguin, 2011.

Rickards, James. *The Death of Money: The Coming Collapse of the International Monetary System.* New York: Portfolio Penguin, 2014.

Ritzmann, Franz. "Money, a Substitute for Confidence? Vaughan to Keynes and Beyond." *American Journal of Economics and Sociology* 58, no. 2 (1999). http://www.questia.com/read/1G1-55084083/money-a-substitute-for-confidence-vaughan-to-keynes.

Robertson, D.H. *Money,* ed. J.M. Keynes. New York: Harcourt Brace and Company, 1922. http://www.questia.com/read/11931888/money.

Rosenberg, Paul. "'That Couldn't Possibly Be True': The Startling Truth About the US Dollar." *CaseyResearch*, February 27, 2015. https://www.caseyresearch.com /that-couldnt-possibly-be-true-the-startling-truth-about-the-us-dollar-2/.

Ross, Stephen A.; Westerfield, Randolph; and Jaffe, Jeffrey. *Corporate Finance,* 10th ed. New York: McGraw-Hill, 2013.

Rothbard, Murray N. "The Gold Standard Act of 1900 and After." Mises Institute, March 24, 2018. https://mises.org/library/gold-standard-act-1900-and-after.

Rothbard, Murray N. *The Mystery of Banking.* Auburn, AL: The Ludwig von Mises Institute. https://mises.org/library/mystery-banking/html.

Rosenzweig, Roy. "Wizards, Bureaucrats, Warriors, and Hackers: Writing the History of the Internet." *American History Review* 103, no. 5, 1998. 1530–1552.

Samuelson, Robert J. "Rethinking the Great Recession." *Wilson Quarterly* 35, no. 1 (Winter 2011): 16–24.

Scaliger, Charles. "Does Money Really Need to Be Controlled by Enlightened Experts?" *New American,* October 10, 2016, 28. http://www.questia .com/read/1G1-467830985/does-money-really-need-to-be-controlled-by-enlightened.

Schaefer, Steve. "Five Biggest U.S. Banks Control Nearly Half Industry's $15 Trillion in Assets." *Forbes,* December 3, 2014. https://www.forbes.com/ sites/steveschaefer/2014/12/03/five-biggest-banks-trillion-jpmorgan-citi-bankamerica/#1da4cd5db539.

Sharma, Rakesh. "Star Wars: The Economics of the Galactic Empire." *Investopedia,* May 4, 2018. https://www.investopedia.com/articles/investing/120815/star-wars-economics-galactic-empire.asp.

Shaw, Edward S. *Money, Income, and Monetary Policy.* Chicago: R.D. Irwin, 1950. http://www.questia.com/read/3800456/money-income-and-monetary-policy.

Simmons, Edward C. "The Elasticity of the Federal Reserve Note." *American Economic Review* 26, no. 4 (December 1936): 683–690. https://www.jstor.org/ stable/1807996.

"Simply, How Bretton Woods Reordered the World." *New Internationalist*, July 1994. http://www.questia.com/read/1P3-441782421/simply-how-bretton-woods-reordered-the-world.

Snowdon, Brian, and Vane, Howard R. *The Development of Modern Macroeconomics: A Macroeconomics Reader*. London: Routledge, 1997. http://www.questia .com/read/104188394/a-macroeconomics-reader.

Son, Hugh. "JP Morgan Is Rolling Out the First US Bank-Backed Cryptocurrency to Transform Payments Business." *CNBC*, February 14, 2019. https:// www.cnbc.com/2019/02/13/jp-morgan-is-rolling-out-the-first-us-bank-back ed-cryptocurrency-to-transform-payments–.html?te=1&nl=dealbook&emc= edit_dk_20190214.

Spross, Jeff. "The Forgotten Recession That Irrevocably Damaged the American Economy." *The Week*, April 18, 2016. https://theweek.com/articles/618964/ forgotten-recession-that-irrevocably-damaged-american-economy.

Spurlock, Morgan. *Inside Man*, episode, "Bitcoin." https://www.youtube.com/ watch?v=-5vkzqvgP6M.

Stanley, Aaron. "Winklevoss Twins See Bitcoin as 'Better than Gold.'" *Financial Times*, November 30, 2016. https://www.ft.com/content/a9d4b73a-abdd-11e6-ba7d-76378e4fef24.

Stevens, Greg. "A Guide to Star Trek Economics." *Kernel*, September 4, 2013. https://kernelmag.dailydot.com/features/report/4849/a-guide-to-star-trek-economics/.

Swan, Melanie. *Blockchain: Blueprint for a New Economy*. Sebastopol, CA: O'Reilly Media, 2015.

Swanson, Donald F., and Trout, Andrew P. "Alexander Hamilton, 'the Celebrated Mr. Neckar,' and Public Credit." *William and Mary Quarterly* 47, no. 3 (July 1990): 442–430. https://www.jstor.org/stable/2938096.

Swanson, Donald F., and Trout, Andrew P. "Alexander Hamilton's Economic Policies After Two Centuries." *New York History* 72, no. 3 (July 1991): 284–297. https://www.jstor.org/stable/23175280.

Swanson, Donald F. "'Bank-Notes Will Be but as Oak Leaves': Thomas Jefferson on Paper Money." *Virginia Magazine of History and Biography*, January 1993, 37–52. https://www.jstor.org/stable/4249329.

Sylla, Richard; Wright, Robert E.; and Cowen, David J. "Alexander Hamilton, Central Banker: Crisis Management during the U.S. Financial Panic of 1792." *Business History Review* 83, no. 1 (Spring 2009): 61–86. https://www.jstor.org/ stable/40538573.

Tabarrok, Alex. "Price Controls and Communism." *MrUniversity*. https://www .mruniversity.com/courses/principles-economics-microeconomics/price-controls-communism-planned-economy.

Taibbi, Matt. "Secrets and Lies of the Bailout." *Rolling Stone*, January 4, 2013. https://www.rollingstone.com/politics/politics-news/secrets-and-lies-of-the-bailout-113270/.

Tanglao, Leezel. "Can Star Trek's World with No Money Work?" *CNN*, October 11, 2015. https://money.cnn.com/2015/10/11/news/economy/new-york-comic-con-star-trek-economics/index.html.

Tapscott, Don, and Tapscott, Alex. *Blockchain Revolution: How the Technology Behind Bitcoin and Other Cryptocurrencies Is Changing the World*. New York: Portfolio/Penguin, 2016.

Tapscott, Don. "How the Blockchain Is Changing Money and Business." *TED*. https://www.ted.com/talks/don_tapscott_how_the_blockchain_is_changing _money_and_business/up-next?language=en.

"The Economic Lessons of Star Trek's Money-Free Society." *Wired*, May 28, 2016. https://www.wired.com/2016/05/geeks-guide-star-trek-economics/.

Timberlake, Richard H. "From Constitutional to Fiat Money: The U.S. Experience." *Cato Journal*, 32, no. 2 (2012). http://www.questia.com/read/1G1-292992182/from-constitutional-to-fiat-money-the-u-s-experience.

Turpin, Jonathan B. "Bitcoin: The Economic Case for a Global, Virtual Currency Operating in an Unexplored Legal Framework." *Indiana Journal of Global Legal Studies* 21, no. 1 (2014): 335–368.

"U.S. Food Retail Industry – Statistics and Facts." *Statista*. https://www.statista .com/topics/1660/food-retail/.

Vilches, Elvira. "Columbus's Gift: Representations of Grace and Wealth and the Enterprise of the Indies." *MLN* 119, no. 2 (March 2004). https://www.jstor .org/stable/3251770.

John R. Walter. "Not Your Father's Credit Union," *Economic Quarterly – Federal Reserve Bank of Richmond* 92, no. 4 (2006). http://www.questia.com/read/ 1P3-1183337561/not-your-father-s-credit-union.

Washington, R.A. "Who Beat Inflation? A Look Back at the Other Great Recession." *The Economist*, March 31, 2010. https://www.economist.com/ free-exchange/2010/03/31/who-beat-inflation.

"Weimar – Crisis of 1923." *BBC*. http://www.bbc.co.uk/schools/gcsebitesize/ history/mwh/germany/crisis1923rev_print.shtml.

Wessel, David. *Red Ink: Inside the High-Stakes Politics of the Federal Budget*. New York: Crown Business, 2012.

Wettereau, James O. "New Light on the First Bank of the United States." *Pennsylvania Magazine of History and Biography*, July 1937, 263–285. https://www .jstor.org/stable/20087054.

Whalen, Christopher. *Inflated: How Money and Debt Build the American Dream*. Hoboken, NJ: John Wiley & Sons, 2011.

Wiedemer, David; Widemer, Robert; and Spitzer, Cindy. *Aftershock: Protect Yourself and Profit in the Next Global Financial Meltdown*, revised and updated, 3rd ed. Hoboken, NJ: John Wiley & Sons, 2011.

Willard, Kristen L; Guinnane, Timothy W.; and Rose, Harvey. "Turning Points in the Civil War: Views from the Greenback Market." *American Economic Review*, 86, no. 4 (September 1996): 1001–1018. https://www.jstor.org/stable/ 2118316.

Wray, Randall, ed. *Credit and State Theories of Money: The Contributions of A. Mitchell Innes.* Cheltenham, UK: Edward Elgar, 2004.

"William Jennings Bryan." *Encyclopaedia Britannica.* https://www.britannica.com/biography/William-Jennings-Bryan.

Wolman, Alexander L. "Zero Inflation and the Friedman Rule: A Welfare Comparison." *Federal Reserve Bank of Richmond Economic Quarterly* 83/84 (Fall 1997). https://pdfs.semanticscholar.org/c0c9/a7cb1e49ffe037f0a542573e483ee54a66ba.pdf.

Zaleskiewicz, Tomasz; Gasiorowska, Agata; Kesebir, Pelin; Luszczynska, Aleksandra; Pyszczynski, Tom. "Money and the Fear of Death: The Symbolic Power of Money as an Existential Anxiety Buffer." *Journal of Economic Psychology* 36 (June 2013): 55–67. https://www.sciencedirect.com/science/article/abs/pii/S0167487013000391

Zingales, Luigi. *A Capitalism for the People: Recapturing the Lost Genius of American Prosperity.* New York: Basic Books, 2012.

About the Author

Tom Anderson is the Founder of Anasova. Anasova is a platform and community that strives to continuously organize and optimize your financial life securely, efficiently and anonymously. Prior to founding Anasova, Tom founded Supernova Lending and Supernova Technology. Supernova is a financial technology company that provides an end-to-end, cloud-based financial technology platform that empowers banks to make secured loans more efficiently to a broader consumer base. Supernova facilitates and automates many of the mission-critical business processes of a bank, including origination, servicing, risk monitoring, payment processing, and loan accounting. The company also hosts the industry's leading wealth management lending education platform. Supernova's solutions are utilized by some of the largest banks in the United States.

Tom is a *New York Times* bestselling author and nationally renowned financial planning expert. His first book, *The Value of Debt*, was a *New York Times* and *USA Today* bestseller and named the No. 2 business book of 2013 by WealthManagement.com. His other books, *The Value of Debt in Retirement* and *The Value of Debt in Building Wealth,* have been featured in the *New York Times, USA Today, Forbes,* the *Washington Post,*

CNBC, Fox Business, and Bloomberg, among multiple other national and international publications.

Tom has worked in investment banking and wealth management for Wells Fargo, Deutsche Bank, Bank of America/Merrill Lynch, and Morgan Stanley. While he was Executive Director, Morgan Stanley Wealth Management, Tom was recognized by *On Wall Street* magazine as a "Top 40 Under 40." Tom has his M.B.A. from the University of Chicago and a B.S.B.A. from Washington University in St. Louis. He lives with his wife and three children in Chicago.

Endnotes

Preface

1. Jessica Dickler, "Most Americans Live Paycheck to Paycheck," *CNBC*, August 30, 2017, https://www.cnbc.com/2017/08/24/most-americans-live-paycheck-to-paycheck.html.
2. Ibid.

Introduction

1. "Richest 1 percent bagged 82 percent of wealth created last year – poorest half of humanity got nothing," *Oxfam International*, January 22, 2018, https://www.oxfam.org/en/pressroom/pressreleases/2018-01-22/richest-1-percent-bagged-82-percent-wealth-created-last-year.
2. Kristian Gjerding, "The Cashless Economy: Why and Where It's Evolving and What Businesses Can Do Now to Prepare," *Forbes*, October 24, 2017, https://www.forbes.com/sites/forbesfinancecouncil/2017/10/24/the-cashless-economy-why-and-where-its-evolving-and-what-businesses-can-do-now-to-prepare/#3ce267873e11.
3. Steve Ingves, "Going Cashless," *International Monetary Fund, Finance & Development*, June 2018, http://www.imf.org/external/pubs/ft/fandd/2018/06/central-banks-and-digital-currencies/point.htm.

4. "Global Payments 2016: Strong Fundamentals Despite Uncertain Times," McKinsey & Company, https://www.mckinsey.com/~/media/McKinsey/Industries/Financial%20Services/Our%20Insights/A%20mixed%202015%20for%20the%20global%20payments%20industry/Global-Payments-2016.ashx.

5. Ryan Brown, "Digital Payments Expected to Hit 726 Billion by 2020 – But Cash Isn't Going Anywhere Yet," October 9, 2017, https://www.cnbc.com/2017/10/09/digital-payments-expected-to-hit-726-billion-by-2020-study-finds.html.

6. Sam Del Rowe, "Mobile Payment Technologies Set to Increase: Reports from Juniper and Forrester Indicate That Use of Mobile Payment Solutions Will Increase for Both Businesses and Consumers," *CRM Magazine*, April 2017, 17, http://www.questia.com/read/1G1-488193746/mobile-payment-technologies-set-to-increase-reports.

7. Hvistendahl Mara, "You Are a Number," *Wired*, January 2018, http://www.questia.com/read/1P4-1984095355/you-are-a-number.

8. H. Quiggin, *A Survey of Primitive Money: The Beginnings of Currency* (London: Methuen & Co., 1949), 25–36.

9. A. Anikin, *Gold – The Yellow Devil* (New York: International Publishers, 1983), 12, http://www.questia.com/read/43146767/gold-the-yellow-devil.

10. Adam Martin, "Remembering Nixon's Gold-Standard Gamble: Interrupting 'Bonanza,'" *The Atlantic,* August 15, 2011, https://www.theatlantic.com/politics/archive/2011/08/nixon-gold-standard-gamble-interrupting-bonanza/354136/.

11. Federal Reserve Bank of Richmond, "Gold & Silver," https://www.richmondfed.org/faqs/gold_silver.

12. "12 Fast Food Prices Then versus Now," by Douglas Ehrman, *Las Vegas Review-Journal,* June 6, 2015, https://www.reviewjournal.com/business/12-fast-food-prices-then-versus-now/.

13. "Igniting the Holocaust – Facing History and Ourselves: Burning Money: Hyperinflation in the Weimar Republic," *Randolph*, https://library.randolphschool.net/c.php?g=237930&p=1581974.

14. Jeffrey Moyo and Norimitsu Onishi, "A Cashless Economy in Zimbabwe? With Little Cash, There's Little Choice," *The New York Times,* November 3, 2016, https://www.nytimes.com/2016/11/04/world/africa/zimbabwe-robert-mugabe-cash-debit-cards.html.

Chapter 1

1. S. Davis, "Greek and Roman Coins and Their Historical Interest," *Acta Classica* 3 (1960) 67–76, published by Classical Association of South Africa, https://www.jstor.org/stable/24591082, p. 67.

2. Peter L. Bernstein, *The Power of Gold: The History of an Obsession* (Hoboken, NJ: Wiley, 2012), 19, http://www.questia.com/read/123791934/the-power-of-gold-the-history-of-an-obsession.

3. Davis, 67.

4. Bernstein, 2–3.

5. Bernstein, 19.

6. Thomas Hoving and Carmen Gómez-Moreno, "Gold," *The Metropolitan Museum of Art Bulletin,* new series, vol. 31, no. 2 (Winter 1972–1973): 69–120, https://www.jstor.org/stable/3258582.

7. Hoving and Gomez-Moreno, 75.

8. Bernstein, 2.

9. Hoving and Gómez-Moreno, 88.

10. Davis, 68.

11. Zay Jeffries, "Gold," *Proceedings of the American Philosophical Society* 108, no. 5 (October 20, 1964): 437–442, published by American Philosophical Society, https://www.jstor.org/stable/985818, 438.

12. Davis, 67.

13. Davis, 69.

14. Bernstein, 48.

15. Jeffries, 438.

16. Davis, 72–74.

17. Debra L. Nousek, "Turning Points in Roman History: The Case of Caesar's Elephant Denarius," *Phoenix* 62, no. 3/4 (Fall–Winter/automne-hiver 2008): 290–307, published by Classical Association of Canada, https://www.jstor.org/stable/25651734, 290.

18. Bernstein, 48.

19. Hans Koning, *Columbus: His Enterprise: Exploding the Myth* (New York: Monthly Review Press, 1991), 56, http://www.questia.com/read/125248315/columbus-his-enterprise-exploding-the-myth.

20. Elvira Vilches, "Columbus's Gift: Representations of Grace and Wealth and the Enterprise of the Indies," *MLN* 119, no. 2 (Hispanic Issue, March 2004): 201–225, published by The Johns Hopkins University Press, https://www.jstor.org/stable/3251770, 207–209.

21. Vilches, 201 202.

22. Vilches, 204.

23. Vilches, 214.

24. Koning, 62.

25. Koning, 84.

26. Vilches, 220.

27. Donald F. Swanson and Andrew P. Trout, "Alexander Hamilton's Economic Policies After Two Centuries," *New York History* 72, no. 3 (July 1991): 284–297, published by Fenimore Art Museum, https://www.jstor.org/stable/23175280, 289.

28. Swanson and Trout, 295.
29. H. Wayne Morgan, "The Origins and Establishment of the First Bank of the United States," *The Business History Review* 30, no. 4 (December 1956): 472–492, https://www.jstor.org/stable/3111717.
30. James Willard Hurst, "Alexander Hamilton, Law Maker," *Columbia Law Review* 78, no. 3 (April 1978): 483–547, https://www.jstor.org/stable/1122042, 487.
31. McGraw, 53.
32. Mitchell, 341.
33. Swanson and Trout, 429.
34. McCraw, 49.
35. Swanson and Trout, 296–297.
36. Donald F. Swanson, "Bank-Notes Will Be but as Oak Leaves: Thomas Jefferson on Paper Money, *The Virginia Magazine of History and Biography* 101, no. 1 (January 1993): 37–52, 37–42.
37. Mitchell, 274.
38. James O. Wettereau, "New Light on the First Bank of the United States," *The Pennsylvania Magazine of History and Biography* 61, no. 3 (July 1937): 263–285, 263.
39. Richard Sylla, Robert E. Wright, and David J. Cowen, "Alexander Hamilton, Central Banker: Crisis Management during the U.S. Financial Panic of 1792," *The Business History Review* 83, no. 1 (Spring 2009): 61–86, 68.
40. Kristen L. Willard, Timothy Guinnane, and Harvey S. Rosen, "Turning Points in the Civil War: Views from the Greenback," *The American Economic Review* 86, no. 4 (September 1996): 1001–1018.
41. Peter L. Bernstein, *The Power of Gold: The History of an Obsession* (Hoboken, NJ: Wiley, 2012), 263, http://www.questia.com/read/123792178/the-power-of-gold-the-history-of-an-obsession.
42. Kenneth W. Dam, "From the Gold Clause Cases to the Gold Commission: A Half Century of American Monetary Law," https://www.jstor.org/stable/1599500?read-now=1&loggedin=true&seq=16#page_scan_tab_contents, 506.
43. "How the End of Bretton Woods Started Our Woes," *The Evening Standard (London, England)*, August 15, 2011, http://www.questia.com/read/1G1-264293376/how-the-end-of-bretton-woods-started-our-woes.
44. Bernstein, 263–265.
45. "William Jennings Bryan," *Encyclopaedia Britannica*, https://www.britannica.com/biography/William-Jennings-Bryan.
46. "Gold Now the Standard," *New York Times,* March 15, 1900, p. 1, https://timesmachine.nytimes.com/timesmachine/1900/03/14/102500611.html?action=click&contentCollection=Archives&module=ArticleEndCTA&region=ArchiveBody&pgtype=article&pageNumber=1.
47. Max Gulker, "The Death of Bimetallism and the Gold Standard Act of 1900," *American Institute of Economic Research*, March 30, 2017, https://www.aier.org/research/death-bimetallism-and-gold-standard-act-1900.

48. "Conferees Agree on Currency Bill," *New York Times*, February 24, 1900, pp. 1–2, https://www.nytimes.com/1900/02/24/archives/conferrees-agree-on-currency-bill-it-declares-unqualifiedly-for-a.html.

49. Murray N. Rothbard, "The Gold Standard Act of 1900 and After," *Mises Institute*, March 24, 2018, https://mises.org/library/gold-standard-act-1900-and-after.

50. Ben S. Bernanke, "A Century of US Central Banking: Goals, Frameworks, Accountability," *The Journal of Economic Perspectives* 27, no. 4 (Fall 2013): 3–16, 4.

51. Bernanke, 4.

52. Edward C. Simmons, "The Elasticity of The Federal Reserve Note," *The American Economic Review* 26, no. 4 (December 1936): 683–690, https://www.jstor.org/stable/1807996, 692.

53. Bernanke, 6.

54. Fred L. Block, "The Origins of International Economic Disorder: A Study of United States Monetary Policy from World War II to the Present" (University of California Press, Berkeley and Los Angeles, 1977), 14–15.

55. Adolph C. Miller, "Whence and Whither in the Gold Standard?" *Proceedings of the Academy of Political Science* 17, no. 1, Economic Recovery and Monetary Stabilization (May 1936): 83–93, https://www.jstor.org/stable/1172418.

56. Barry Eichengreen and Peter Temin, "The Gold Standard and the Great Depression," *Contemporary European History* 9, no. 2 (July 2000): 183–207, https://www.jstor.org/stable/20081742.

57. Eichengreen and Temin, 202.

58. Bernstein, xi.

59. Kenneth W. Dam, "From the Gold Clause Cases to the Gold Commission: A Half Century of American Monetary Law," *University of Chicago Law Review* 50, no. 2 (Spring 1983): 504–532, https://www.jstor.org/stable/1599500?read-now=1&loggedin=true&seq=16#page_scan_tab_contents, 509.

60. Dam, 510.

61. Richard H. Timberlake, "From Constitutional to Fiat Money: The U.S. Experience," *The Cato Journal* 32, no. 2 (2012), http://www.questia.com/read/1G1-292992182/from-constitutional-to-fiat-money-the-u-s-experience.

62. Bernstein, 320–322.

63. J. II. Jones, "The Gold Standard," *The Economic Journal* 43, no. 172 (December 1933): 551–574, https://www.jstor.org/stable/2224503, 554.

64. Bernstein, 323.

65. William J. Luther, "The Battle of Bretton Woods: John Maynard Keynes, Harry Dexter White, and the Making of a New World Order," *Independent Review* 18, no. 3 (2014), http://www.questia.com/read/1G1-353438637/the-battle-of-bretton-woods-john-maynard-keynes.

66. Michael D. Bordo, "The Gold Standard and Other Monetary Regimes," *NBER Reporter*, 1992, http://www.questia.com/read/1G1-12730329/the-gold-standard-and-other-monetary-regimes.

67. Paul W. McCracken, "Economic Policy in the Nixon Years," *Presidential Studies Quarterly* 26, no. 1 (Winter 1996): 165–177, https://www.jstor.org/stable/27551556, 172.

68. Milton Friedman, "Bimetallism Revisited," *The Journal of Economic Perspectives* 4, no. 4 (Autumn 1990): 85–104, https://www.jstor.org/stable/1942723, 86.

69. Dam, 526.

70. "Simply, How Bretton Woods Reordered the World," *New Internationalist*, July 1994, http://www.questia.com/read/1P3-441782421/simply-how-bretton-woods-reordered-the-world.

71. "How the End of Bretton Woods Started Our Woes," *The Evening Standard (London, England)*, August 15, 2011, http://www.questia.com/read/1G1-264293376/how-the-end-of-bretton-woods-started-our-woes.

72. "Silver as an Investment," *Wikipedia*, https://en.wikipedia.org/wiki/Silver_as_an_investment.

73. Elizabeth Eder, "The Golden Solution," *Harvard International Review*, 4, no. 3 (November 1981): 18–19, https://www.jstor.org/stable/42763896.

74. Adam Martin, "Remembering Nixon's Gold-Standard Gamble: Interrupting "Bonanza,'" *The Atlantic*, August 15, 2011, https://www.theatlantic.com/politics/archive/2011/08/nixon-gold-standard-gamble-interrupting-bonanza/354136/.

75. Bernstein, 351.

76. McCracken, 174.

77. Martin.

78. Richard Hofstadter and Beatrice K. Hofstadter, *Great Issues in American History, Vol. III* (New York: Vintage Books, 1982), 511.

79. McCracken, 175.

80. Mundell, 284.

81. C. Lowell Harriss, ed., *Inflation: Long-Term Problems* (New York: Academy of Political Science, 1975), http://www.questia.com/read/101947454/inflation-long-term-problems.

82. Bernstein, 356.

83. Mundell, 335.

84. R.A. Washington, "Who Beat Inflation?" *The Economist*, March 31, 2010, https://www.economist.com/free-exchange/2010/03/31/who-beat-inflation.

85. David Kestenbaum, "How Former Fed Chairman Paul Volcker Tamed Inflation – Maybe for Good," *National Public Radio*, December 15, 2015, https://www.npr.org/2015/12/15/459871005/how-former-fed-chairman-paul-volcker-tamed-inflation-maybe-for-good.

86. Jeff Spross, "The Forgotten Recession that Irrevocably Damaged the American Economy," *The Week*, April 18, 2016, http://theweek.com/articles/618964/forgotten-recession-that-irrevocably-damaged-american-economy.

87. "Silver as an Investment," *Wikipedia*, https://en.wikipedia.org/wiki/Silver_as_an_investment.

Chapter 2

1. Robert A. Leonard, "1: Money and Language," in *Money: Lure, Lore, and Literature*, ed. John Louis Digaetani (Westport, CT: Greenwood Press, 1994), 3, http://www.questia.com/read/33826756/money-lure-lore-and-literature.
2. "Money," Wikipedia, https://en.wikipedia.org/wiki/Money.
3. "Currency and Coin Services," Federal Reserve, https://www.federalreserve.gov/paymentsystems/coin_currcircvolume.htm.
4. "How Much Money Is There in the World?" World Economic Forum, December 29, 2106, https://www.facebook.com/worldeconomicforum/videos/how-much-money-is-there-in-the-world/10154018639106479/.
5. Sue Chang, "Here's All the Money in the World, in One Chart," *MarketWatch*, November 28, 2017, https://www.marketwatch.com/story/this-is-how-much-money-exists-in-the-entire-world-in-one-chart-2015-12-18.
6. "Money Makes the World Go Round," *USA TODAY*, November 1995, p. 9, http://www.questia.com/read/1G1-17606148/money-makes-the-world-go-round.
7. Tomasz Zaleskiewicz, Agata Gasiorowska, Pelin Kesebir, Aleksandra Luszczynska, and Tom Pyszczynski, "Money and the Fear of Death: The Symbolic Power of Money as an Existential Anxiety Buffer," *ScienceDirect*, Feburary 8, 2013, pp. 55–67, https://www.sciencedirect.com/science/article/abs/pii/S0167487013000391.
8. "Money Fights the Fear of Death," *BusinessTech*, June 7, 2013, https://businesstech.co.za/news/general/39520/money-fights-the-fear-of-death/.
9. Geoffrey Ingham, "Money Is a Social Relation," *Review of Social Economy* 54, no. 4 (1996), http://www.questia.com/read/1G1-19115414/money-is-a-social-relation.
10. Franz Ritzmann, "Money, a Substitute for Confidence? Vaughan to Keynes and Beyond," *The American Journal of Economics and Sociology* 58, no. 2 (1999), http://www.questia.com/read/1G1-55084083/money-a-substitute-for-confidence-vaughan-to-keynes.
11. Ritzmann.
12. Ghislain Deleplace, "Problems and Paradoxes of Money," *UNESCO Courier*, January 1990, http://www.questia.com/read/1G1-8561011/problems-and-paradoxes-of-money.
13. D. H. Robertson, *Money*, ed. J. M. Keynes (New York: Harcourt Brace and Company, 1922), 11, http://www.questia.com/read/11931888/money.
14. Bonamy Price, "What Is Money?" *Fraser's Magazine*, no. 602 (February 1880): 248–60, 248, https://search.proquest.com/openview/069615c7110f1baa/1?pq-origsite=gscholar&cbl=1795.
15. A. Mitchell Innes, "The Credit Theory of Money," *Banking Law Journal* 31 (December/January 1914): 151–168, http://wfhummel.net/innes.html.
16. L. Randall Wray, *Credit and State Theories of Money: The Contributions of A. Mitchell Innes* (Cheltenham, UK: Edward Elgar, 2004), 52.

17. A. Mitchell Innes, "What Is Money?" *Banking Law Journal* 30 (May 1913): 377–408, http://www.newmoneyhub.com/www/money/mitchell-innes/what-is-money.html.

18. Ludwig von Mises, *The Theory of Money and Credit* (1912).

19. Ibid, 147.

20. Ibid.

21. Paul Rosenberg, "'That Couldn't Possibly Be True': The Startling Truth About the US Dollar," *CaseyResearch*, February 27, 2015, https://www.caseyresearch.com/that-couldnt-possibly-be-true-the-startling-truth-about-the-us-dollar-2/.

22. Edward S. Shaw, *Money, Income, and Monetary Policy* (Chicago: R.D. Irwin, 1950), 9, http://www.questia.com/read/3800456/money-income-and-monetary-policy.

23. Hugh R. Catherwood, "The U.S. National Debt," *The Government Accountants Journal* 49, no. 2 (2000), http://www.questia.com/read/1P3-55109496/the-u-s-national-debt.

24. Charles Scaliger, "Does Money Really Need to Be Controlled by Enlightened Experts?" *The New American*, October 10, 2016, p. 28, http://www.questia.com/read/1G1-467830985/does-money-really-need-to-be-controlled-by-enlightened.

25. Marc Joffe, "How Ugly Is America's Balance Sheet?" *The Fiscal Times*, July 24, 2017, https://www.thefiscaltimes.com/Columns/2017/07/24/Just-How-Ugly-Americas-Balance-Sheet

26. Antony Davies, "Going for Broke: Deficits, Debt, and the Entitlement Crisis," *Independent Review* 20, no. 4 (2016), http://www.questia.com/read/1G1-449314256/going-for-broke-deficits-debt-and-the-entitlement.

27. From the testimony of Laurence Kotlikoff before the Senate Budget Committee and as summarized by the Brookings institute in the article The Federal Debt is Worse Than You Think, Ron Haskins, April 8, 2015 https://www.brookings.edu/opinions/the-federal-debt-is-worse-than-you-think/.

28. Antony Davies and James R. Harrigan, "Debt Myths, Debunked," *U.S. News,* December 1, 2016, https://www.usnews.com/opinion/economic-intelligence/articles/2016-12-01/myths-and-facts-about-the-us-federal-debt.

29. Davies and Harrigan.

30. L. Randall Wray, ed., *Credit and State Theories of Money: The Contributions of A. Mitchell Innes*, (Cheltenham, UK: Edward Elgar, 2004).

31. Robert A. Leonard, "1: Money and Language," in *Money: Lure, Lore, and Literature*, ed. John Louis Digaetani (Westport, CT: Greenwood Press, 1994), 10, http://www.questia.com/read/33826773/money-lure-lore-and-literature.

Chapter 3

1. Murray N. Rothbard, *The Mystery of Banking* (Auburn, AL: The Ludwig von Mises Institute), 39.

2. Rothbard, 91.
3. Rothbard, 88.
4. Niall Ferguson, *The Ascent of Money: A Financial History of the World* (New York: The Penguin Press), 2008, 51–59.
5. Rothbard, 42–43.
6. Ferguson, 50–51.
7. Ferguson, 61–62.
8. Rothbard, 238.
9. Rothbard, 147.
10. Rothbard, 54.
11. A. Mitchell Innes, "The Credit Theory of Money," *Banking Law Journal* 31 (December/January 1914): 151–168, http://wfhummel.net/innes.html.
12. Riccardo Bellofiore, "Between Wicksell and Hayek: Mises' Theory of Money and Credit Revisited," *American Journal of Economics and Sociology* 57, no. 4 (1998), http://www.questia.com/read/1G1-53449312/between-wicksell-and-hayek-mises-theory-of-money.
13. John R. Walter, "Not Your Father's Credit Union," *Economic Quarterly – Federal Reserve Bank of Richmond* 92, no. 4 (2006), http://www.questia.com/read/1P3-1183337561/not-your-father-s-credit-union.
14. Walter.
15. "About Credit Unions," League of Southeastern Credit Unions & Affiliates, https://www.lscu.coop/about/about-credit-unions/.
16. B. Dan Berger, "Credit Unions: A History of Stepping Up," https://www.cutimes.com/2018/08/31/credit-unions-a-history-of-stepping-up/?slreturn=20190016162353.
17. Aaron Klein, "'Everyone' Is the Wrong Way to Define Credit Union Members," *Brookings*, July 10, 2017, https://www.brookings.edu/opinions/everyone-is-the-wrong-way-to-define-credit-union-members/.

Chapter 4

1. Jaromir Benes and Michael Kumhof, "The Chicago Plan Revisited" (International Monetary Fund working paper, authorized for distribution by Douglas Laxton, August 2012), 15.
2. Brian Doherty, "The Life and Times of Milton Friedman: Remembering the 20th Century's Most Influential Libertarian," *Reason*, March 2007, http://www.questia.com/read/1G1-159238152/the-life-and-times-of-milton-friedman-remembering.
3. Tim Collins, "The Rise of Bitcoin Was Predicted by Nobel Prize Winning Economist Milton Friedman in an Interview Recorded 18 Years Ago, Footage Reveals," *Daily Mail,* October 20, 2017, https://www.dailymail.co.uk/sciencetech/article-5000260/Bitcoin-predicted-Milton-Friedman-18-years-ago.html

4. Benes and Kumhof, 1.
5. William R. Allen, "Irving Fisher and the 100 Percent Reserve Proposal," *Journal of Law and Economics* 36, no. 2 (1993): 703–717, http://www.jstor.org/stable/725805, 707.
6. Allen, 711–712.
7. Benes and Kumhof, 17.
8. Benes and Kumhof, 4.
9. Edward Nelson and Anna J. Schwartz, "The Impact of Milton Friedman on Modern Economics: Setting the Record Straight on Paul Krugman's 'Who Was Milton Friedman?'" (Working Paper 13546, October 2007), 26; https://www.investors.com/news/management/leaders-and-success/economist-milton-friedman-championed-free-markets-and-individualism/.
10. Nelson and Schwartz, 3.
11. Nelson and Schwartz, 9.
12. Michael D. Bordo and Hugh Rockoff, "The Influence of Irving Fisher on Milton Friedman's Monetary Economics" (Rutgers University paper prepared for the AEA Session on Irving Fisher and Modern Economics: 100 Years After the Purchasing Power of Money, Denver, January 8, 2010), 4–5, http://citeseerx.ist.psu.edu/viewdoc/download;jsessionid=CF3C959AD00B985D086474688AE41088?doi=10.1.1.364.5640&rep=rep1&type=pdf.
13. Doherty.
14. Alexander L. Wolman, "Zero Inflation and the Friedman Rule: A Welfare Comparison," *Federal Reserve Bank of Richmond Economic Quarterly*, 3, https://pdfs.semanticscholar.org/c0c9/a7cb1e49ffe037f0a542573e483ee54a66ba.pdf.
15. Timothy Cogley, "What Is the Optimal Rate of Inflation?" (Federal Reserve Bank of San Francisco, September 19, 1997), https://www.frbsf.org/economic-research/publications/economic-letter/1997/september/what-is-the-optimal-rate-of-inflation/.
16. Greg Ip and Mark Whitehouse, "How Milton Friedman Changed Economics, Policy and Markets," *Wall Street Journal*, November 17, 2006, https://www.wsj.com/articles/SB116369744597625238
17. F.A. Hayek, *Denationalisation of Money: The Argument Refined: An Analysis of the Theory and Practice of Concurrent Currencies*, 3d ed. (London: The Institute of Economic Affairs, 1990), 13, https://nakamotoinstitute.org/static/docs/denationalisation.pdf.
18. Hayek, 14.
19. William J. Luther, "Friedman vs. Hayek on Currency Competition" (American Institute for Economic Research, August 22, 2014), https://www.aier.org/article/sound-money-project/friedman-vs-hayek-currency-competition.
20. Hayek, 33.
21. Hayek, 110.
22. Hayek, 131.

23. Hayek, 23.
24. Hayek, 92.
25. Hayek, 37.
26. Hayek, 36.
27. Hayek, 130.
28. Hayek, 137.
29. "US Dollar," *Priced in Gold*, http://pricedingold.com/us-dollar/.
30. Hayek, 46–47.
31. Hayek, 59–62.
32. Hayek, 48–49.
33. Hayek, 60.

Chapter 5

1. Satoshi Nakamoto, "Bitcoin: A Peer-to-Peer Electronic Cash System," October 31, 2008, https://nakamotoinstitute.org/bitcoin/.
2. William J. Luther, "Bitcoin and the Future of Digital Payments," *Independent Review* 20, no. 3 (Winter 2016): 397–404, https://www.jstor.org/stable/24562161, 397.
3. Luther, 399.
4. Luther, 399.
5. Denis T. Rice, "The Past and Future of Bitcoins in Worldwide Commerce," *Business Law Today* (2013): 1–4, http://www.jstor.org/stable/businesslawtoday.2013.11.06.
6. Morgan Spurlock, "Inside Man," "Bitcoin," https://www.youtube.com/watch?v=-5vkzqvgP6M.
7. Jonathan B. Turpin, "Bitcoin: The Economic Case for a Global, Virtual Currency Operating in an Unexplored Legal Framework," *Indiana Journal of Global Legal Studies* 21, no. 1 (2014): 335–368, 352.
8. Stanley, Aaron, "Winklevoss Twins See Bitcoin as 'Better Than Gold,'" *Financial Times*, November 30, 2016, https://www.ft.com/content/a9d4b73a-abdd-11e6-ba7d-76378e4fef24.
9. Brian Doherty, "In Search of the Elusive Bitcoin Billionaire: Bitcoin Is Booming. Libertarians Were There First. So Where Are All the Cryptocurrency Tycoons?" *Reason* 49, no. 8 (January 2018), http://www.questia.com/read/1G1-519584225/in-search-of-the-elusive-bitcoin-billionaire-bitcoin.
10. Cameron Harwick, "Cryptocurrency and the Problem of Intermediation," *Independent Review* 20, no. 4 (Spring 2016): 569–588, 571.
11. Adrian Chen, "Much Ado About Bitcoin," *New York Times*, November 26, 2013, https://www.nytimes.com/2013/11/27/opinion/much-ado-about-bitcoin.html?hp&rref=opinion.
12. Ethereum, www.ethereum.org.

13. Hugh Son, "JP Morgan Is Rolling Out the First US Bank-Backed Cryptocurrency to Transform Payments Business," *CNBC*, February 14, 2019, https://www.cnbc.com/2019/02/13/jp-morgan-is-rolling-out-the-first-us-bank-backed-cryptocurrency-to-transform-payments–.html?te=1&nl=deal book&emc=edit_dk_20190214.

14. Luther, 399.

15. Matthew Frankel, "How Many Cryptocurrencies Are There?" *Motley Fool*, March 16, 2018, https://www.fool.com/investing/2018/03/16/how-many-cryptocurrencies-are-there.aspx.

16. "Cryptocurrencies Have Shed Almost $700 Billion Since January Peak," *CNBC*, November 23, 2018, https://www.cnbc.com/2018/11/23/crypto currencies-have-shed-almost-700-billion-since-january-peak.html.

17. https://coinmarketcap.com/, as of March 25, 2019.

18. Frankel.

19. Nellie Bowles, "Everyone Is Getting Hilariously Rich, and You're Not," *New York Times*, January 13, 2018, https://www.nytimes.com/2018/01/13/style/bit coin-millionaires.html?em_pos=large&emc=edit_li_20180113&nl=nyt-living& nlid=12940167&ref=headline&te=1&_r=0.

20. SEC v. W. J. Howey Co., 328 US 293 (1946), US Supreme Court, https:// supreme.justia.com/cases/federal/us/328/293/.

21. Aaron Hankin, "Winklevoss Twins' Gemini Trust Launches World's First Regulated Stablecoin," *MarketWatch*, September 10, 2018, https://www .marketwatch.com/story/winklevoss-twins-gemini-trust-launches-worlds-first-regulated-stablecoin-2018-09-10.

22. Ibid.

23. Ibid.

Chapter 6

1. Alex Tabarrok, "Price Controls and Communism" (video), https://www .mruniversity.com/courses/principles-economics-microeconomics/price-controls-communism-planned-economy.

2. Mike Collins, "The Big Bank Bailout," *Forbes*, July 14, 2015, https:// www.forbes.com/sites/mikecollins/2015/07/14/the-big-bank-bailout/# 453ee0022d83; John Carney, "The Size of the Bank Bailout: $29 Trillion," *CNBC*, December 14, 2011, https://www.cnbc.com/id/45674390.

3. Steve Schaefer, "Five Biggest U.S. Banks Control Nearly Half Industry's $15 Trillion In Assets," *Forbes*, December 3, 2014, https://www.forbes.com/ sites/steveschaefer/2014/12/03/five-biggest-banks-trillion-jpmorgan-citi-bankamerica/#231f8d90b539.

4. Matt Taibbi, "Secrets and Lies of the Bailout," *Rolling Stone*, January 4, 2013, https://www.rollingstone.com/politics/politics-news/secrets-and-lies-of-the-bailout-113270/.

5. Courtney Reagan, "What's Behind the Rush into the Low-Margin Grocery Business," *CNBC*, June 6, 2013, http://www.cnbc.com/id/100794988.

6. "U.S. Food Retail Industry – Statistics & Facts," *Statista*, https://www.statista .com/topics/1660/food-retail/.

7. "Number of Restaurants in the United States from 2011 to 2018," *Statista*, https://www.statista.com/statistics/244616/number-of-qsr-fsr-chain-independent-restaurants-in-the-us/.

Chapter 7

1. Harry Markowitz, Francis Gupta, and Frank J. Fabozzi, "Modern Portfolio Theory," *Journal of Investing* (Fall 2002): 211.

2. "This Year's Laureates Are Pioneers in the Theory of Financial Economics and Corporate Finance," The Royal Swedish Academy of Sciences, October 16, 1990, 15, https://www.nobelprize.org/prizes/economic-sciences/1990/ press-release/.

3. Mark Hebner, "The Separation Theorem," *Index Fund Advisers*, July 28, 2013, 120, https://www.ifa.com/articles/separation_theorem/.

4. Francis Armstrong III, "Tobin's Separation Theorem," *Padadin Research & Registry*, https://www.paladinregistry.com/advisor/Francis.Armstrong/ tobin-s-separation-theorem.

Chapter 9

1. Doug Eberhardt, "What Really Backs the U.S. Dollar?" *Seeking Alpha*, June 28, 2009, https://seekingalpha.com/article/145722-what-really-backs-the-u-s-dollar.

2. "FSB Publishes 2017 G-SIB List," *Financial Stability Board*, November 2017, http://www.fsb.org/2017/11/fsb-publishes-2017-g-sib-list/.

3. B. Dan Berger, "Credit Unions: A History of Stepping Up," *CU Times*, August 31, 2018, https://www.cutimes.com/2018/08/31/credit-unions-a-history-of-stepping-up/?slreturn=20190016162353.

4. Gil Press, "A Very Short History of the Internet and the Web," *Forbes*, January 2, 2015, https://www.forbes.com/sites/gilpress/2015/01/02/a-very-short-history-of-the-internet-and-the-web-2/#ffd518c7a4e2.

5. Roy Rosenzweig, "Wizards, Bureaucrats, Warriors, and Hackers: Writing the History of the Internet," *The American Historical Review* 103, no. 5 (1998): 1530–1552,1532–1533.

6. Press.

7. Yashpalsinh Jadeja and Kirit Modi, "Cloud Computing – Concepts, Architecture and Challenges," 2012 International Conference on Computing,

Electronics and Electrical Technologies (ICCEET), May 24, 2012, pp. 877–880, https://ieeexplore.ieee.org/abstract/document/6203873.

8. V.V. Arutyunov, "Cloud Computing: Its History of Development, Modern State, and Future Considerations," *Scientific and Technical Information Processing* 39, no. 3 (July 2012): 173–178, 173.

9. Michael Miller, *Cloud Computing: Web-Based Applications That Change the Way You Work and Collaborate Online* (Que Publishing, 2009), 42

10. Mary Ann Bell, "Cloud Crowd: You Belong Whether You Know It or Not!" *Multimedia & Internet@Schools*, July–August 2009, http://www.questia.com/read/1G1-203230755/cloud-crowd-you-belong-whether-you-know-it-or-not.

11. Don Tapscott and Alex Tapscott, *Blockchain Revolution: How the Technology Behind Bitcoin Is Changing Money, Business, and the World* (New York: Portfolio/Penguin, 2016), 5, https://books.google.com/books?hl=en&lr=&id=NqBiCgAAQBAJ&oi=fnd&pg=PT11&dq=bitcoin&ots=sRwOyK16AA&sig=XdV6RWXMlQG38QblHkFqHprzXtY#v=onepage&q=bitcoin&f=false.

12. Trevor I. Kiviat, "Beyond Bitcoin: Issues in Regulating Blockchain Transactions," *Duke Law Journal* 65, no. 3 (2015), http://www.questia.com/read/1G1-439635382/beyond-bitcoin-issues-in-regulating-blockchain-transactions.

13. Melanie Swan, *Blockchain: Blueprint for a New Economy* (Sebastopol, CA: O'Reilly Media, 2015),

14. Andreas M. Antonopoulos, *Mastering Bitcoin: Unlocking Digital Cryptocurrencies* (Sebastopol, CA: O'Reilly Media, 2015), 24.

15. Tapscott and Tapscott, 81.

16. Tapscott and Tapscott, 42.

17. Swan, 51.

18. "How Blockchain Technology Works. Guide for Beginners," *Cointelegraph*, https://cointelegraph.com/bitcoin-for-beginners/how-blockchain-technology-works-guide-for-beginners#hash-function.

19. Ethereum, www.ethereum.org.

20. "Wikipedia: Introduction," *Wikipedia*, https://en.wikipedia.org/wiki/Wikipedia:Introduction.

21. "Hyperledger," *Wikipedia*, https://en.wikipedia.org/wiki/Hyperledger.

22. "Hyperledger: Blockchain Collaboration Changing the Business World," *IBM*, https://www.ibm.com/blockchain/hyperledger.

23. Ibid.

24. "What Is Blockchain?" *IBM*, https://www.ibm.com/blockchain/what-is-blockchain.

Chapter 10

1. "Capital Markets," *Investopedia*, https://www.investopedia.com/video/play/capital-markets/.

2. "Money-Market Fund 'Breaks the Buck,'" *New York Times*, September 17, 2008, https://dealbook.nytimes.com/2008/09/17/money-market-fund-says-customers-could-lose-money/.

3. "Commercial Paper," *Investopedia*, https://www.investopedia.com/terms/c/commercialpaper.asp.

4. "US Repo Market Fact Sheet, 2018," *SIFMA*, September 18, 2018, https://www.sifma.org/resources/research/us-repo-market-fact-sheet-2018/.

5. "Euro Repo Index," *RepoFundsRate*, February 1, 2019, http://www.repofundsrate.com/.

6. "Repurchase Agreement (Repo)," *Investopedia*, https://www.investopedia.com/terms/r/repurchaseagreement.asp.

7. Robert J. Samuelson. "Rethinking the Great Recession," *Wilson Quarterly* 35, no. 1 (1976): 16.

Chapter 11

1. "The Economic Lessons of Star Trek's Money-Free Society," *Wired*, May 28, 2016, https://www.wired.com/2016/05/geeks-guide-star-trek-economics/.

2. A.M. Gittlitz, "'Make It So': 'Star Trek' and Its Debt to Revolutionary Socialism," *The New York Times,* July 24, 2017, https://www.nytimes.com/2017/07/24/opinion/make-it-so-star-trek-and-its-debt-to-revolutionary-socialism.html.

3. Greg Stevens, "A Guide to Star Trek Economics," *The Kernel*, September 4, 2013, https://kernelmag.dailydot.com/features/report/4849/a-guide-to-star-trek-economics/.

4. Leezel Tanglao, "Can Star Trek's World with No Money Work?" CNN, October 11, 2015, https://money.cnn.com/2015/10/11/news/economy/new-york-comic-con-star-trek-economics/index.html.

5. *Wired.*

6. Rakesh Sharma, "Star Wars" The Economics of the Galactic Empire," Investopedia, May 4, 2018, https://www.investopedia.com/articles/investing/120815/star-wars-economics-galactic-empire.asp.

7. "Currency," Wookieepedia, http://starwars.wikia.com/wiki/Currency.

8. Sharma.

9. Shannon Quinn, "What the 'Star Wars' Movies Can Tell Us About Our Finances," *Moneywise*, May 28, 2018, https://moneywise.com/a/the-not-so-far-far-away-economics-of-the-star-wars-galaxy

10. Christopher Miller and George R. Hamell, "A New Perspective on Indian-White Contact: Cultural Symbols and Colonial Trade," *The Journal of American History* 73, no. 2 (1986): 311-28. 311.

11. Stephen Donnelly, "Fur, Fortune, and Empire: The Epic History of the Fur Trade in America," *Historical Journal of Massachusetts* 39, no. 1/2 (2011), 22.

12. Ann M. Carlos and Frank D. Lewis, *Commerce by a Frozen Sea: Native Americans and the European Fur Trade* (Philadelphia: University of Pennsylvania Press, 2010), 8.
13. Donnelly, 48.
14. "Why Bitcoin Uses So Much Energy," *The Economist*, July 9, 2018.
15. Timothy B. Lee, "New Study Quantifies Bitcoin's Ludicrous Energy Consumption," *ARSTechnica*, May 17, 2018.
16. Mix, "Bitcoin Mining Consumes More Electricity than 20+ European Countries," *The Next Web*, November 23, 2017.

Chapter 12

1. Mitchell Innes, "The Credit Theory of Money," *Banking Law Journal* 31 (December/January 1914), https://www.community-exchange.org/docs/The%20Credit%20Theoriy%20of%20Money.htm.
2. "Mass Versus Weight," *Wikipedia*, https://en.wikipedia.org/wiki/Mass_versus_weight.
3. Luke Baker, "How Much Does a Kilogram Weigh? Depends on Your 'Plank Constant,'" *Reuters*, November 16, 2018, https://www.reuters.com/article/us-science-kilogram/how-much-does-a-kilogram-weigh-depends-on-your-planck-constant-idUSKCN1NL21P.
4. Patrick McBriarty, "For Bridge Lovers, Chicago Is the Greatest Show on Earth," *Chicago Architecture*, March 31, 2014, https://www.chicagoarchitecture.org/2014/03/31/for-bridge-lovers-chicago-is-the-greatest-show-on-earth/.
5. "Movable Bridges Types, Design and History," *History of Bridges*, http://www.historyofbridges.com/facts-about-bridges/movable-bridge/.
6. Von Mises, *Theory of Money and Credit*, §8, p. 8.
7. "Historical Crude Oil Prices (Table)," *Inflationdata*, https://inflationdata.com/articles/inflation-adjusted-prices/historical-crude-oil-prices-tablc/.

Chapter 13

1. Milton Friedman, "Letter to the Editor: Roots," *Wall Street Journal,* October 30, 1992, https://miltonfriedman.hoover.org/friedman_images/Collections/2016c21/WSJ_10_30_1992.pdf.
2. Milton Friedman, "M1's Hot Streak Gave Keynesians a Bad Idea," *Wall Street Journal,* September 18, 1986, https://miltonfriedman.hoover.org/friedman_images/Collections/2016c21/WSJ_09_18_1986.pdf.
3. Harris Dellas and George S. Tavlas, "Milton Friedman and the Case for Flexible Exchange Rates and Monetary Values," *Bank of Greece*, October 2017, https://www.bankofgreece.gr/BogEkdoseis/Paper2017236.pdf.

4. Milton Friedman, "The Case for a Monetary Rule," *Newsweek*, February 7, 1972, 67.

5. Milton Friedman, "Defining Monetarism," *Newsweek*, July 12, 1982, 64.

6. "Milton Friedman Assesses the Monetarist Legacy and the Recent Performance of Central Banks," Milton Friedman interviewed by Robert Pringle, *Central Banking* (London) 13 (August 2002): 15–23.

7. Milton Friedman, "Introduction," *The Road to Serfdom,* by F.A. Hayek (Chicago: University of Chicago Press, 1994), ix–xx, https://miltonfriedman .hoover.org/friedman_images/Collections/2016c21/1994RoadSer.pdf.

8. Milton Friedman, "The Keynes Centenary: A Monetarist Reflects," *Economist*, June 4, 1983, 17–19, https://miltonfriedman.hoover.org/friedman_images/ Collections/2016c21/Economist_06_04_1983.pdf.

9. Milton Friedman, Sidney Hook, Rose Friedman, and Roger Freeman, "Market Mechanisms and Central Economic Planning," in *Market Mechanisms and Central Economic Planning* (Washington, D.C.: American Enterprise Institute, 1981), 3, https://miltonfriedman.hoover.org/friedman_images/Collections/ 2016c21/AEI_1981.pdf.

10. Brian Snowdon and Howard R. Vane, eds., "The Development of Modern Macroeconomics," in *A Macroeconomics Reader* (London: Routledge, 1997), 8, http://www.questia.com/read/104188394/a-macroeconomics-reader.

11. Milton Friedman, "My Evolution as an Economist," in *Lives and Laureates: Seven Nobel Economists*, ed. William Breit and Roger W. Spencer (Cambridge: MIT Press, 1986), 77–92, https://miltonfriedman.hoover.org/friedman_ images/Collections/2016c21/MIT_1986.pdf.

Chapter 14

1. F.A. Hayek, *Denationalisation of Money: The Argument Refined: An Analysis of the Theory and Practice of Concurrent Currencies*, 3d ed. (London: The Institute of Economic Affairs, 1990), https://nakamotoinstitute.org/static/docs/ denationalisation.pdf, 135.

2. Ibid.

3. Ibid.

4. Ibid.

5. Ibid.

6. Ibid.

7. Ibid.

8. Ibid.

9. Ibid.

10. Ibid.

Appendix B

1. Kimberly Amadeo, "Current US Federal Budget Deficit," *The Balance*, January 17, 2019, https://www.thebalance.com/current-u-s-federal-budget-deficit-3305783.

2. Greg Richter, "Ex-Comptroller General Walker: Real National Debt Triple What Most Think," *Newsmax*, November 8, 2015, https://www.newsmax.com/newsmax-tv/david-walker-national-debt/2015/11/08/id/701187/.

3. Joe English, "The Biggest Threat to America's Future Is Its Debt," *Chicago Tribune*, February 10, 2018, https://www.chicagotribune.com/news/opinion/letters/ct-government-debt-trillion-spending-20180209-story.html.

4. Tom Murse, "History of the US Federal Budget Deficit," *ThoughtCo.*, June 4, 2018, https://www.thoughtco.com/history-of-us-federal-budget-deficit-3321439.

5. "Debt Crusader: David Walker Sounds the Alarm for America's Financial Future," *Journal of Accountancy* 207, no. 3 (2009), http://www.questia.com/read/1G1-194962798/debt-crusader-david-walker-sounds-the-alarm-for-america-s.

6. Matthew Frankel, "9 Baby-Boomer Statistics That Will Blow You Away," *The Motley Fool*, July 29, 2017, https://www.fool.com/retirement/2017/07/29/9-baby-boomer-statistics-that-will-blow-you-away.aspx.

7. Jeanne Sahadi, "Social Security Must Reduce Benefits in 2034 if Reforms Aren't Made," *CNN*, June 5, 2018, https://www.cnn.com/2018/06/05/politics/social-security-benefit-cuts/index.html.

Index